OXFORD
UNIVERSITY PRESS

fourth edition

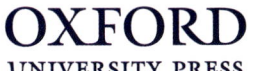

English File

Intermediate Plus

Student's Book

WITH ONLINE PRACTICE

Christina Latham-Koenig
Clive Oxenden
Kate Chomacki

Paul Seligson and Clive Oxenden are the original co-authors of *English File 1* and *English File 2*

Contents

		GRAMMAR	**VOCABULARY**	**PRONUNCIATION**
1				
6	**A** Why did they call you that?	pronouns	names	vowel sounds
10	**B** Life in colour	adjectives	adjective suffixes	word stress
14	**Practical English** Episode 1	reporting lost luggage		
2				
16	**A** Get ready! Get set! Go!	present tenses	packing	/s/, /z/, and /ɪz/
20	**B** Go to checkout	possessives	shops and services	r and final -r
24	**Revise and Check** 1&2			
3				
26	**A** Grow up!	past simple, past continuous, or *used to*?	stages of life	-*ed* endings, sentence rhythm
30	**B** Photo albums	prepositions	photography	word stress
34	**Practical English** Episode 2	renting a car		
4				
36	**A** Don't throw it away!	future forms: *will / shall* and *be going to*	rubbish and recycling	/aɪ/ and /eɪ/
40	**B** Put it on your CV	first and second conditionals	study and work	word stress
44	**Revise and Check** 3&4			
5				
46	**A** Screen time	present perfect simple	television	/w/, /v/, and /b/
50	**B** A quiet life?	present perfect continuous	the country	vowel sounds, sentence rhythm
54	**Practical English** Episode 3	making a police report		

		GRAMMAR	**VOCABULARY**	**PRONUNCIATION**
6				
56	**A** What the waiter really thinks	obligation, necessity, prohibition, advice	at a restaurant	word pairs with *and*
60	**B** Do it yourself	*can*, *could*, and *be able to*	DIY and repairs, paraphrasing	consonant clusters
64	**Revise and Check** 5&6			
7				
66	**A** Take your cash	phrasal verbs	cash machines, phrasal verbs	linking
70	**B** Shall we go out or stay in?	verb patterns	live entertainment	homographs
74	**Practical English** Episode 4	talking about house rules		
8				
76	**A** Treat yourself	*have something done*	looking after yourself	sentence stress
80	**B** Sites and sights	the passive, defining and non-defining relative clauses	wars and battles, historic buildings	silent consonants
84	**Revise and Check** 7&8			
9				
86	**A** Total recall	reported speech	word building	word stress
90	**B** Here comes the bride	third conditional and other uses of the past perfect, adverbs	weddings	sentence stress
94	**Practical English** Episode 5	giving directions in a building		
10				
96	**A** The land of the free?	*be*, *do*, and *have*: auxiliary and main verbs	British and American English	stress on *be*, *do*, and *have*
100	**B** Please turn over your papers	revision of verb forms	exams	revision of sounds
104	**Revise and Check** 9&10			

106	Communication	132	**Grammar Bank**	164	**Appendix**
115	Writing	152	**Vocabulary Bank**	165	**Irregular verbs**
124	Listening			166	**Sound Bank**

3

Course overview

English File

Welcome to **English File fourth edition**. This is how to use the Student's Book, Online Practice, and the Workbook in and out of class.

Student's Book

All the language and skills you need to improve your English, with Grammar, Vocabulary, Pronunciation, and skills work in every File. Also available as an eBook.

Use your Student's Book in class with your teacher.

Workbook

Grammar, Vocabulary, and Pronunciation practice for every lesson.

Use your Workbook for homework or for self-study to practise language and to check your progress.

ACTIVITIES AUDIO VIDEO RESOURCES

Go to **englishfileonline.com** and use the code on your Access Card to log into the Online Practice.

LOOK AGAIN
- Review the language from every lesson.
- Watch the videos and listen to all the class audio as many times as you like.

PRACTICE
- Improve your skills with extra Reading, Writing, Listening and Speaking practice.
- Use the interactive video to practise Practical English.

CHECK YOUR PROGRESS
- Test yourself on the language from the File and get instant feedback.
- Try an extra Challenge.

SOUND BANK
- Use the Sound Bank videos to practise and improve your pronunciation of English sounds.

Online Practice

Look again at Student's Book language you want to review or that you missed in class, do extra *Practice* activities, and *Check your progress* on what you've learnt so far.

Use the Online Practice to learn outside the classroom and get instant feedback on your progress.

englishfileonline.com

Course overview 5

1A Why did they call you that?

> What's your first name?
>
> It's Charlotte, but usually people call me Charlie.

G pronouns **V** names **P** vowel sounds

1 VOCABULARY names

a Read about the people and match photos A–H to the texts. Compare with a partner and together, work out the meaning of the **bold** words and phrases.

 A Marie Curie
 B Winona Ryder
 C Tolkien
 D Paul McCartney
 E J.K. Rowling
 F Miley Cyrus
 G Ed Sheeran
 H Lupita Nyong'o

1. **H** Her **full name** is Lupita Amondi Nyong'o. She was born in Mexico and her parents gave her a Spanish name which **is short for** Guadalupe.
2. ☐ He was an English writer, poet and university professor, and author of *The Lord of the Rings*. His full **initials** were J.R.R.T, but he was known as Ronald to his family.
3. ☐ Her **maiden name** was Sklodowska, but she was awarded the Nobel Prize under her **married name**.
4. ☐ Her name comes from her childhood **nickname** of 'Smiley'. She **changed her name** legally, from Destiny, in 2008.
5. ☐ After she became a famous novelist, she published detective stories under the **pseudonym** Robert Galbraith.
6. ☐ She is an award-winning actress who **is named after** a city near where she was born, in the state of Minnesota, USA.
7. ☐ His **first name** is James, after his father, but his family used his **middle name** to avoid confusion.
8. ☐ His first three albums are called + (*Plus*), x (*Multiply*), and ÷ (*Divide*). His name is Edward, but he**'s called** Ed **for short**.

b 🔊 1.2 Listen and check.

c Tell a partner about someone you know who…
- has a nickname.
- is named after a place.
- is named after a famous person.
- is called something for short.
- has a very old-fashioned name.
- has changed his / her name.

2 PRONUNCIATION
vowel sounds

a 🔊 1.3 Look at the first names in the chart. Listen and (circle) the name which doesn't have the sound in the sound picture.

1	🐟	Chris Bill Linda Diana	5	e	Adele Edward Leo Jessica
2	🐑	Peter Steve Emily Eve	6	eɪ	Sam Grace James Kate
3	æ	Alex Amy Andrew Anna	7	əʊ	Tony Joe Nicole Sophie
4	ɔː	George Paula Charlotte Sean	8	aɪ	Caroline Mia Mike Simon

b With a partner, decide if the names in **a** are men's names, women's names, or both. Write **M**, **W**, or **B** next to each name. Are any of them short for another name?

c 🔵 **Communication** Middle names quiz **p.106** Do the quiz.

3 READING

a With a partner, guess which countries or regions these names are from. Do you think they are first names or surnames?

| Yeon Seok | Rakhmaninov | López Ramírez |
| Aarushi | Li | Abdul Ahad | Jones |

b Read the article and check your answers to **a**. Are the first names from the list male or female?

c Read the article again. In which country or countries…?
1 does the surname come before the first name
2 do people have no surname
3 do people have more than one surname
4 do people have a middle name connected to their father's name
5 do some people stop using the surname they were born with
6 are people given names depending on when they were born

d What is the naming custom in your country? Has it changed over the years? Do you think it ought to change?

4 LISTENING & SPEAKING

a 🔊 1.4 Listen to four people talking about their name. For each person, write their name and tick (✓) if they are happy with it.

b Listen again and answer the questions for each person.
1 Why did their parents choose that name for them?
2 Do they have a nickname?
3 Would they like to change their name?

c Answer the questions in groups.

> What's your first name?
> Why did your parents call you that?
> Do you have a middle name?
> Do you have a nickname, or are you called something for short?
> Do you use your initials or your full name when you sign your name?

> Do you like your name? Why (not)? Would you like to change it? What to?
> Are there any names you don't like at all? Why do you dislike them?
> Do you think it's an advantage or a disadvantage to…?
> – have a very long name
> – have a very unusual name
> – be named after a celebrity

Naming customs around the world

1 **KOREA** Names in Korea are written with the surname first, and the first name usually has two parts. So, if Yeon Seok has the surname Lee, his name is written Lee Yeon Seok. Two-part first names are never shortened; that is, Lee Yeon Seok will always be called Yeon Seok, not Yeon.

2 **RUSSIA** Russian names have three parts: a first name, a patronymic (a middle name based on the father's first name), and the father's surname. If Viktor Aleksandrovich Rakhmaninov has two children, his son's name might be Mikhail Viktorevich Rakhmaninov and his daughter's name might be Svetlana Viktorevna Rakhmaninova (the 'a' at the end of all three names shows that she is female).

3 **SPANISH-SPEAKING COUNTRIES** In most Spanish-speaking countries, people have a first name (sometimes in two parts, e.g. Maria José, Juan Carlos) and two surnames, their father's and their mother's, for example, Maria José López Ramírez. In Spain, traditionally the father's surname goes first, followed by the mother's, but nowadays the order can be reversed. However, both surnames are always used and on any form, people will be asked for their surnames, not their surname.

4 **INDIA** India has many religions and languages which influence the naming customs. Hindu first names are usually based on the position of the planets at the date and time of birth, but the names are often shortened by family and friends. For example, a brother and sister may have the formal names Aditya and Aarushi, but family and friends may call them Adi and Ashi for short.

5 **CHINA** Chinese names are made up of three 'characters': a one-character surname followed by a two-character first name, e.g. Li Xiu Ying. A child's official name is used for their birth certificate and for school, but Chinese children often have a different name that is used among friends and classmates.

6 **AFGHANISTAN** Afghan names traditionally consist of only a first name. Male first names are usually Arabic double names, e.g. Abdul Ahad, and women are generally given Persian names, e.g. Jasmine. Surnames are chosen only when needed. Commonly, this is when people have contact with the Western world. The surname may be related to the tribe the person comes from, their place of birth, or their profession, e.g. 'Doctor'. This may result in people within the same family having different surnames.

7 **THE UK** Since the 15th century, British women have taken their husband's surname when they get married, so when Sophie Jones marries Peter Elliot, she becomes Mrs Sophie Elliot. However, 14% of married women now choose to keep their maiden name. If they do so, couples sometimes then combine their surnames for their children, so if Sophie decided to keep the surname Jones, their children might have the surname Jones-Elliot or Elliot-Jones.

7

5 GRAMMAR pronouns

a Talk to a partner. What are the two most popular brand names in your country for phones, sportswear, and cars? Do you know what country the brands are from, or what the names mean?

b Read about how the Kindle got its name. Do you think it's a good name? Why (not)?

> **The Kindle eBook reader** first appeared in 2007, and since then, millions of **them** have been sold. But how did **it** get its unusual name? Amazon's founder, Jeff Bezos, asked an American designer, Michael Cronan, to think of a name for the new device. Bezos told **him** that **he** didn't want a high-tech name because Amazon's customers loved traditional paper books. Cronan and his wife talked to each other about the warm, comfortable feelings people get from reading. Finally, he chose the word 'kindle', which means 'to light a fire'. Cronan thought that **it** would make people think of the excitement they feel when they are enjoying **their** favourite book. The name was also inspired by a line from the French novelist Victor Hugo: 'to read is to light a fire'.

c Read the text again. With a partner, say what the highlighted pronouns refer to.

d ⓖ p.132 Grammar Bank 1A

e ◉ 1.6 Listen and change the word order. Change the direct object to *it* or *them*.

1 ◁)) Give me **the book**.   (Give **it** to me.
2 ◁)) Give her **the shoes**. (Give **them** to her.

f Think of a couple you know well (friends or family). Tell your partner about them. Give the information below and anything else you know about them. Try to get all the pronouns right!

> names   jobs   children   pets
> appearance   personality   how they met

> I'm going to tell you about my neighbours. **His** name is Mario and **hers** is Sara. **She**'s a writer and **he**'s an accountant. **They** don't have any children, but **they** have a dog. **Its** name is Beppo…

6 LISTENING

a Look at the brand names in the photos. What do you associate with these brands? How do you think the names are pronounced in English?

b ◉ 1.7 Listen and check the pronunciation. Which ones are pronounced differently in your language?

c Work in pairs. Which of the brand names, A–H, do you think these are? Don't write the letters yet.

1 ___ It means 'three stars' in the local language.
2 ___ It means 'snow white' in Latin.
3 ___ It's a combination of three words.
4 ___ It's named after a character in a book.
5 ___ It's a translation of the name of a Viking king.
6 ___ It's named after a Greek goddess.
7 ___ They are named after the people who started the companies.

d ◉ 1.8 Now listen to a radio programme about naming and match photos A–H to 1–7 in **c**. Did you guess them correctly?

e Listen again and answer the questions.
1 What two words does the name Microsoft come from?
2 In what year was the name Samsung chosen?
3 What was Nike's original name?
4 Why did the Starbucks founders want a name beginning *St-*?
5 What two Viking letters is the Bluetooth symbol made of?

f Think of some popular brands from your country. Do you know where the names come from?

7 SPEAKING

a *Kickstarter.com* is a website that helps people raise money for creative projects, including new product ideas. Read about one product from the website. Do you think it's a good idea? Why (not)?

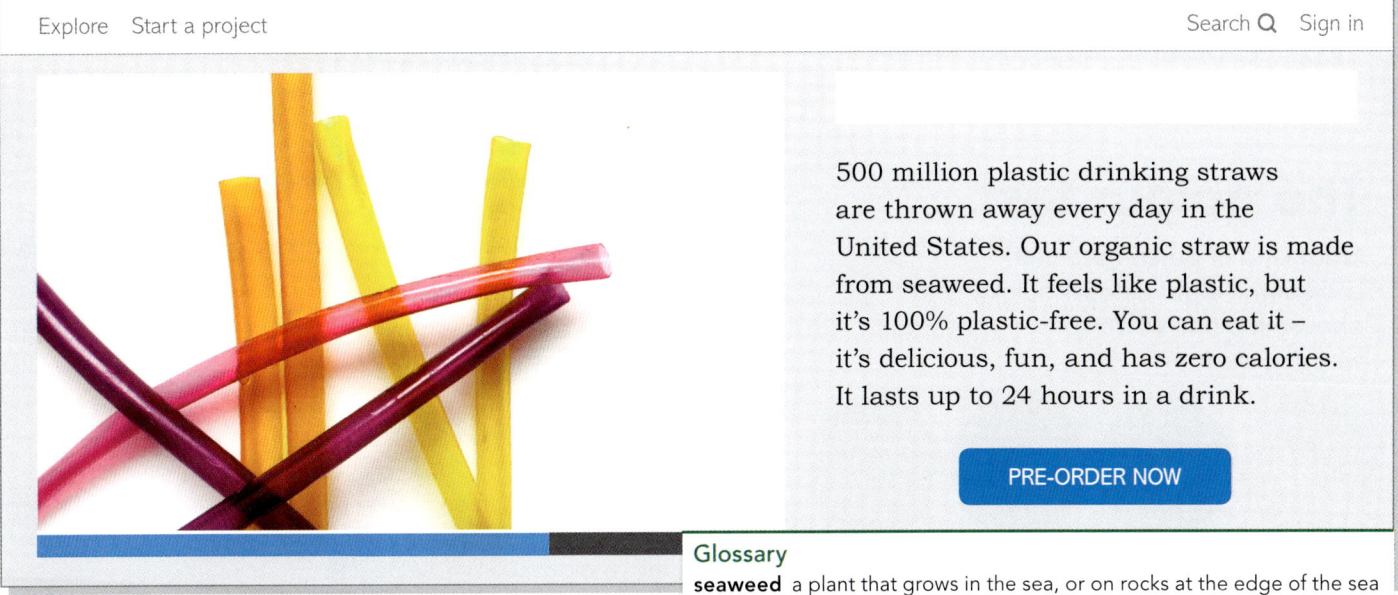

Explore   Start a project   Search 🔍 Sign in

500 million plastic drinking straws are thrown away every day in the United States. Our organic straw is made from seaweed. It feels like plastic, but it's 100% plastic-free. You can eat it – it's delicious, fun, and has zero calories. It lasts up to 24 hours in a drink.

PRE-ORDER NOW

Glossary
seaweed a plant that grows in the sea, or on rocks at the edge of the sea

b With a partner, look at some possible names for the product in **a**. Which name do you think is the best? What aspects of the product does it highlight?

Diet straw   Eco-straw   Lolistraw   Seastraw

c Read about three more products from the website. In small groups, invent a name for each product. Look at the photos and the highlighted words and phrases in the product descriptions, and think about…

- what the product is for.
- why it's special.
- how you want people to feel about the product.
- the sound and length of the name.

🔍 **Making suggestions**
What about…?   How about…?
We could call it…

Accepting suggestions
That's a good idea.
Yes, let's call it that.

Rejecting suggestions
I think it's too…
That's not bad, but…

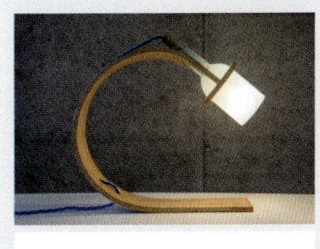

We make nice things that are good for the planet. We created this amazing lamp for a student competition. It produces warm light from a low energy bulb. The lamp is made from a wine bottle from a local restaurant and oak wood from local trees. The lamp is very easy to take apart and all the parts are entirely recyclable.

These are the first snack bars that improve your brainpower. They are high in healthy fats and low in carbohydrates and are made only from natural ingredients. They come in three delicious flavours using nuts, fruit, and chocolate; much better for you than snacks with lots of salt, sugar, or caffeine.

Our simple building system is for creative people of all ages. You can make almost anything you can think of, in either 2D or 3D, from a picture or a model, to large, complex sculptures, and even furniture. The small magnetic coloured blocks click together easily and are available in a wide range of modern colours. Use it in your workplace, at home, or simply as a fun hobby. Start small, but dream big.

d Present your names to the rest of the class. Have a class vote to choose the best names.

Go online to review the lesson

9

1B Life in colour

> What's your favourite colour?
>
> I really like bright blue.

G adjectives V adjective suffixes P word stress

1 VOCABULARY adjective suffixes

a Do the colour test.

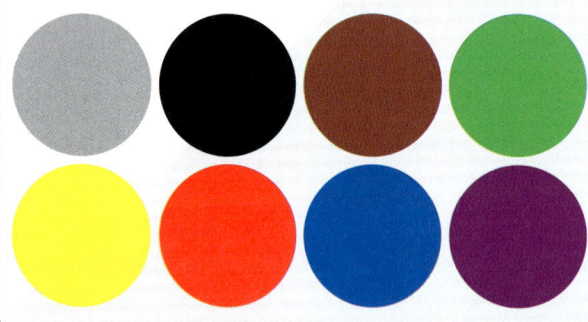

The colour test

What kind of person are you?
Look at the eight colours quickly and choose the one you like best. Think about why you like it.

b **G Communication** The colour test p.106
Read about the colour you chose.

c Answer the questions in pairs.
  1 What colour did you choose in the test? Do you both agree with your results?
  2 What colour(s) do you wear most? Do you think they say anything about your personality? Are there any colours you would never wear?

> **Talking about results**
> According to the test, I'm…
> It says that I'm…
> That's quite accurate. / That's definitely me.
> That's not me. / That isn't accurate at all.

d Complete some adjectives from the colour test with the correct ending: *-able*, *-ate*, *-ive*, *-ous*, or *-ful*.

  am**bi**ti_____   **pas**sion_____   **sen**sit_____
  soci_____   suc**cess**_____

e **V** p.152 **Vocabulary Bank** Adjective suffixes

2 PRONUNCIATION word stress

> **Word stress on adjectives formed with suffixes**
> When an adjective is formed from a root word and a suffix, the stress is always on a syllable of the root word, and not on the suffix, e.g. *rely* – *re**li**able*. The stress stays the same when a negative prefix is added, e.g. *unre**li**able*.

a Underline the stressed syllable in the **bold** adjectives in the questions below.
  1 Do you think you are a **cre|a|tive** person? Why (not)?
  2 Are you very **po|sse|ssive** of anything, e.g. your phone or your laptop? Why don't you like other people using it?
  3 Have you ever felt **en|vi|ous** of a brother or sister? Why (not)?
  4 Were you a **re|be|lli|ous** child or teenager? What kinds of things did you do?
  5 Who is the most **gla|mo|rous** person you know? What makes him / her like that?
  6 What are your most **com|for|ta|ble** clothes? When do you wear them?
  7 What kind of **un|heal|thy** food do you really like eating?
  8 What do you think is a **sui|ta|ble** present to take if somebody invites you for a meal at their house?
  9 What's the most **im|pre|ssive** monument or building you've ever seen? Why did you like it so much?
  10 Have you ever been to a very **lu|xu|ri|ous** hotel or restaurant? Where? Was it worth the money?

b 🔊 1.12 Listen to the adjectives and check. Then listen again and repeat them.

c Work with a partner. **A** ask **B** questions 1–5. Then **B** ask **A** questions 6–10.

3 LISTENING

a What colour do you associate with the following? Why?

  calmness   happiness   luck   power   safety

b Read some facts about colour. In pairs, discuss which colour from the list could go in each gap.

  black   blue   brown   green   orange
  pink   purple red   white   yellow

10

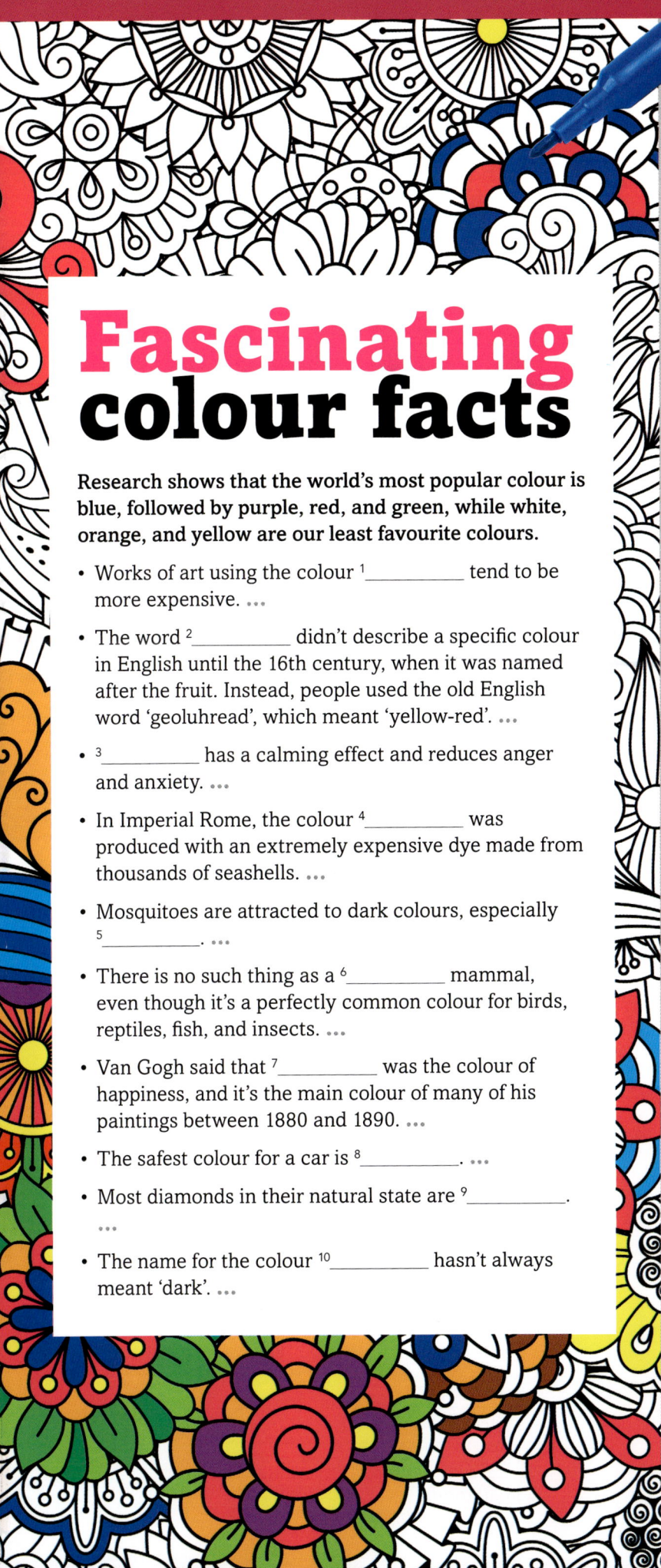

Fascinating colour facts

Research shows that the world's most popular colour is blue, followed by purple, red, and green, while white, orange, and yellow are our least favourite colours.

- Works of art using the colour ¹_____ tend to be more expensive. ...

- The word ²_____ didn't describe a specific colour in English until the 16th century, when it was named after the fruit. Instead, people used the old English word 'geoluhread', which meant 'yellow-red'. ...

- ³_____ has a calming effect and reduces anger and anxiety. ...

- In Imperial Rome, the colour ⁴_____ was produced with an extremely expensive dye made from thousands of seashells. ...

- Mosquitoes are attracted to dark colours, especially ⁵_____. ...

- There is no such thing as a ⁶_____ mammal, even though it's a perfectly common colour for birds, reptiles, fish, and insects. ...

- Van Gogh said that ⁷_____ was the colour of happiness, and it's the main colour of many of his paintings between 1880 and 1890. ...

- The safest colour for a car is ⁸_____. ...

- Most diamonds in their natural state are ⁹_____. ...

- The name for the colour ¹⁰_____ hasn't always meant 'dark'. ...

c 🔊 1.13 Listen to a podcast about colour and check your answers to **b**. How many did you get right?

d Listen again. Which colour does the speaker say…?
1 can be seen clearly in most types of weather
2 isn't used to describe a hair colour
3 originally meant 'to shine'
4 might be seen more strongly by someone who has a certain illness
5 is not a good colour to wear outside on a summer evening
6 could once only be worn by a very powerful person
7 is a lucky colour in some countries
8 might be a good colour to use in a hospital
9 is the colour of something found in South Africa in 1985
10 certain types of animals can't see

e Which facts might make you think more carefully about your choice of colours?

4 SPEAKING

Talk to a partner.

What colours do these words remind you of? Can you explain why?

spring   summer   autumn   winter
work   holiday   money   love   hate

What colours would you choose for these things? Why?

smart shoes   a phone case   a bag
a suitcase   a car   a sofa

Do you know anyone who…?
- wears very colourful clothes
- never wears colourful clothes
- dyes his / her hair an unusual colour
- wears one colour most of the time
- is colour-blind (unable to see the difference between some colours, especially red and green)

What are they like?

5 GRAMMAR adjectives

a Complete some more colour facts with a word from the list.

as   in   more   most   much   ones   than   the

1 According to a recent survey, the world's _____ popular colour is blue.
2 White meat is considered healthier _____ red meat.
3 Black tulips are often more expensive than pink _____.
4 The blue whale is the largest creature _____ the world.
5 Insurance for a red car can be a bit _____ expensive than for other colours.
6 White tigers are _____ less common than ordinary tigers.
7 Black tea isn't generally as good for you _____ green tea.
8 According to a survey, _____ most popular car colour in Europe is white.

b **G** p.133 Grammar Bank 1B

c Talk to a partner. Choose three topics or questions from each section.

COMPARE THEM!
1 restaurant food and home-made food
2 being an only child and having lots of brothers and sisters
3 people from the north and south of your country
4 walking or running outdoors and going to the gym
5 studying in the morning and studying at night
6 going on holiday abroad and going on holiday in your country

I think restaurant food is better than my home-made food because I'm not a very good cook, but it's much more expensive and it usually isn't as healthy…

EXTREMES!
1 What is ____ film you've ever seen? (sad) Did you cry?
2 Which sportsperson do you think is ____ role model? (positive) Why do you think so?
3 Which is ____ tourist attraction in your town or area? (popular) Which do *you* think is ____? (good)
4 What's the ____ place you've ever been to? (far) Why did you go there?
5 Who is ____ person you know? (generous) Why do you think so?
6 Which subject did you find ____ at school? (boring) Why didn't you like it?

I think the saddest film I've ever seen is Brokeback Mountain. I've seen it twice and I cried both times.

6 READING

a Look at the photos of three rooms. Which colour scheme do you like best? What do you think are the best colours for a) a bedroom, b) a bathroom, c) a study?

b Read the article quickly. Which room in **a** most closely follows the advice in the article?

c Read the article again. Complete the chart for each room. Which three colours are not always suitable for bedrooms?

	Suitable colours
a bedroom	
a living room	
a dining room	
a kitchen	
a study	
a bathroom	

How colour affects our mood

Since ancient times, colour has been linked to the way we think and feel. For early humans, the red of fire signalled danger. Later, artists used coloured glass in church windows to represent different feelings, for example, green symbolized hope. In modern times, the colours we use to paint the walls in our houses can affect our mood. So which colours should we use when we are decorating?

Red is an optimistic colour. It's a good colour for a dining room, because it makes people feel sociable. It stimulates conversation and makes you feel hungry. But as it's a strong colour, it can sometimes be a bit too much, and even give people headaches. You could just paint one wall red, or use it for accessories such as lamps and curtains. However, never use red in a baby's bedroom, as it may stop the baby from sleeping. **Pink**, on the other hand, is often used in bedrooms. It's traditionally the colour of love – a pale shade can be peaceful and restful, while a darker shade can suggest passion. Some people think it's a very 'girlie' colour, so adding in areas of dark grey or black to this colour scheme can help make it more generally attractive.

If you want a warm, comforting effect, try **orange**. It's also good for dining rooms, as it's said that it helps you digest your food. However, like red, it's a strong colour and can make a room look smaller, so only use it in a room that gets plenty of light. A colour that's great for smaller spaces, on the other hand, is **yellow**. It's a happy, energetic colour, and is a good colour for a kitchen, as apparently, it discourages insects! It's not very restful though, so it's best not to use it for a bedroom.

Purple is good for rooms where you work, for example, a study or a bedroom, because it's a very creative, stimulating colour. However, it's another colour that can make it difficult for people to relax after a busy day, so if you use it in a bedroom, it's a good idea to combine it with a lighter shade or another colour. **Blue** is also suitable for a study, because it helps you to think and concentrate, as well as being calm and restful. It's a popular colour for bathrooms, and bedrooms too, where a lot of people spend 'thinking time'. Another calming colour is **green**, and it's also good for a bedroom or living room. Green makes people feel relaxed and less stressed, but it can make them lazy, so if you don't want people to go to sleep on the sofa, choose cushions and carpets in a bright colour like red or orange.

For people who prefer neutral colours, **brown** can be a good choice. Although it can be boring, it's a safe, reliable colour in a living room, and you can paint one wall green or blue if you want a bit of extra mental stimulation! Other neutral colours, like **white**, **grey**, and **beige**, are always in fashion. White is the most flexible. It's safe and clean, and you can add any other colours to make the room look brighter. However, white isn't great for a bedroom if you want to relax there – a survey showed that people with a white bedroom tended to work in bed at least three times a week. Finally, the most dramatic, and perhaps eccentric, choice of bedroom wall colour is **black**. In fact, it works in any room in moderation, for example, one black wall.

d Talk to a partner. Why does the article suggest…?
1 only using red for one wall
2 adding grey or black to a pink room
3 only using orange in a light room
4 using yellow in a kitchen
5 combining different shades of purple in a bedroom
6 having red or orange accessories in a green living room
7 having a green or blue wall in a brown living room
8 not using white for a bedroom
9 using black

e Look at some adjectives from the article to describe colours. Match them to 1–3.

pale / light green   bright green
dark green

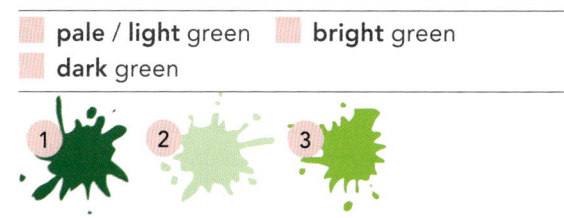

Use the adjectives to describe these colours.

beige   cream   khaki   maroon
navy   scarlet   turquoise

f Are there any rooms in your house that are painted the 'right' or 'wrong' colours, according to the article? Do you think you should change them?

7 SPEAKING & WRITING

a You're going to describe your favourite room in your house to a partner. Think about these things.
- why it's your favourite room
- the colours of the walls and accessories, e.g. curtains, blinds, cushions, carpets
- the furniture that's in the room, e.g. sofa, armchairs, etc.
- any paintings or posters
- what you can see from the window
- anything else in the room

While you listen to your partner, ask questions to help you imagine what their room is like.

b W p.115 Writing Describing a room Write a description of your favourite room.

Go online to review the lesson

EPISODE 1 Practical English A bad start

reporting lost luggage

1 ▶ JENNY IS BACK IN LONDON

a **1.17** Jenny works in New York for the magazine *NewYork 24seven*. She has just arrived in London. Watch or listen to her talking to Andrew. How does he help her? What problem does she have at the end?

b Watch or listen again. Mark the sentences **T** (true) or **F** (false). Correct the **F** sentences.
1 Jenny is in the UK for business and pleasure.
2 Andrew was on holiday in New York.
3 Jenny's husband (Rob) is working in San Francisco.
4 Andrew gives Jenny back her laptop.
5 He introduces himself, and says his surname is Paton.
6 Jenny's flight to London was delayed.

Why do you think a man was watching Jenny and Andrew? What do you think he is going to do?

2 ▶ REPORTING LOST LUGGAGE

a **1.18** Watch or listen to Jenny reporting her missing suitcase. Answer the questions.
1 How long is Jenny staying in the UK?
2 What does her suitcase look like?
3 What's in it?
4 How long will it probably take for Jenny to get her case back?

b Watch or listen again. Complete the **You hear** phrases.

You hear	You say
Can I help you?	Yeah, my suitcase hasn't arrived.
¹_____ flight were you on?	Flight RT163 from JFK.
I'll take your ²_____ and then I can issue you with a reference number. Can I have your name, please?	My name's Jenny Zielinski. That's Z-I-E-L-I-N-S-K-I.
And you're a ³_____ to the UK.	That's right.
How ⁴_____ are you staying for?	Ten days.
OK. How many ⁵_____ are you missing?	Just one – a suitcase.
Can you ⁶_____ it for me?	Well, it's kind of greyish blue…and hard plastic, I think.
And what ⁷_____ is it?	Oh, it's medium size, like this. And it has wheels.
Anything else?	Yeah, there's a small lock and a label with my name and phone number on it.
And what was ⁸_____ the suitcase?	Just about everything! Clothes, toiletries, all my personal belongings, really.
Can I have your ⁹_____ in the UK?	Just a minute. It's The Grange, Marsh Lane, Long Crendon, Oxfordshire.
And a ¹⁰_____ number?	Yes, it's 001 202 494 012.
And finally, can you ¹¹_____ this?	Of course. Do you have any idea where it is? I mean, do you think it's still in New York?
It's possible. We're very ¹²_____ for the inconvenience. Here's your reference number. You can track the progress of your luggage ¹³_____, or just give us a call. But we should be able to get it back to you within 24 hours.	That'd be great. Thank you.

c ◉ 1.19 Watch or listen and repeat some of the **You say** phrases. Copy the rhythm and intonation.

d Practise the conversation in **b** with a partner.

e 👥 In pairs, role-play the conversation.

> **A** You are a passenger on flight BA1722 from San Francisco. You have just landed at London Heathrow Airport and your luggage hasn't arrived, so you go to Lost Luggage to report it. **B** works at the Lost Luggage counter. Use the **Useful language** box to help you to describe your luggage.
>
> **B** You work at the Lost Luggage counter at London Heathrow Airport. **A**'s luggage hasn't arrived. Take **A**'s details and give a reference number.

f Swap roles.

> 🔍 **Useful language: describing luggage**
> **Type of luggage:** *suitcase / case, sports bag, backpack / rucksack*
> **Colour:** *It's dark / light / greyish blue, etc.*
> **Material:** *It's made of hard plastic / canvas / synthetic material, etc.*
> **Size:** *It's small / medium size / large.*
> **Extras:** *It has four wheels / a logo / a label, etc.*

3 ▶ AT HENRY'S HOUSE

a ◉ 1.20 Watch or listen to the rest of Jenny's day. What other problem does she have?

b Watch or listen again. Answer the questions.
1 Is Rob having a good time in Alaska? Why (not)?
2 What is Jenny drinking?
3 Whose computer is she using? Why?
4 Who is Luke?
5 When is Jenny going to see him? Why?
6 What is Henry going to lend Jenny?

Who is Selina Lavelle? Why do you think Grant (the man who was following them) is watching Henry's house?

c Look at the **Social English** phrases. Can you remember any of the missing words?

> 💬 **Social English**
> 1 Henry (And) it's _____ to see you.
> 2 Jenny It's _____ to see you too.
> 3 Henry No, no, _____ me take that.
> 4 Jenny It's weird, _____ it?
> 5 Rob I really _____ you.
> 6 Jenny Oh no! That's _____.
> 7 Rob It's not your _____, is it?
> 8 Rob Oh _____! You'll look great in those, Jenny!

d ◉ 1.21 Watch or listen and complete the phrases. Then watch or listen again and repeat.

e Complete conversations A–G with **Social English** phrases 1–8. Then practise them with a partner.

A	Nobody's answering the door. How strange.	Yes.
B	▢ It's too heavy for you to carry.	Thanks so much.
C	Did you know there was a fire at the station last night?	No, I didn't. ▢ Was anybody hurt?
D	I'm in New York today, and then I fly to Atlanta for a few days.	When will you be home? ▢
E	Do you like my new bag?	▢ It's really beautiful!
F	I'm exhausted. First I missed my train, and then the next one was delayed.	Poor you. ▢
G	Hi! Welcome back! ▢	▢ You're looking very well!

CAN YOU...?
▢ report lost luggage
▢ greet someone you haven't seen for some time
▢ sympathize with someone about a problem

Go online to watch the video, review the lesson, and check your progress

2A Get ready! Get set! Go!

> What time does your flight leave?
>
> At 9.00. I'm getting a taxi to the airport at 6.00.

G present tenses | V packing | P /s/, /z/, and /ɪz/

1 VOCABULARY packing

a What type of holiday is a 'city break'? If you could go on one this month, where would you most like to go to?

b Imagine you're going on the city break in **a**. You can only take a small suitcase. Talk to a partner. Which of the things in the photo below would you definitely pack?

> I'd definitely pack trainers, an umbrella,...

c **V** p.153 **Vocabulary Bank** Packing

d Now imagine you're going on a beach holiday. Make a list of the ten things you would definitely pack. Then compare your list with a partner. What differences are there?

2 PRONUNCIATION /s/, /z/, and /ɪz/

a Look at the words below. What sound do the pink letters have, or ?

slippers   scissors

b ◆ 2.4 Listen and check. Practise saying the words.

c What sound do the pink letters have in these words? Write five words in each column.

batteries   cards   flip-flops   passport   pyjamas
razor   swimsuit   sunscreen   toothpaste   visa

🐍	🦓

d ◆ 2.5 Listen and check. Practise saying the words. In what position is *s* never pronounced /z/?

e Circle the words where the final *-es* is pronounced /ɪz/.

beaches   brushes   cases   clothes   headphones
magazines   shoes   sunglasses

f ◆ 2.6 Listen and check. Practise saying the words. When is *-es* pronounced /ɪz/?

3 LISTENING

a Have you ever forgotten to pack something really important when you went on holiday (e.g. a document)? What was it? What did you do?

b Read the introduction to an article. What do you think are the top three things that British travellers most often forget to pack?

| Home | News | Sport | TV | Health | Science | **Travel** | Money |

British people spend millions of pounds replacing forgotten holiday items

By TRAVEL REPORTER

41% of people forget to pack at least one essential item when they go on holiday, according to a survey of British travellers. In total, almost 15 million important holiday items are left behind each year, and travellers spend £118 million buying these things again once they reach their destination.

Oh no, I forgot my charger.

Adapted from the Daily Mail

c ◉ 2.7 Listen to the top ten items in reverse order, and write them down. Did you guess the top three correctly?

d You're going to listen to a travel journalist giving advice about how to pack. In pairs, try to predict what the missing words are in tips 1–8.
1 Don't pack _____ _____.
2 Keep some space in your suitcase for _____.
3 Pack in the right _____.
4 Make sure your _____ arrive looking good.
5 Keep your _____ and _____ together.
6 Use _____ bags.
7 Think about airport _____.
8 Buy a travel _____.

e ◉ 2.8 Listen to the tips and check. Did you predict any of them correctly?

f ◉ 2.9 Now listen to all the journalist's advice and answer the questions.
1 What should you do with one third of the clothes you were planning to pack?
2 What kinds of things might you want to buy on holiday?
3 Where should you pack the clothes you're planning to wear on the first day of your holiday?
4 How should you pack a) T-shirts, b) shirts?
5 Where should you put your chargers and adaptors?
6 What should you pack inside your shoes?
7 What should you pack at the top of your hand luggage?
8 Why is it important to also print out documents that you have on your phone?

g Do you already do any of these things? Which tip do you think is the most useful?

4 SPEAKING

a Read the questionnaire and think about your answers.

How good are you at preparing for a holiday?

 Planning
- How much research do you do before you decide where to go, where to stay, and how to travel? What websites do you use?
- How far in advance do you book flights and accommodation? If you're travelling by plane, do you check your luggage allowance?
- Do you usually ask people to look after your house (or pet, plants, etc.) while you're away? Do you try to leave the house clean and tidy before you go?
- If you are travelling by car, do you always get your car serviced before you leave? Do you plan the route in advance?

 Packing
- When do you start packing? Do you make a list of what to pack?
- Do you usually pack too much or too little? Have you ever had to pay for excess baggage?
- Have you ever packed anything fragile which was broken when you arrived? How well had you packed it?
- Where do you normally put important travel documents?

✈ **Leaving**
- How early do you like to arrive at the airport or station? Have you ever missed a flight, train, or bus?
- Have you ever realized at the last moment that one of your travel documents was out of date? What did you do?
- How far in advance do you normally check in for a flight?

b Answer the questions with a partner. Ask for more information and give examples. Which of you is better prepared for a holiday?

I don't do much research. I usually ask friends to recommend somewhere to go. Then I book a cheap flight and a room on Airbnb.

17

5 GRAMMAR present tenses

a Caroline's going on holiday to Ibiza. Circle the correct verb form to complete her messages to her friends. Tick (✓) if both forms are possible.

> Just arrived at the airport. ¹ *I wear / I'm wearing* a sun hat and flip-flops and ² *I look like / I'm looking like* a typical tourist. Ibiza, here I come!
> 08.58

> Oh no! I can't find my boarding pass! My flight ³ *boards / is boarding* at 11.00…30 minutes from now…
> 10.30

> Great news. Just found my boarding pass in the book ⁴ *I read / I'm reading*. ⁵ *I have / I'm having* a quick drink in the bar.
> 10.35

b Compare with a partner. Explain why you think each form is correct.

c **G** p.134 Grammar Bank 2A

d **C** Communication Caroline's holiday plans A p.107 B p.111 Ask and answer questions to complete a holiday calendar.

e Make questions with the present simple or present continuous. Then ask and answer with a partner.

Holidays
- / you / prefer summer holidays or winter holidays? Why?
- Which places / you / think about going to for your next holiday?
- Why / you / want to go there?

Weekends
- What / you / usually do at the weekend?
- What / you / do this weekend?

Today
- What time / this class / finish? Where / you / go after class today?
- What / you / do / this evening? Where / you / have dinner?

6 READING

a Are there any things that you do on holiday that you don't usually do in normal life? Think about the things below.

activities   daily routine   food and drink
shopping   spending money

> *I don't usually do much exercise, but when I'm on holiday, I go for a lot of walks, and if I'm at the beach, I swim every day.*

b Read the article once. Does it mention any of the things you answered in **a**?

We only do them on holiday

We all have them. Strange little rituals that have become an important part of any holiday, and if you don't do them, it somehow doesn't feel quite right…

Go on an airport shopping spree
This could be because you like a bargain. It could also be because you get to the airport and realize that you packed at the last minute and ¹☐. Whatever the reason, the hour before your flight is usually spent buying more travel adaptors, sweets, another pair of headphones, and unnecessary clothes.

Pay too much for hotel extras
You never eat macadamia nuts at home. But when you find them in a little jar beside the minibar, you have to eat them. Whether it's a tiny but ridiculously expensive tub of Pringles, or an overpriced and mediocre cocktail at the bar, you don't seem to have a problem paying far too much for little extras at your hotel. It may be because you're tired after the journey, or just because you're on holiday, but suddenly ²☐.

Steal things (sort of)
Of course you don't take bathrobes or towels, but after being charged so much for those macadamia nuts, you try to get your revenge on the hotel by taking little things – espresso capsules, shampoo, shower gel…sometimes even a sewing kit, that ³☐.

Talk to strangers

On holiday, suddenly everyone wants to make new friends. How many times have you started talking to the people at the next table at a restaurant in your town? Probably never. But walk into a beachside taverna, and ⁴☐.

Change your eating habits

Your normal breakfast routine goes completely out the window. Goodbye cornflakes, hello smoked salmon, eggs, toast, and a big slice of cake from the hotel buffet. You're also thrilled when you find strange and exciting foods at the local supermarket and you want to try them all, even though ⁵☐.

Sleep in the afternoon

Maybe it's because the shops have closed. Maybe ⁶☐. Maybe it's all that breakfast. Whatever the reason, afternoon naps only become a fixture twice a year: at Christmas and on holiday.

Buy pointless postcards, and other rubbish

There must be millions of postcards out there that people buy and never send. They're a great reminder of your holiday, but when you get home, you put them in a shoebox under the bed and never look at them again. You also have the urge to buy cheap souvenirs from street stalls. 'A fridge magnet of the Eiffel Tower? A solar-powered Japanese sumo-wrestler figure?' 'Yes, sure, ⁷☐…'

Visit obscure museums

Can you imagine your partner suggesting a Saturday afternoon trip to the local ethnographical museum to see a wonderful new ceramics exhibition? Definitely not. But on a city break, suddenly the most obscure cultural attractions develop a magnetic pull. 'Darling, the guidebook says it's one of Hungary's six best museums, so ⁸☐…'

Adapted from the Daily Telegraph

c Read the article again. Complete it with phrases A–H.

A I'll take three
B it's too much sun
C you don't seem to care about prices
D we absolutely must go
E you aren't as prepared as you should be
F you aren't normally adventurous at home
G you'll never ever use
H you're suddenly super-sociable

d Look at the highlighted phrases. With a partner, try to explain what they mean in your own words.

e Talk to a partner. Do you ever do any of these things on holiday? Give examples and reasons why you do them.

7 SPEAKING

a Look at the pairs of holiday options in the box. On your own, decide which one you prefer in each pair, and think of reasons why.

Would you rather…?

have one long holiday		several short holidays
have a holiday abroad		in your own country
travel north		south
go somewhere you've been before		somewhere new
go on holiday with family	OR	with friends
stay in one place		travel around
stay in a hotel		rent a house or flat
have an active holiday		a relaxing holiday
see interesting monuments and museums		interesting wildlife and scenery
go somewhere where there are good shops		somewhere where there is good food

b Now compare in small groups. Explain your reasons. Do you all like the same kind of holiday?

> 🔍 **Expressing preferences**
> **I'd rather have** one long holiday.
> **I'd prefer to have** several short holidays.

8 WRITING

Ⓦ p.116 Writing Holiday messages Write a series of messages to post to friends.

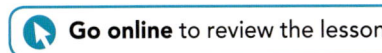

2B Go to checkout

> Where did you get your scarf?
> From a website that a friend of mine recommended.

G possessives **V** shops and services **P** r and final -r

1 GRAMMAR possessives

a Look at the photos. For each one, say:
When was the last time you bought one (or some)?
Did you buy them in a shop or online? Why?

b Are there any things in the photos that you would never buy online? Why not?

c Read sentences 1–6. Do they refer to shopping in a physical shop or shopping online?
1 Excuse me, could you tell me where to find childrens books?
2 I'm going to get Carlos present from Amazon. I know there's a book he wants.
3 When we've finished shopping, we're going to Martas – she lives near the shopping centre.
4 A Is this your husbands new car?
   B Yes. He got it on eBay – it was a fantastic bargain.
5 When my sisters sweater arrived, it was the wrong size, so she had to send it back.
6 My two daughters friends all shop at the new boutique on the corner – it's the 'in' place, apparently.

d With a partner, look at the highlighted words and phrases in c, and add an apostrophe (') in the correct place.

e **G** p.135 Grammar Bank 2B

2 PRONUNCIATION r and final -r

a ◉ 2.17 Listen and repeat the words and sound.

| receipt | room | children |
| parents | wrong | write |

b ◉ 2.18 Listen to the pairs of sentences. Then (circle) the correct word to complete the pronunciation rule.
1 a It's her shop. b It's her own shop.
2 a The bank's on the corner.
  b The bank's on the corner of the road.
3 a He's my brother. b He's my brother-in-law.
4 a Is that umbrella yours? b Is that your umbrella?
5 a It's our business. b It's our own business.

> **Final -r**
> Final -r is pronounced /r/ when the next word begins with a *vowel* / *consonant* sound.

c Listen again and practise saying the sentences.

d ◉ 2.19 Listen and write five sentences. Then listen again and mark where -r is pronounced /r/.

3 LISTENING

a Look at a list of things people love and hate about online shopping. Tick (✓) the things from each section that you strongly agree with. Compare with a partner.

Online shopping is here to stay
Do you love it or hate it – or both?

THINGS WE LOVE
- [ ] You don't have to carry heavy bags any more.
- [ ] It's easy to send presents to people.
- [ ] You can do your shopping from work without anyone noticing.
- [ ] You can buy things from shops that aren't near you.
- [ ] You can do your shopping in your pyjamas, when it's cold and raining outside.
- [ ] Things are often cheaper than if you buy them in a shop.
- [ ] You don't have to push your way through crowds of people.
- [ ] Online shops are open 24/7.

THINGS WE HATE
- [ ] You do less exercise and interact less with other people.
- [ ] You can't get advice from a specialist shop assistant.
- [ ] You can't feel things or see exactly what they look like.
- [ ] Your shopping is always delivered when you're out.
- [ ] Supermarkets often substitute an item you ordered for something you don't want.
- [ ] Things are often bigger or smaller than you wanted because you didn't read the detailed description.
- [ ] Clothes or shoes often don't fit, or don't suit you because you weren't able to try them on.
- [ ] If something isn't right, it can be a problem sending it back or getting it changed.

b ◆) 2.20 You're going to listen to five people talking about what they love or hate about online shopping. First, listen and complete some extracts. Are the phrases positive or negative?

1 It's just a huge _____.
2 It's so _____.
3 That's a real _____.
4 It was a real _____.
5 I _____ the fact that…
6 It's _____ being able to…
7 That's so _____.

c ◆) 2.21 Now listen to the people talking. Which 'loves' and 'hates' from the list in **a** does each speaker refer to? Write the speaker's number next to the things they mention.

d Listen again and answer the questions with the speaker's number.
Who…?
- [ ] likes knowing exactly when things he or she has bought are going to arrive
- [ ] once bought a large quantity of something by mistake
- [ ] has one particular item he or she often has to return
- [ ] enjoys looking on shopping websites
- [ ] thinks it's easier to deal with problems in real shops

e Are there any other things you love or hate about online shopping?

4 SPEAKING

Choose three of the topics and tell a partner about them. Give as much information as you can.

Talk about a time when you…	made a mistake and bought the wrong thing online	bought a present for someone online
had to wait a long time for something to be delivered	ordered something that didn't fit and had to send it back	bought something online much more cheaply than in a shop
found that something you bought online was very different from what you were expecting		ordered something online that never arrived

🔍 **Showing interest**
Ask questions about what people say to show interest and keep the conversation going, or react to what they're saying.

Really?   Then what happened?
What was it like?   That's amazing!
What did you do?   How annoying!

21

5 VOCABULARY & SPEAKING shops and services

a Look at the photos. Where do you think these people work? What do they sell?

b **V** p.154 **Vocabulary Bank** Shops and services

c Talk to a partner. What's the difference between…?
1 a stationer's and a newsagent's
2 a dry-cleaner's and a launderette
3 an estate agent's and a travel agent's
4 'the shop's closing' and 'the shop's closing down'

d Interview a partner with the questions below.

My local shops

1 What kinds of shops are there near where you live? Do you use them much? If not, where do you usually do your shopping?
2 What shops have opened up or closed down near you? Are you pleased or sorry about it?
3 What chain stores are there near you (H&M, Zara, etc.)? Do you shop there? How do you feel about them? Are they in competition with local shops?
4 Are there many small independent shops in your country? Do you think it's important to support them? Why (not)?
5 Do you have charity shops where you live? What kinds of things do they sell? Have you ever bought anything from one?

6 READING

a Look at the title of the article and the photo. What do you think the article will be about?

b Read the article once. Were you right?

c Read the article again. Choose a, b, or c.
1 People queued outside Waterstones in Piccadilly because they wanted to _____.
 a take part in a Harry Potter book event
 b meet the author of the Harry Potter books
 c buy the fifth Harry Potter book
2 Waterstones was also celebrating the fact that _____.
 a a wizard was visiting the store
 b the chain was now making money
 c the bookshop owned by James Daunt was closing down
3 One of the things Daunt did to transform Waterstones was to _____.
 a choose the books himself
 b make stores smaller
 c give stores more independence
4 Daunt thinks a good bookseller should _____.
 a have read every book in their store
 b be able to recommend suitable books to customers
 c be able to copy what Amazon is doing
5 Daunt feels confident about the future of bookshops because he thinks that _____.
 a they provide something which online booksellers cannot
 b bookshops are the most important part of the community
 c online shopping will not last forever

d Look at the highlighted words and phrases from the article and their meanings. Can you remember the missing words? Find the phrases in the article and check your answers.
1 In many of the chain's 275 _____ across the UK
 = shops belonging to the same chain in different parts of the UK
2 it was _____ in profit
 = making money again
3 had many _____ customers
 = customers who always go to the same shop
4 his first task was to _____ costs
 = save money in order to increase profit
5 Waterstones _____ more than 150,000 titles
 = has (books) in the shop

e James Daunt says that 'people will always want to go to shops'. Do you agree? Why (not)?

22

David and Goliath, or Waterstones versus Amazon...

Queues outside the Waterstones bookshop in Piccadilly.

At 6.00 p.m. on Thursday, in Waterstones in Piccadilly, London, staff were running around with bowls of jelly beans and bottles of raspberry lemonade. Five minutes later, people of all ages started to come through the doors, some dressed up as characters from the books – a small girl even produced an owl cage! 'I'm reading the fifth book again at the moment', said 28-year-old Alex. 'This is the third event I've been to. Last year they transformed the second floor into Diagon Alley.' In many of the chain's 275 branches across the UK, similar scenes were taking place. 'Our first wizards have arrived for #harrypotterbooknight', tweeted staff at the Bradford store.

But Harry Potter night wasn't the only cause for celebration for staff and customers. The previous day, Waterstones had announced that it was back in profit for the first time since 2011, under the leadership of its very own wizard, James Daunt. Daunt was already a successful bookseller, who had many loyal customers. He was brought in to rescue the Waterstones chain when it was about to close down.

When Daunt took over Waterstones, his first task was to cut costs. Then he had to make the stores more attractive and improve the lighting. Coffee shops were opened inside the stores, and events were held, such as the now-famous Harry Potter nights, or talks by authors. But the biggest change was that Daunt gave each individual store the power to choose what books to sell, and to choose the prices for different books. This made a big difference. Sales went up because shops were stocking more books that appealed to local customers.

Another of his changes was training really knowledgeable staff. 'If a customer can tell me what was the last really good book they read, I know exactly what to sell them next,' Daunt says. Given that Waterstones stocks more than 150,000 titles, this is not an easy thing to do – but it is something that is helping Waterstones to differentiate itself from Amazon.

Daunt is optimistic about the future of bookshops. 'People love buying books,' he said. 'It's a physical pleasure that customers don't get when they shop online. If we keep creating shops that do that, it doesn't matter what goes on online. High streets and shops are part of the heart of the community. People will always want to go to shops.'

Glossary

David and Goliath a situation in which a weaker person fights a much stronger one; from a story in which a giant, Goliath, is killed by a boy, David, with a small stone
jelly bean a kind of small coloured sweet
Diagon Alley the name of a street full of shops in the Harry Potter stories
high street the main street of a town where you can find shops, banks, and other businesses

7 VIDEO LISTENING

a Are there any markets near you? Do you ever go to them? Do you have a favourite stall?

b Watch the documentary about a farmers' market. How is it different from other markets? Do you have similar markets in your country?

c Read the sentences. With a partner, decide if the missing information is a word or a number.
   1 There are now more than _____ farmers' markets in Britain.
   2 Some are held every week, some every fortnight, and some every _____.
   3 At farmers' markets, customers buy directly from the _____.
   4 Food in supermarkets often spends a long time in _____ or warehouses.
   5 Winchester market takes place _____ a month.
   6 It has more than _____ stalls.
   7 All the food there comes from the _____ area.
   8 Lyburn Farmhouse Cheesemakers is a _____-run business.
   9 They can have up to _____ cheeses maturing at any one time.
   10 Everything about Lyburn cheese is local – the employees, the customers, and even the _____.

d Watch the documentary again and complete the information in **c**.

e What food or drink is produced in the area where you live? Do you agree that it's important to buy local produce?

Go online to watch the video and review the lesson

1&2 Revise and Check

GRAMMAR

Circle a, b, or c.

1 I emailed ____ the photos.
   a her   b she   c hers
2 What are ____ surnames?
   a them   b theirs   c their
3 He made ____.
   a for me coffee   b coffee for me
   c coffee to me
4 My sister ____.
   a lent them to us   b them lent to we
   c lent to us them
5 The red shoes are nice, but I prefer those ____.
   a blue one   b blues ones
   c blue ones
6 He's ____ man I've ever met.
   a the bossiest   b the most bossy
   c the more bossy
7 She's ____ in her new job than she was before.
   a much more happy   b more happier
   c much happier
8 The film was ____ than the book.
   a a bit better   b bit better
   c a bit more better
9 ____ a word he says.
   a I'm not believing   b I don't believe
   c I'm not believe
10 You look worried – what ____ about?
   a are you thinking
   b you are thinking
   c do you think
11 Where ____ dinner tonight?
   a do we have   b are we having
   c we have
12 ____ our cousins next weekend.
   a We're visiting   b We're visit
   c We visit
13 I love looking at other ____ family photos.
   a people's   b peoples'   c people'
14 What's the ____ where you were born?
   a village's name   b village name
   c name of the village
15 We grow all ____.
   a my own vegetables
   b our own vegetables
   c ours own vegetables

VOCABULARY

a Complete the sentences with an adjective from the **bold** word.
1 My grandmother is extremely _____. **glamour**
2 I'm so sorry I was late – it was very _____ of you to wait for me. **consider**
3 Martin is very _____. I'd trust him to complete the job well. **rely**
4 She's very _____. She won't do anything stupid. **sense**
5 He's always been _____ – he loves painting. **create**
6 Their car's not really _____ for a family of four. **suit**
7 Our hotel room was _____. **luxury**
8 Work is very _____ at the moment. **stress**
9 It's a bit _____ to carry so much money. **risk**
10 Her Russian is very _____. **impress**

b Complete the words.
1 There are a lot of mosquitoes – where's the i_____ r_____?
2 The plugs in the USA are different. We're going to need an a_____.
3 I brought my toothbrush, but I don't have any t_____.
4 It always takes me ages to p_____ my suitcase.
5 Angela can't go swimming. She hasn't brought her sw_____.
6 You don't need to take your dr_____ l_____ – we won't want to hire a car in Paris.
7 **A** Did you bring any nail sc_____? **B** Look in my washbag.
8 I looked in the g_____ and found this great seafood restaurant.

c Where can you buy these things? Write the name of the shop.
1 meat _____
2 a newspaper _____
3 bread _____
4 flowers _____
5 aspirin _____
6 a house _____ _____
7 fish _____
8 potatoes _____

PRONUNCIATION

a Practise the words and sounds.

Vowel sounds   **Consonant sounds**

f**i**sh   tr**ee**   c**a**t   h**or**se   **e**gg   **r**ight   **k**ey   **s**nake   **z**ebra

b **p.166–7 Sound Bank** Say more words for each sound.

c What sound in **a** do the pink letters have in these words?
1 **ea**sy   2 h**ea**dphones   3 s**c**issors   4 **ch**emist's   5 s**t**all

d Underline the stressed syllable.
1 i|ni|tials   3 lu|xu|ri|ous   5 fish|mon|ger's
2 a|ffor|da|ble   4 un|der|wear

CAN YOU understand this text?

a Read the article once. Which Underground stations were named after things which were made there?

Where did these Tube station names come from?

If you travel on the London Underground, you will notice that the names of many of the stations are rather strange. Here is ¹___ well-known station names.

The name with one of the oldest origins is **Tooting Bec**. It goes back more than 1,300 years, to ²___. Many English towns still contain words from Old English: the suffix '-ham' (as in Birmingham) meant 'settlement', while '-ton' (as in Brighton) referred to a farm. The ending '-ing' meant 'belonging to someone', so Tooting means a place belonging to the Saxon chief Tota. Bec comes from France. When the Normans invaded England in 1066, they took over a lot of properties and gave them new names. The abbey of Bec-Hellouin in Normandy was given the land that once belonged to Tota.

At some point in its long history, **Covent Garden** lost the letter 'n'. Now it is one of London's best-known tourist attractions, but ³___ which was owned by monks from Westminster Abbey. They called it 'the garden of the Abbey and Convent', or 'Convent Garden'. King Henry VIII destroyed the monastery in the 1500s and some large houses were built there. It was also a fruit market from the 1650s to the 1970s.

The **Elephant & Castle** station in south London probably gets its name from a group of medieval craftsmen who made knives and swords. Their symbol showed an elephant carrying a castle. It is thought that the elephant referred to the ivory that they used for their knife handles. The castle was possibly included to ⁴___, because few Europeans at the time would have known what this animal looked like.

Like Oxford Circus, the 'circus' part of **Piccadilly Circus** refers to a roundabout where different streets meet. The other half of its name is centuries old. A 'piccadill' is a large collar that ⁵___ – often worn by Queen Elizabeth I, for example. One London tailor, Robert Baker, made a fortune selling piccadills and built a large house called Piccadilly Hall in the area in 1611. When the roundabout was built in 1819, it was named Piccadilly Circus, and the same name was given to the Underground station when it opened in 1906.

Glossary
sword a weapon with a long metal blade and a handle
ivory a hard material like bone that forms the tusks of elephants
collar the part around the neck of a shirt, dress, etc.

b Read the article again and complete it with phrases A–F. There is one phrase you do not need.
A when the Anglo-Saxons lived in Britain
B show the size of an elephant
C the fascinating history behind some
D the name means 'a river crossing'
E in the 13th century, it was an orchard and garden
F was very fashionable in the late 16th century

CAN YOU understand these people?

🔊 2.24 Watch or listen and choose a, b, or c.

1 Tilly 2 Tory 3 Claudia 4 Maria 5 Diarmuid

1 Tilly's name is short for ____.
 a Ottilie
 b Otillie
 c Otilie
2 Tory ____ her purple and white bedroom.
 a really likes
 b has just changed
 c isn't happy with
3 When Claudia travels, she usually ____.
 a packs a lot
 b prefers to take hand luggage
 c packs well in advance
4 Maria ____ when she's on holiday.
 a is often tired
 b goes for walks in the evening
 c likes really quiet places
5 Diarmuid buys ____ online.
 a everything
 b everything except clothes
 c everything except food

CAN YOU say this in English?

Tick (✓) the box if you can do these things.
Can you...?
1 ☐ talk about a brand name that you think works well and say why
2 ☐ say which colour clothes you usually wear, and which you would never wear and why
3 ☐ talk about five things you always pack when you travel, and why you need them
4 ☐ give two advantages and two disadvantages of shopping online

3A Grow up!

> What were you like as a teenager?
>
> I used to have long hair, and I played in a rock group.

G past simple, past continuous, or *used to*? **V** stages of life **P** *-ed* endings, sentence rhythm

1 VOCABULARY stages of life

a Match the phrases and photos.

He's / She's…
- a <u>ba</u>by /ˈbeɪbi/
- a <u>to</u>ddler /ˈtɒdlə/
- a <u>chi</u>ld /tʃaɪld/
- a pre-<u>teen</u> /ˌpriː ˈtiːn/
- a <u>tee</u>nager /ˈtiːneɪdʒə/
- in his / her early twenties (= 20–23)
- in his / her mid-thirties (= 34–36)
- in his / her late forties (= 47–49)
- re<u>ti</u>red /rɪˈtaɪəd/

> 🔍 **middle-aged, old, elderly**
>
> The word *middle-aged* means different things to different people, but usually refers to a person in their forties or fifties.
>
> *old* and *elderly* mean the same thing, but *elderly* is more polite. It is not considered polite to call a person *old*, especially to their face.

b 🔊 3.1 Listen and check.

c Which stage of life do you associate with…?
- being forgetful
- being cheeky /ˈtʃiːki/
- being moody
- being naughty /ˈnɔːti/
- crying a lot
- getting a mortgage
- going clubbing
- having tantrums /ˈtæntrəmz/
- listening to pop music
- playing games
- settling down
- watching cartoons
- wearing jeans

> *I think being forgetful is typical of elderly people.*
>
> *I think it can be any age. I'm forgetful, too!*

d Think of people you know who are in three of the different stages of life in **a**. Tell your partner about them.

> *My sister Ana is in her mid-thirties. She's married and has a six-month old baby. She used to work as a nurse, but now she's at home looking after her son.*

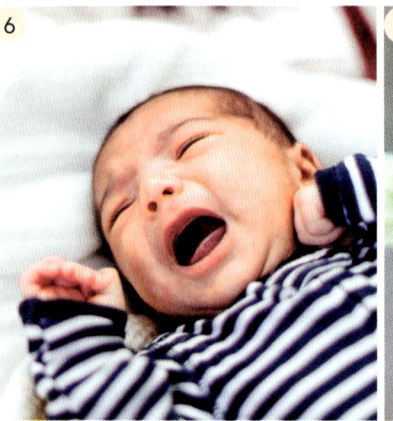

2 READING

a Look at the cartoon and read the information box. At what age do you think someone becomes 'a grown-up'?

> *grow up*
>
> *grow up* means to become an adult. A *grown-up* is used, often by children, as an informal word for an adult. *Grown-up* can also be used as an adjective.

b Read the first paragraph of an article about being grown-up. Answer the questions with a partner.
  1 How long is the period of 'emerging adulthood'?
  2 What are the characteristics of this stage of life?
  3 According to the article, what do owning a vacuum cleaner and having a mortgage have in common?

c **Ⓒ Communication** A real grown-up? **A** p.107 **B** p.111 Read and tell your partner about Carol or Hugo.

d What do you think are the three things that most show that you are (or aren't) a grown-up? Have you grown up yet?

3 LISTENING

a What kinds of things do you think teenagers are better at than adults?

b 🔊 **3.2** Listen to Part 1 of a local radio news report and answer the questions.
  1 What is the Mosquito Tone and who can hear it?
  2 Were both the presenters able to hear it?
  3 Were you able to hear it? If yes, how did it make you feel?

c 🔊 **3.3** Listen to Part 2 of the news report. Where is the Mosquito Tone being used? Why? Is everybody in favour of it?

d Listen to Part 2 again. What does the interviewee say about these things?
  1 how teenage gangs behave in shopping centres
  2 what shop owners say about the Mosquito Tone
  3 why some people think the Mosquito Tone is unfair to teenagers
  4 why the Mosquito Tone doesn't stop the problem
  5 how some teenagers are taking advantage of the Mosquito Tone

e If you were a shop owner, would you use the Mosquito Tone? Why (not)?

So you think you're a grown-up? Think again.

Are you 29 or older?
Then you're officially an adult. Well done. In a research study, 29 was the age at which most people thought they finally felt like a proper grown-up. But you're a legal adult when you're 18, so that's about 11 years to live through what psychologists call 'emerging adulthood', that is, the stage when you don't yet have children, don't live in your own house, and don't earn enough money to be financially independent. Some people say that buying your first house or having your first child represent real adulthood, as these mean you are a responsible person. A few years ago, a bank did a survey to find out the top things that proved you were a grown-up. Number one was having a mortgage and number two was no longer relying on your parents for money. Other things included having a pension plan, doing a weekly food shop, and getting married. A less obvious sign was owning a vacuum cleaner!

So when do you become a real grown-up?
We asked two journalists...

Adapted from The Times

4 SPEAKING

a Read the questions and answer for you. Then compare in groups. Did you do the things early or late?

  At what age did you…?
  start nursery school   _____
  learn to swim or ride a bicycle   _____
  find out that Father Christmas wasn't real   _____
  get your first mobile phone   _____
  start going out in the evening with friends   _____
  use public transport on your own   _____
  get paid for doing some work   _____

b Now discuss the following questions in groups.

> **What do you think is the best age for…?**
> • first going on holiday without your parents
> • starting to learn a musical instrument
> • starting to use social media
> • starting to save money
> • moving out of your parents' home
> • having your first baby
> • retiring

27

5 GRAMMAR past simple, past continuous, or *used to*?

a What were you like as a child? Choose two adjectives from the list, and add one of your own. Compare with a partner.

accident-prone clever lazy lonely naughty nervous
noisy quiet serious shy sociable well-behaved

b Read the posts on an online forum. Who…?
1. knew how to do something grown-up at an early age
2. has a job that started as a childhood hobby
3. created problems for his or her mother
4. remembers being very frightened by an animal

What kind of child were you…and have you changed?

David, 47 I loved being an only child. I was never lonely; I enjoyed spending time on my own, doing what I wanted, when I wanted. I ¹*was liking / used to like* reading, going for walks and bike rides in the countryside, and birdwatching. I also collected insects and I ²*used to keep / kept* them in the garden to learn how they grew and behaved. Now I am a professional biologist, so I still enjoy those things! I'm still very happy spending time on my own, but I enjoy the company of others much more now.

Magda, 22 I was quite sociable as a child and I really enjoyed playing with my friends. But I used to be a bit shy about meeting new people and also quite afraid of some things. Once when I was little, I remember we went for a walk, and I ³*was holding / held* an ice cream and a big black dog ran over and bit the whole top off. As a result, I didn't like dogs or going for walks for many years. 'Dog ate my ice cream' has become a bit of a family joke. After I ⁴*started / was starting* university, I became much more confident. Now I still enjoy spending time with friends, but I like spending time on my own, too. I also love dogs. So maybe I've changed a lot!

Alex, 59 I am one of five brothers and sisters – I'm the second youngest. I ⁵*was having / used to have* tantrums as a two-year-old, but I was very independent. When I was three, my mum ⁶*went / used to go* into hospital to have my younger brother, and I was the only one in the house who knew how to turn the washing machine on. Actually, I haven't changed much. I'm almost 60 now – I've been strongly independent all my life and I even have the occasional tantrum.

Stephen, 23 I ⁷*used to be / was always* very messy when I was younger. I used to throw my clothes around everywhere, and Mum never knew which was clean and which was dirty washing. However, now that I'm older, I'm very tidy – mess really stresses me out! Also, I ⁸*always hated / was always hating* going to school, but now I'm doing a postgraduate course at university. But in some ways, I haven't changed at all. I was quite a thoughtful, sensitive person when I was young, and I'm the same now.

c With a partner, circle the correct form of the highlighted verbs, or tick (✓) if both forms are possible.

d Ⓖ p.136 Grammar Bank 3A

e Think about your answers in **a**. Have you changed much? Then write a short post like the ones on the forum about you. Use the correct verb forms.

6 PRONUNCIATION -ed endings, sentence rhythm

a 🔊 3.6 Listen to the three different pronunciations of the -ed ending. Listen again and repeat.

1	/t/	I us**ed** to be shy. I lik**ed** reading.
2	/d/	I've chang**ed** a lot. I enjoy**ed** playing with my friends.
3	/ɪd/	I start**ed** university. I collect**ed** insects.

b 🔊 3.7 Listen to some more regular past simple verbs. How is the -ed ending pronounced? Tick (✓) the correct box.

	/t/	/d/	/ɪd/
1 I hat**ed** eating vegetables.			
2 We look**ed** alike.			
3 I tri**ed** everything.			
4 We liv**ed** abroad.			
5 I hop**ed** to pass.			
6 We decid**ed** to move.			

c Practise saying the sentences in **b**.

> 🔍 **Past or present?**
> When the -ed ending is pronounced /t/ or /d/, it can often be difficult to hear whether a regular verb is in the past or present tense. This is especially true when the next word begins with a *t* or *d* and the two words are linked, e.g. *I hoped‿to pass*. Use the context to help you.

d 🔊 3.8 Listen and write six sentences. Are the verbs in the present or past?

e 🔊 3.9 Listen and repeat the questions and sentences below. Copy the rhythm. What kinds of words are stressed or unstressed?
1. A **Where** did you **live** when you were a **child**?
   B We **lived** in a **village** in the **country**.
2. I **used** to **love playing football** when I was at **primary school**.
3. This **happened** when I was **ten**. I was with my **parents** and we were **shopping**.

7 SPEAKING

With a partner, do the tasks in each section. Try to use good sentence rhythm.

EVENTS IN YOUR LIFE

Ask and answer past simple questions.

1 Where ▢ you born? (be)
  Where ▢ you ▢ when you ▢ a child? (live, be)
2 How old ▢ you when you ▢ primary school? (be, start)
  ▢ you ▢ your first day? (enjoy)
  What ▢ you ▢? (do)
3 When ▢ the first time you ▢ abroad? (be, travel)
  Where ▢ you ▢? (go)

Where were you born? *I was born in a small town called Morella.*

WHEN YOU WERE YOUNGER

Talk about the things in the list. Use the correct form of *used to*. How are you different now?

- a toy you used to play with a lot
- a game or sport you used to enjoy
- what you used to look like and how you used to dress
- school subjects you used to love / hate
- a singer / group you used to listen to a lot
- something you used to be afraid of

I had a teddy bear when I was small and I used to take him everywhere.

AN INCIDENT IN YOUR CHILDHOOD

Choose one of the topics below. Think about how old you were, what you were doing at the time, and what happened. Then tell your partner about the incident.

Think about a time when…
- you hurt yourself quite badly.
- your parents caught you being very naughty.
- you got lost.
- you had a scary experience.
- you had a disappointing birthday.
- you had a problem at school.
- you had a really big argument with your parents.

This happened when I was about seven. I was playing with my friends and we were climbing trees…

Go online to review the lesson

29

3B Photo albums

G prepositions **V** photography **P** word stress

> Who's this photo of?
> It's my sister, standing in front of our house.

1 VOCABULARY photography

a Look at the photo in the article. In which city do you think it was taken?

b Read the article quickly and check your answer to **a**. Why are selfies becoming a problem?

The dangerous art of the selfie
Jane Wakefield

A lot of people have died this year while ¹*making / taking* selfies. In Moscow, a university graduate died after trying to take a selfie while he was hanging from a bridge. In Australia, a very fragile and unstable rock that looks like a wedding cake was closed to the public because too many people were climbing it to take wedding photos of themselves. And in Colorado, USA, officials had to close a park after several people were caught getting a little too close to the wildlife. 'We've seen people using selfie sticks to ²*do / take* a photo of themselves with the bears ³*in the foreground / in the background*. Sometimes they get as close as three metres,' said recreation manager Brandon Ransom. So why are some people willing to risk their life to take the ultimate selfie? Lee Thompson's selfie ⁴*on top of / in front of* the Christ the Redeemer statue in Rio de Janeiro went viral. 'People see how pictures like mine spread across the world, and they see a way to make themselves famous for 15 minutes,' he said.

Lee Thompson

Adapted from the BBC website

c Read the article again and (circle) the correct highlighted word or phrase.

d **V** p.155 **Vocabulary Bank** Photography

e Have you ever taken a dangerous selfie? Do you have any photos of yourself in front of a famous monument?

2 PRONUNCIATION word stress

a ◆ 3.12 Under<u>line</u> the stress in words 1–7. Listen and check. Practise saying the words.
1 pho|to
2 pho|to|graph
3 pho|to|gra|pher
4 pho|to|gra|phy
5 pho|to|gra|phic
6 pho|to|ge|nic
7 pho|to|shop

b Now under<u>line</u> the stressed syllable in the **bold** words.
1 There's a tree in the **back|ground**.
2 In the **fore|ground**, there's a girl.
3 You can see a house in the **dis|tance**.
4 There's a man **be|hind** her.
5 In the **bo|ttom** right-hand **cor|ner**, there's a dog.

c ◆ 3.13 Listen and check. Practise saying the sentences.

d **C Communication** Spot the differences **A** p.107 **B** p.112 Describe the picture and find the differences.

3 LISTENING

a In pairs, think about the last photo that you took. Where were you? What was the photo of? Did you use a camera or your phone?

b Read about Darja Bilyk and look at some photos from her website. Which one…?
1 ☐ is a portrait
2 ☐ is a landscape
3 ☐ uses light in an interesting way
4 ☐ is taken from an unusual angle
5 ☐ is a still life

Which photo do you like best?

Darja Bilyk is 26 years old and was born and grew up in Moscow. She believes that a good photographer should be able to take great photographs of everything – landscapes, portraits, or family photos – even without expensive photographic equipment. The things that she looks for are atmosphere and mood. You can see her work by visiting her website, or following her on Instagram.

c 🔊 3.14 Listen to Darja giving some tips about how to take good photos with your phone. Number the tips 1–10 in the order she gives them.

- ▨ Don't think twice.
- ▨ Don't stick to one style.
- ▨ Don't use zoom.
- ▨ Light is important.
- ▨ Learn about your phone camera.
- ▨ Be ready.
- ▨ Make your pictures come alive.
- ▨ Select and edit.
- ▨ Use the grid.
- ▨ Choose unique angles.

d Listen again. Complete some details from each tip.
1 Keep your phone in _____ mode, so it's ready when you unlock it.
2 You can always _____ a picture if you don't like it.
3 Know the _____ and _____ of your phone camera.
4 If you want to take a _____, move nearer.
5 You can improve a boring photo if you use _____ well.
6 It's also important to be able to take photos _____ using the grid.
7 Try taking a photo from a _____ view.
8 Learn to develop your unique _____.
9 Use _____ to help you to edit your photos.
10 Print your photos, don't just look at your photos on a _____.

e Are there any of Darja's tips that you might use next time you take a photo?

4 SPEAKING & WRITING

a Talk to a partner.
1 What do you normally take photos with? Does it take good photos? Do you ever use special features like panoramic photos or slo-mo videos?
2 Do you prefer taking photos of scenery or portraits of people? What else do you take photos of?
3 Do you think you're good at taking photos? Why (not)?
4 Do you usually edit your photos? How?
5 Do you post photos on social media sites? Which ones? What kinds of photos? How do you feel if other people post photos of you?
6 Do you like being photographed? Why (not)?

b Ⓦ p.117 Writing An article Write an article with tips on how to do something.

5 GRAMMAR prepositions

a Read the description of a photo. With a partner, complete the gaps with a preposition from the list.

at (x2)   in   of (x2)   over   next to   to

I took this photograph when we were flying ¹_____ the Great Wall of China – I was going back ²_____ the USA after a holiday in Beijing. I was sitting ³_____ the window, so I had a great view. I'm not usually very good ⁴_____ taking photographs, but I'm quite proud ⁵_____ this one. It was a long flight, and by the time we finally arrived home ⁶_____ Washington, DC, I was exhausted. But when I look ⁷_____ this photograph, it reminds me ⁸_____ the fantastic trip I had to China.

b ◯ 3.15 Listen and check.

c G p.137 **Grammar Bank 3B**

d Complete 1–10 with a preposition. Then choose four topics and tell your partner about them.

1 a photo you took that you are very proud _____
2 someone in your family who you really like talking _____
3 something you're really looking forward _____ at the moment
4 something your country is famous _____
5 a person who you sometimes argue _____
6 a beautiful sight that you once flew _____
7 what you have _____ the walls of your bedroom
8 someone you could rely _____ in a crisis
9 something you usually ask _____ when you eat out
10 somewhere you had to walk _____ a large number of steps

A photo that I'm very proud of is one I took last summer…

6 LISTENING & SPEAKING

a ◯ 3.19 You're going to listen to Chris, Tom, and Kate talking about a holiday photo they really like. Look at the photos. Then listen and match them to speakers 1–3. Were all the photos taken by the speakers?

A ☐

B ☐

C ☐

b Listen again. Take notes about each person's answers to questions 1–5.
1 Where was the photo taken? Who took it?
2 Who were you with?
3 What was happening, or had just happened?
4 Why do you like the photo?
5 Where do you keep the photo?

c Think of an interesting photo you took on holiday. Tell a partner about it. Include your answers to 1–5.

d Show your partner some photos on your phone and tell him or her about them.

7 READING

a Look at the list below. How do you usually store the photos you've taken?
- on your phone, tablet, etc.
- on the internet, e.g. in iCloud or Dropbox
- on a separate hard drive or CD-ROM
- on an online photo site
- on paper / in an album / on the wall

b Read the article about storing digital photos and complete 1–5 with a heading from the list. There is one heading you do not need.

A **Safe in the cloud?**
B **Digital cameras vary**
C **Digital files can deteriorate**
D **Photo sites come and go**
E **Technology becomes obsolete**
F **Hard drives don't last forever**

c Read the article again. Match the storage method to the problem it has.

1 ☐ .jpg files
2 ☐ hard drives
3 ☐ CD-ROMs and flash drives
4 ☐ CD-ROM drives
5 ☐ iCloud or Dropbox
6 ☐ photo sites

a only last for about five years
b only last for 10 to 20 years
c are damaged when they're copied
d can close down
e may not exist in the future
f can be damaged by storms

d Match the **bold** verbs or phrases from the article to their meaning.

1 ☐ to **store** photos l.08
2 ☐ to **back up** photos l.13
3 ☐ to **go offline** l.26
4 ☐ to **upload** a photo l.29
5 ☐ to **cancel** your account l.36

a to disconnect from the internet
b to transfer to another computer
c to no longer continue
d to make a copy
e to keep or preserve

e After reading the article, will you do anything differently to protect your photos?

How safe are your digital photos?

In the past, your grandmother probably kept her photos in a box, or in an old album, and sadly, over time, these memories faded or disappeared. But with today's technology, that shouldn't be a problem. A digital photo lasts forever, right? Actually, think again.
05 Although it is still a good idea to keep all of your photos as digital computer files, there are plenty of things that can damage or even destroy those high-tech memories.

1

Very few people realize this can happen, but if you store your photos as .jpgs (the most common file format), the file will actually
10 deteriorate every time you copy and edit it. Experts disagree about how much damage this can do, but the damage is real.

2

Your files may be safe on your hard drive, but how long until your hard drive dies? The average lasts just five years. You could back up your photos on a CD-ROM or flash drive, but they don't last forever either
15 – about 10–20 years at most, experts say.

3

Let's say all goes well and your CD-ROM or flash drive full of photos lasts for 20 years. By then, will there still be any CD-ROM drives in the world that can read the disc? Will you be able to insert your flash drive into a modern computer? Today's high-tech storage solution is
20 tomorrow's useless floppy disk.

4

People talk about saving their photos in a magical place on the internet, like Apple's iCloud, or Dropbox. But this just means they are in a company's data centre on – guess what? – lots of hard drives, which could die or corrupt just as easily as your own. During
25 a thunderstorm, a cloud storage centre in the USA was hit, and major sites like Netflix, Pinterest, and Instagram went offline for almost a whole day. Thousands of files were lost.

5

Websites like Flickr and Instagram let you quickly upload photos and share them with others. But bear
30 in mind that a photo site which is popular now could one day go out of business, taking your photos with it. What's more, if you upload photos to these sites, there is someone other than you who controls your access. While it is generally not in their interest
35 to stop you accessing your files, they can and sometimes do. They can even cancel your account.

So what should you do? Experts say you should make lots of copies of your photos and save them in many different ways – on your computer, on
40 a back-up drive, online, and even as traditional printed photos. It may be too late to save Grandma's photos, but you can still save yours.

Glossary
floppy disk a flexible disk covered in hard plastic, which used to be used for storing computer data

 Go online to review the lesson

EPISODE 2 Practical English All kinds of problems

renting a car

1 ▶ HENRY'S CAR

a ◉ 3.20 Watch or listen to Jenny and Henry. Where does Henry want to take her? Why can't he? How is Jenny going to get there?

b Watch or listen again and circle the correct answer.
1 Jenny's suitcase *still hasn't been found / has been found*.
2 Henry thinks Jenny *will like Luke / won't understand Luke*.
3 Henry's car *has a flat tyre / has two flat tyres*.
4 He thinks the car was damaged by *neighbours / vandals*.
5 Jenny *doesn't know / knows* Luke's address.
6 Jenny had previously decided to *travel by public transport / rent a car*.
7 She offers to *make dinner for Henry / take Henry out to dinner*.
8 Jenny *waits / doesn't wait* while Luke looks at her laptop.

Glossary
a spare (tyre) /speə ˈtaɪə/ an extra tyre in a car
the AA a breakdown service in the UK

> **British and American English**
> *rent a car* = American English
> *rent a car* OR *hire a car* = British English

Who do you think vandalized Henry's car?
Who is the man who arrives at Henry's house as Jenny leaves?

2 ▶ RENTING A CAR

a ◉ 3.21 Watch or listen to Jenny renting a car. Answer the questions.
1 How long does Jenny rent a car for?
2 Which car does the assistant recommend?
3 Where does she want to leave the car?

What do you think is significant about the news on the TV? Do you think Jenny noticed it?

b Watch or listen again. Complete the **You hear** phrases in the conversation on p.35.

c ◉ 3.22 Watch or listen and repeat some of the **You say** phrases. Copy the rhythm and intonation.

d Practise the conversation in **b** with a partner.

e 👥 In pairs, role-play the conversation.
A You're a visitor to the UK who wants to rent a car for a week. Talk to the assistant and choose the car you want. Use the **Useful language** box to help you.
B You're the assistant at a car rental company. Help **A** choose a car and get all of **A**'s details. Use the **Useful language** box to help you.

f Swap roles.

> **Useful language: describing cars**
> **Kinds of drive:** *automatic* or *manual*
> **Car types:** *economy (small cars)*
> *compact (small, but larger than economy)*
> *family (medium size)*
> *luxury (large cars, 4x4s, sports cars)*
> *convertibles (open-top cars)*
> *people carriers (for more than five people)*
> **Extras:** *air conditioning, satnav*

You hear	You say
Hello. Can I help you?	Oh, hi. I'd like to rent a car, please.
Have you ¹_____ from us before?	No.
OK, could I ²_____ your driving licence, please? Great. So what ³_____ of car are you looking for?	Oh, nothing too big. It's just for me.
OK, so a compact. ⁴_____-door?	Yeah, that'll be fine.
For how long?	Nine days.
Automatic or ⁵_____?	An automatic, please.
Any additional ⁶_____?	No, just me.
Great. Well, we have several ⁷_____ I can show you, but I'd recommend the Vauxhall Corsa. It's ⁸£_____ per day and that includes insurance.	That sounds promising. Can I take a look?
Of course, but first I'd like to run through some of the basics. The ⁹_____ tank is full when you start, so if you return it with a full tank, there's no extra ¹⁰_____.	Great.
But if you get any ¹¹_____ tickets or speeding fines, you have to pay for them yourself.	Fair enough! Would it be possible to leave the car at the airport?
No problem, but that's a one-way rental, so there's an additional charge of ¹²£_____.	OK.
And one last thing – have you driven in ¹³_____ before?	Yes, I have. So driving on the left's not a problem.
That's good. OK, let's go out and take a look at the car. We can go through the paperwork afterwards.	Great.

3 WHERE IS HENRY?

a ◉ 3.23 Watch or listen to Jenny's afternoon and evening. What has happened to a) her laptop, b) her suitcase? What does she hear on the news?

b Watch or listen again and mark the sentences **T** (true) or **F** (false). Correct the **F** sentences.
1 Henry is in his study when Jenny comes back.
2 Jenny reminds Henry about the dinner.
3 She isn't surprised by Luke's news about her computer.
4 Luke thinks that Henry has probably gone to the university to work.
5 Henry is always late for everything.
6 Jenny is feeling tired because of jet lag.
7 When she wakes up, Henry is back.
8 She phones Rob to say goodnight.

Who do you think was responsible for what happened on the news? What do you think has happened to Henry?

c Look at the **Social English** phrases. Can you remember any of the missing words?

> **Social English**
> 1 Henry   I'm _____ I can't take your call at the moment.
> 2 Henry   Please leave your message after the _____.
> 3 Luke   Hi, Jenny. What's _____?
> 4 Jenny   _____ on…my suitcase has arrived!
> 5 Jenny   Well, at _____ it's back.
> 6 Jenny   I'm _____ tired.
> 7 Jenny   Thanks, Luke. See you _____.

d ◉ 3.24 Watch or listen and complete the phrases. Then watch or listen again and repeat.

e Complete conversations A–F with **Social English** phrases 1–7. Then practise them with a partner.

A	Mark, do you think you could come over? I've got a problem.	Sure. ☐ You sound a bit stressed.
B	Would you like to go out to dinner?	To be honest, ☐ Could we just get a takeaway?
C	So shall I book tickets for the 7th?	☐ – I'll just check in my diary.
D	Hi. You've reached Jack Carling's phone. ☐ ☐	Hi Jack, it's Sarah. Can you give me a ring as soon as possible?
E	What time will you be back?	In a couple of hours. ☐
F	What an awful day! It hasn't stopped raining.	Yes. But ☐ we didn't have to go anywhere.

CAN YOU…?

☐ describe a car
☐ rent a car
☐ record a voicemail greeting and leave a message

> **Go online** to watch the video, review the lesson, and check your progress

35

4A Don't throw it away!

> Are you going to throw away that pasta?
>
> No, I'll have it for dinner.

G future forms: *will / shall* and *be going to*   **V** rubbish and recycling   **P** /aɪ/ and /eɪ/

1 VOCABULARY rubbish and recycling

a How often do you or your family throw away food? What kinds of things? How do you feel about it?

b Read the infographic. Then match the <mark>highlighted</mark> words and phrases to the definitions below.

Over 1/3 of all food produced globally <mark>goes to waste</mark>.

<mark>Surplus</mark> food in supermarkets is **less than 2%** of total food waste (though the supermarket business is directly responsible for much food waste in the <mark>supply chain</mark>).

There are nearly one billion hungry people in the world. They could be fed on **less than a quarter** of the food that is wasted in the USA, UK, and Europe.

In most developed countries, **over half** of all <mark>food waste</mark> takes place in the home.

25% of the world's fresh water <mark>supply</mark> is used to grow food that is never eaten.

There will be 2.3 billion more people on the planet by 2050 – this will require a **60–70%** increase in global food production. Or we can just stop throwing away our food!

1 _____ food that is no longer needed and is thrown away
2 _____ is thrown away
3 _____ the amount of sth that is available to be used
4 _____ the process from when sth is first made to when it is bought or used
5 _____ an amount that is extra or more than you need

c With a partner, discuss which facts a) didn't surprise you, b) surprised you a lot, c) you think are really shocking.

d **V** p.156 **Vocabulary Bank** Rubbish and recycling

2 PRONUNCIATION /aɪ/ and /eɪ/

a Look at the sound pictures. What are the words and sounds? Write the words from the list in the correct column.

aw**ay**   d**a**te   re**a**pply   rec**y**cle   repl**ay**
requ**i**re   sell-b**y**   s**i**te   s**u**pply   tr**ay**   w**a**ste

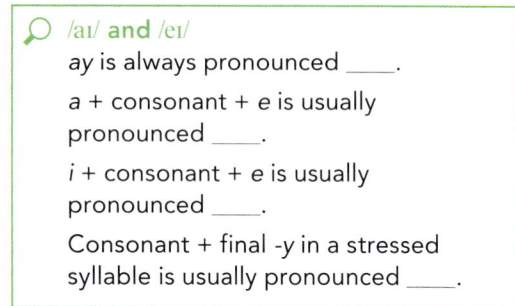

b ▶ 4.5 Listen and check. Practise saying the words.

c Complete the rules with the phonetic symbols /aɪ/ or /eɪ/.

> 🔍 /aɪ/ and /eɪ/
>
> *ay* is always pronounced ____.
> *a* + consonant + *e* is usually pronounced ____.
> *i* + consonant + *e* is usually pronounced ____.
> Consonant + final *-y* in a stressed syllable is usually pronounced ____.

d Look at more words containing the sounds /aɪ/ or /eɪ/ which have irregular spellings. How do you pronounce them?

br**ea**k   b**uy**   cl**i**mate   **ey**es   fl**i**ght
g**uy**   h**ei**ght   n**ei**ghbour   str**aig**ht   surv**ey**
w**ei**ght   w**i**-fi

e ▶ 4.6 Listen and check. Practise saying the words.

36

3 LISTENING

a Read Part 1 of an interview with Tessa Cook, co-founder of OLIO, an app to help reduce food waste. With a partner, try to predict the missing words.

Tessa Cook

Can you explain what OLIO is, exactly?
So, OLIO is a free app which connects ¹n_____ with each other and with local ²b_____ so that surplus food can be shared and not thrown away.

What kinds of food?
It could be food that's near its ³s_____-_____d_____ in local shops, or home-grown vegetables that you're not going to eat, or bread from your ⁴b_____ that hasn't been sold at the end of the day, or the food that's in your ⁵f_____ when you're about to go away. Any food that people have that they're not going to use.

And how does the app work?
It's super easy! If you have some food that you want to ⁶sh_____, you simply open the app, add a ⁷ph_____ and a description, and say when and where the food can be collected from. And if you're looking for some food, you just put in your postcode and send a ⁸m_____ to the person who's offering the food you want, and then you arrange a time to go and collect it.

b 🔊 4.7 Listen to Part 1 and check your answers to **a**.

c 🔊 4.8 Now listen to Part 2 and answer the questions.
   1 Why has Tessa always been worried about food waste?
   2 What circumstances inspired her to come up with the idea for the app?
   3 How did her friend Saasha react when Tessa told her about the idea?

d 🔊 4.9 Finally, listen to Part 3. Why does Tessa mention the following?

| £700 worth of food | one in three people | 12 people | two weeks |
| half a bag of onions | 9th July 2015 | 41 countries | within an hour |

e Do you think the app is a good idea? Would you use it? Why (not)?

4 SPEAKING

a Read the questions and think about your answers.

b Discuss the questions in groups of three or four.

Zero waste

- What three things could you and your family do in order to throw away less food?
- Do you ever eat anything that's past its sell-by date? Why (not)? Has anything ever happened?
- Do you ever buy special food offers of the type 'Buy one, get one free'? Do you usually finish both?
- Do you ever take leftover food home from a restaurant?
- What do you think restaurants or supermarkets in your town should do with unused food? Do you know if any of them ever do it?
- How would your neighbours react if you offered them leftover food? Why?
- What kinds of food do you think have too much packaging? When do you think packaging is really necessary?

37

5 GRAMMAR future forms: will / shall and be going to

a Complete the conversations with will / shall or be going to and the correct form of the verb.

1 A Could you take the rubbish out? It's beginning to smell.
  B I _____ it as soon as this programme finishes. (do)
2 A _____ you _____ that pasta? You've hardly eaten any. (finish)
  B I can't, I'm just not hungry. But don't throw it away. I _____ it for lunch tomorrow. (have)
3 A Don't put bottles in the black bin. You need to put them in the recycling bin.
  B Sorry, I forgot. I _____ it again. (not do)
4 A This lasagne's been in the fridge for three days. _____ I _____ it away? (throw)
  B No, don't waste it. Put it in the freezer.
5 A I'm a bit worried about this yogurt. The sell-by date was yesterday.
  B Don't worry, it _____ fine. (be)

b ▶ 4.10 Listen and check. Practise the conversations with a partner.

c G p.138 Grammar Bank 4A

d Talk to a partner. Practise making plans and predictions. Choose topics from the lists.

Talk about a plan you have…
- to waste less food.
- to improve your diet.
- to spend less money.
- for learning a new skill.
- for this evening or weekend.

Make a prediction about…
- the environment (e.g. pollution, climate change).
- a sporting event.
- a TV drama series you are watching.
- someone in your family (his / her life, plans).
- something in the recent news.

I'm going to plan my meals for the week and only buy what I need. (*What a good idea!*)

🔍 **Responding to plans and predictions**
Plans
I'm going to… | What a good idea!
| How nice!
| Are you? So am I.

Predictions
I don't think… will / is going to…
I think there'll be…
I think so, too. | I hope so.
I don't think so, either. | I hope not.

6 READING & SPEAKING

a What kinds of things do you recycle? Do you ever feel guilty about not recycling enough? Why (not)?

b How much do you know about recycling? Do the quiz on p.39 with a partner.

c Now read the article about recycling and check your answers to **b**. How many did you get right?

d Read the article again. Match each paragraph to the summary of what it's about.
  A ___ It's time to change our shopping habits.
  B ___ One country has stopped importing and recycling plastic waste because it isn't of a good enough quality.
  C ___ People are starting to understand that plastic is a major problem.
  D ___ People don't really know what can be recycled.
  E ___ Some containers have parts which cannot be recycled.
  F ___ The food industry doesn't provide the right information clearly.

e What do you think is the main message of the article? Choose a, b, or c.
  a We don't recycle enough of our waste and need to make more of an effort.
  b We put out our waste to be recycled, but sometimes we are making matters worse.
  c We need local authorities to do more to help us to recycle correctly.

f Complete the second word in these compound nouns from the article.
  1 water b_____
  2 recycling b_____
  3 ready-meal tr_____
  4 wrapping p_____
  5 baby f_____
  6 pasta s_____

g Have you noticed any of the problems mentioned in the article?

h Talk to a partner. Do you think that the following will happen in the future? Why (not)?
- all food will be produced without plastic packaging
- supermarkets will stop selling all types of plastic bags to their customers at the checkout
- food producers will improve the labelling on their packaging
- people in your country will recycle 75% of their waste

Why your recycling isn't working

Do you know what can be recycled – and what can't?

Try our quiz.

1 Which part of this water bottle can be recycled, the cap or the bottle?

2 Which of these two plastic trays can be recycled, the white one or the black one?

3 Which of these two kinds of wrapping paper can be recycled, the glittery one or the red and brown one?

4 Which of these two containers of pasta sauce can be recycled, the glass jar or the plastic pouch?

5 Which of these two toothpaste containers can be recycled, the plastic pump-action bottle or the tube?

6 What does the number '4' in this symbol tell you?

1 'Since its invention some 100 years ago, plastic has become an integral part of our daily lives,' said naturalist David Attenborough in the final episode of the highly praised BBC series *Blue Planet II*. 'But every year, some eight million tons of it ends up in the ocean…and there it can be lethal.' Slowly, it seems, we may at last be waking up to the fact that something that makes our lives easier in the short term has consequences that can last thousands of years.

2 One of our main convenience items is plastic water bottles. They are a major contributor to waste in the UK, and we use ten million of them a day. Although the bottles themselves can be recycled, the caps cannot. The problem doesn't stop with plastic bottles. According to new research, almost a fifth of the waste that people put into recycling bins cannot, in fact, be recycled. The reason for this is that the packaging is often made up of several components, many of which are not recyclable.

3 People often believe that something is recyclable when it's not. Take, for example, that black plastic ready-meal tray that you normally put with your bottles and newspapers, or your glittery Christmas wrapping paper – these cannot be recycled, though white trays and plain wrapping paper can be. Plastic pouches, such as the ones used for baby food or pasta sauce, can't be recycled, so it's better to buy them in glass jars, which can be. Toothpaste tubes also can't be recycled, but the pump-action bottles can be.

4 Unclear labelling is often to blame. Recycling information on packaging varies dramatically. Sainsbury's supermarket, for example, labels on its own-brand packaging exactly which parts can and cannot be recycled. Some manufacturers, on the other hand, include no information. Even the recycling symbol itself is confusing, because people don't know what the numbers mean. A 1 or 2 means that a product can be widely recycled, 3 indicates PVC, which is not widely recycled, 4 is polyethylene, and 5 is polypropylene, both of which can only be recycled in some centres. 6 and 7 are not widely accepted for recycling.

5 Last year, more than half of the plastic waste that the UK exported for recycling was sent to China. China has now banned imports of 'foreign garbage', because it is receiving too much poor-quality plastic, contaminated with non-recyclable items. It's a worrying prospect. There are fears that it might not be possible to find alternative destinations for all our recyclable waste. As a result, plastic may end up being burnt, or put in landfill, or more will end up in the sea.

6 Perhaps we should stop assuming that everything that looks recyclable actually is. Instead, we need to start buying products that come in packaging that we are sure can be recycled, or better still, we should try to avoid packaging altogether.

Adapted from The Times

4B Put it on your CV

G first and second conditionals **V** study and work **P** word stress

> Why do you want to go to university?
>
> Because if I get a degree, I'll be able to earn more money.

1 VOCABULARY & PRONUNCIATION
study and work; word stress

a Write four words from the list in each circle.

A levels   campus   classroom   CV   degree
experience   graduate (*noun*)   head teacher
professor   pupil   qualifications   reference

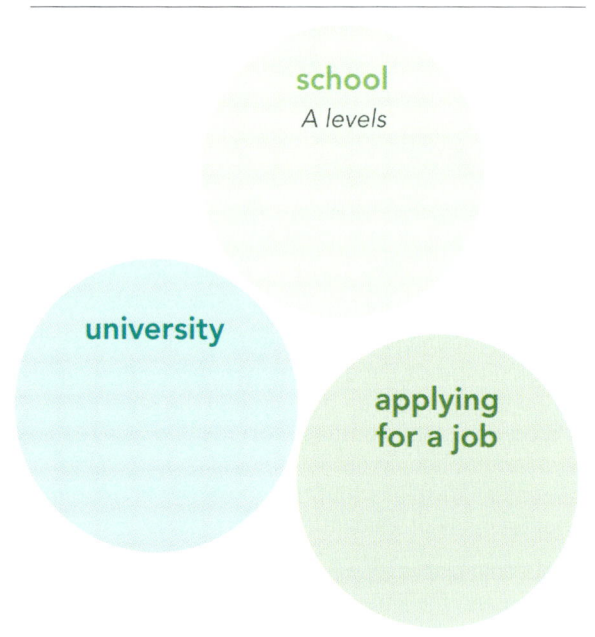

- school — *A levels*
- university
- applying for a job

b **V** p.157 **Vocabulary Bank** Study and work

c Underline the stressed syllable in these words.

a|ttend   di|sser|ta|tion   PhD
post|gra|du|ate   pro|fe|ssor   qua|li|fi|ca|tions
re|fe|rence   re|si|dence   scho|lar|ship
se|mi|nar   tu|to|ri|al   un|der|gra|du|ate
va|can|cy

d ◉ 4.15 Listen and check. Practise saying the words.

e Work in pairs. What is the difference between…?

1. an undergraduate and a postgraduate
2. a Master's degree and a PhD
3. a campus and a hall of residence
4. a professor and a tutor
5. a seminar and a webinar
6. a tutorial and a lecture
7. qualifications and skills
8. a CV and a covering letter / email

2 SPEAKING

Discuss the statements in small groups. Do you agree?

- You should choose a university subject you enjoy, not one which you think may get you a good job.
- People shouldn't have to pay to go to university.
- You will have a better experience if you don't go to university in your home town.
- It's not very useful to study for an arts degree because you will never get a well-paid job.
- Students shouldn't get part-time jobs while they are at university.
- For most young people, an apprenticeship is a better option than going to university.

> **Agreeing / Disagreeing and giving opinions**
> I completely agree / disagree with that.
> I don't agree with that at all.
> I think that's true because…
> Maybe that's true.
> Personally, I think…
> I'd say that…

3 LISTENING

a Would you ever consider doing a job for no pay? Why (not)?

b Read the article from a students' website about internships. Why are some internships paid and some not? Are internships a good or a bad thing, according to the article?

c ◉ 4.16 Listen to the first part of a radio programme, where Jake Butler of savethestudent.org talks about internships. Circle the correct answer.

1. The situation for interns is *better / worse* than in the past.
2. It is sometimes *legal / illegal* not to pay interns.
3. The law says that interns who have been promised jobs in the future *don't have to / have to* be paid.
4. A company *doesn't have to / must* pay interns who are substituting for paid employees.
5. School-age students doing work experience *have to / don't have to* be paid.
6. If an intern is not being paid, he or she should *have fixed working hours / choose his or her own hours*.

Glossary
National Minimum Wage the lowest wage that an employer is allowed to pay by law

National Living Wage the lowest wage that an employer is allowed to pay by law if a worker is over 25

SAVE THE STUDENT! | FINANCE BANKING MAKE MONEY SAVE MONEY

The **ultimate** guide to internships

Thinking about applying for an internship? Make sure you know the facts before you get started.

An internship is generally somewhere in the middle between work experience and an apprenticeship.

It can be more like work experience if it involves shadowing other members of staff, having the opportunity to ask a lot of questions, and learning about the company and industry. This kind of internship is often unpaid. Other internships can be more similar to an apprenticeship, if you're being trained within a particular department, are contributing to the company by producing work, and are getting paid (at least a little).

Either way, an internship can be a great opportunity for a student or graduate, or someone who wants to change their career. Benefits include having the chance to try out a job without committing to it, making connections, and having something to put on your CV. A couple of years ago, a report revealed that almost half of employers said they wouldn't consider candidates who didn't have work experience, regardless of their university qualifications.

Rosie   Lauren

d ◉ 4.17 Listen to the second part of the programme, where two women talk about their experiences of internships. What was each of them paid, if anything?

e Listen again and make notes for each woman about:
   1 the kind of work they did.
   2 the good side of internships.
   3 the bad side.

f Discuss the questions.
   1 Do you think unpaid internships are fair? Why (not)?
   2 Do the following things exist in your country?
      • work experience while you are still at school
      • apprenticeships
      • internships
      Have you ever done any of these things? Do you know anyone who has had a good or bad experience of them?
   3 If you had the chance to do an internship in any industry, which industry would you choose?

4 GRAMMAR first and second conditionals

a ◉ 4.18 Listen to the ends of two job interviews. Complete the conditional sentences. Who do you think is going to get the job?
   1 If we _____ you the job, when _____ you _____ to start?
   2 If we _____ you the job, you _____ a lot of training.

b **G** p.139 Grammar Bank 4B

c ◉ 4.21 Listen and write five first conditional sentences giving advice to people looking for work. Do you agree?

d Imagine you were in these situations. What would you do? Use a second conditional sentence and say why.
   1 You are offered a great job abroad.
   2 Your partner is offered a job abroad, but you don't want to move.
   3 You have to choose between a well-paid but boring job and a very interesting but badly-paid job.
   4 You are offered a good job while you are still studying.
   5 You have to choose between working at night or at weekends.

   If I was offered a great job abroad, I'd probably take it because I'd have the opportunity to learn about a new culture.

5 READING

a In your country, do students sometimes have part-time jobs during the evening, weekends, or holidays? What sort of part-time jobs are common?

b Read the article. For each person, underline a sentence that shows whether they learnt something from the job or not. Who is the most positive about their job?

c Read the article again. Answer with A–E.
Which person…?
1 ____ felt that the job was badly-paid
2 ____ liked the parts of the job where he / she could rest
3 ____ started very early and finished very late
4 ____ enjoyed spending time with the other workers
5 ____ was very unsuccessful in one of his / her jobs

d Find one word or phrase related to money in each paragraph for these definitions.

A _____ an informal word for money
B _____ money that children get from their parents every week
C _____ got money for doing a job
D _____ a regular amount of money that you earn, usually every week
E _____ the place where you pay, e.g. in a supermarket

e Which of the part-time jobs mentioned would you most / least like to do?

Glossary
shelf-stacker a person who puts things on shelves in a supermarket
sell sth door to door visit houses to ask people if they want to buy something
do a round do a job with a particular route, e.g. a postman

The best part-time job I ever had...

Dog walker, babysitter, shelf-stacker – most of us would have one of these classic part-time jobs on our CV. But did we really learn anything from the experience?

A Sir Ranulph Fiennes, *explorer*

When I was 16, I wanted to buy a canoe and needed £85. I washed the buses at Midhurst bus station between 3.00 a.m. and 7.00 a.m. during the week. Then I washed the dishes at the Angel Hotel from 6.00 p.m. to 10.00 p.m. I was paid £11 per week in all, and that's how I got the cash. It's too long ago to know if I actually learned anything from the experience.

B Russell Kane, *comedian*

I did two humiliating Saturday jobs. The first was selling vacuum cleaners door to door. I didn't sell a single one. The other job was working with my granddad for a frozen-food delivery service. I doubt that a Saturday job really teaches you anything. Where I come from, it's automatic – at age 11 you get a job. It wasn't, 'Hey man, I'm really learning the value of work.' It was, 'If I want money, I must work for it.' My dad never gave me a penny of pocket money after the age of 11.

C Tony Ross, *illustrator and author*

In the fifties, when I was a boy, I used to work at the post office over Christmas. It was fantastic fun. I earned enough to buy an old motor scooter. My favourite part was going in the lorry to collect the mailbags from the station because you didn't have to walk the streets all day. The other good thing was doing a round with your own house in it, because then you could stop for a cup of tea. I learned the basics of working for money, like arriving on time and enjoying it no matter what. It was a good introduction because very few people work for fun.

D Clive Stafford Smith, *lawyer*

I worked for a sand and gravel company when I was 16. It was cold, damp, and so boring that I cried. I've learned various important things from that job. First, I know I'm very lucky to have a job now that I truly love. I also learned that it's crazy to pay bankers millions while paying a low wage to people at gravel companies. It's terrible work and no one should have to do it. Anyone who says differently should be forced to work at that gravel company for a year.

E Adele Parks, *author*

When I was doing my A levels, I worked in our local supermarket for two years, stacking shelves. I was 16 then, and in a job like that, you make the decision whether this is what you want to do for the rest of your life. I spent a lot of time chatting to the other guys and girls who had permanent jobs. I am good at talking and telling stories, and I think I learned it there because one of the things about stacking shelves or being at the checkout is that you have lots of opportunities to talk to people. That's what I liked best.

Adapted from The Times

6 SPEAKING

In pairs, discuss the questions about work and studies. Follow the arrows to ask the questions that are most relevant to your partner.

Part-time work

Have you ever done a part-time or holiday job? What was it? → Why did you choose it? Did you enjoy it? → What did you learn from the job?

If you're studying now…

What qualification are you studying for?
↓
Do you think you will continue studying when you finish your present course?
↓
What jobs do you think you might get with your qualification?
↓
Do you know anyone who has a job you'd like to have? Which job? Why?
↓
What jobs would you definitely not like to do? Why?

If you're working now…

Why did you apply for your current job?
↓
What qualifications did you need?
↓
Why do you think you got the job?
↓
Would you like to change jobs? Why (not)?
↓
If you could go back in time and choose a different career, what would you choose?

7 ▶ VIDEO LISTENING

a Watch an interview with a student who has a part-time job. What does Milly want to do when she leaves college? How did her part-time job change her life?

b Watch again and mark the sentences **T** (true) or **F** (false). Correct the **F** sentences.
 1 Milly is studying at the Royal Academy of Music.
 2 Her mother was a good singer.
 3 She was optimistic when she started her Master's degree.
 4 One of Milly's problems is the cost of living in London.
 5 Her part-time job involves playing with professional musicians.
 6 Milly only had 48 hours to prepare for the concert.
 7 The audience was not impressed that the performer was a music student.
 8 There was a lot of publicity about Milly immediately after the concert.
 9 The media attention wasn't as exciting as the actual concert for Milly.
 10 Milly still does the part-time job.

c What does Milly say and do that makes you think she might be successful in her career?

8 WRITING

W p.118 Writing A LinkedIn profile
Create your own profile for LinkedIn or a similar site.

Go online to watch the video and review the lesson

43

3&4 Revise and Check

GRAMMAR

Circle a, b, or c.

1 I couldn't answer my phone because I ____.
   a drove   b used to drive   c was driving
2 We ____ to a lot of different shops yesterday.
   a went   b used to go   c were going
3 She ____ get up so late.
   a didn't use   b didn't use to   c didn't used to
4 When I was young, I ____ playing football.
   a love   b was loving   c used to love
5 Go ____ the steps until you get to the bottom.
   a down   b on   c along
6 We're very pleased ____ our holiday photos.
   a with   b to   c of
7 A Are we going out?
   B It ____ the weather.
   a depends   b depends on   c depends of
8 I'm really sorry. I promise ____ late again.
   a I'm not   b I won't be   c I'm not going to be
9 A These bags are so heavy!
   B ____ you with them.
   a I help   b I'm going to help   c I'll help
10 A We've booked a week in Venice in April.
    B Where ____ stay?
    a do you   b will you   c are you going to
11 This job looks interesting. ____ I apply?
    a Shall   b Do   c Will
12 I ____ to work abroad unless the pay was very good.
    a don't want   b won't want   c wouldn't want
13 I might get the job if I ____ more experience.
    a will have   b had   c would have
14 If you ____ to earn some money, you shouldn't become an intern.
    a will need   b need   c needed
15 You won't get into university ____ harder.
    a unless you don't study   b if you study   c unless you study

VOCABULARY

a Write a word or phrase connected with age.
   1 15 years old _____   4 over 65 _____
   2 21 or 22 _____   5 58 _____
   3 18 months old _____   6 44 or 45 _____

b Circle the correct word or phrase.
   1 My sister's a very good *photographer / photograph*.
   2 It's very dark in here, so you'll need to use *zoom / flash*.
   3 This is me, *in the centre / in front of* the Taj Mahal.
   4 There's my dog, in the *bottom right-hand / right-hand bottom* corner.
   5 Here's a photo of us on the beach – you can see our hotel in the *foreground / background*.

c Write words for the definitions.
   1 a person whose job is to take the rubbish away _____
   2 the material often used to make boxes _____
   3 the top of a jar _____
   4 a large plastic bag for putting rubbish in _____
   5 a plastic or paper cover for a chocolate bar _____
   6 a large area of land where waste is put _____

d Complete the words.
   1 Don't forget to include a c_____ letter with your CV.
   2 I'm living in a hall of r_____ in my first year at university.
   3 He won't get the job. He doesn't have enough q_____.
   4 You need to apply for a work p_____ to work in the USA.
   5 Most university students attend l_____ every day.
   6 I'm trying to get a job, but there are very few v_____.
   7 We'd like to invite you to a_____ an interview on 3rd March.
   8 The Humanities f_____ is the largest at this university.

PRONUNCIATION

a Practise the words and sounds.

Vowel sounds   Consonant sounds

train bike bird   tie dog television shower chess jazz

b 🅟 p.166–7 Sound Bank Say more words for each sound.

c What sound in **a** do the pink letters have in these words?
   1 j**a**r   2 l**e**cture   3 w**or**k p**er**mit   4 v**a**cancy   5 **a**pply

d Underline the stressed syllable.
   1 re|tired   3 pho|to|gra|pher   5 pro|fe|ssor
   2 o|ppo|site   4 re|cy|cle

44

CAN YOU understand this text?

a Look at the title of an article about a 'zero waste' store and the photo. What kind of store do you think it is? Read the article once and check.

Leading the fight against a 'plastic planet'

In the past few weeks, Richard Eckersley has noticed a change in the type of people who come into his shop. In 2017, the former Manchester United footballer set up Earth.Food.Love in Totnes, Devon, with his wife, Nicola. It's the UK's first 'zero waste' store – the food is in big jars and boxes and people bring their own containers. 'A lot of new people are coming in – people who have not necessarily been interested in environmental issues before', he says.

Recently, the government called for supermarkets to introduce plastic-free aisles. But Eckersley says many consumers are already way ahead of politicians. 'We are getting calls every week from people who want to do something similar.' He and Nicola have helped people set up stores in Wales, Birmingham, and Bristol. Ingrid Caldironi had a similar idea. She set up a plastic-free shop in London last year, which has been so popular that it is soon moving to a bigger site.

Eckersley and Caldironi are members of an anti-plastics movement in the UK that has been growing as a result of the BBC's *Blue Planet* series and a general worry about the damage plastic is doing to the environment. But big supermarkets have so far not tried very hard to reduce their plastic waste. Sian Sutherland, founder of the campaign 'A Plastic Planet', says, 'The most exciting thing is that politicians and industry are no longer saying that recycling will solve the problem. Banning the use of plastic packaging for food and drink products is the only answer.' Walking down the aisles of the supermarket where everything from pizza to fresh fruit and vegetables is covered in plastic, Sutherland says urgent action is needed. 'It is really quite overwhelming,' she says. 'I can buy gluten-free, fat-free, African food, Asian food, but I can't buy food without plastic.'

Plastic pollution is causing widespread global damage. More than one million plastic bottles are bought around the world every minute, and most end up in landfill or the sea. The contamination is so extensive that tap water around the world also contains plastic. Back in Devon, Eckersley says, 'After my daughter was born, it made me think about what future lies ahead for her. I wanted to say that at least I tried to make a difference.'

Adapted from The Guardian

b Read the article again. Mark the sentences **T** (true) or **F** (false). Correct the **F** sentences.
1 Richard Eckersley gives away boxes of food.
2 All the new customers at Earth.Food.Love are people who are active in fighting for the environment.
3 People phone Eckersley to ask for help with their shops.
4 There are no 'zero waste' shops in London.
5 The food industry is confident that recycling is better than banning plastic packaging.
6 Nowadays, it's easier to find gluten-free food than plastic-free food.
7 Plastic bottles are one of the biggest problems.
8 Eckersley became more interested in environmental issues after he became a father.

CAN YOU understand these people?

4.22 Watch or listen and choose a, b, or c.

1 Erica   2 Keith   3 Shreeya   4 Emma   5 Thomas

1 Erica ____ when she was a child.
a used to annoy people
b has stopped being as inquisitive as
c has completely changed from
2 Keith ____.
a usually uses a normal camera
b takes more videos than photos nowadays
c only takes photos of his children
3 Shreeya tries to avoid using plastic by ____.
a always having a packed lunch
b shopping in small local shops
c using her own refillable water bottle
4 Emma is studying osteopathy because ____.
a someone suggested it as a career
b a family member was an osteopath
c she recovered from injuries thanks to osteopathy
5 Thomas says that ____.
a he rarely met interesting people
b customers often treat waiters quite badly
c he didn't enjoy his part-time jobs

CAN YOU say this in English?

Tick (✓) the box if you can do these things.
Can you...?
1 ☐ talk about what you were like as a child
2 ☐ describe one of your favourite photographs
3 ☐ talk about what you are going to do personally to reduce waste
4 ☐ complete the sentence so that it's true for you and say why. *If I had to choose between going to university or getting a job, I would…*

Go online to watch the video, review Files 3 & 4, and check your progress

5A Screen time

How long has *MasterChef* been on TV?

It's been on for a long time, at least ten years.

G present perfect simple **V** television **P** /w/, /v/, and /b/

1 VOCABULARY television

a ▶ 5.1 Listen to extracts from six TV programmes. Match each extract to a type of programme.

a ▢ chat show   d ▢ sitcom
b ▢ documentary e ▢ live sport
c ▢ crime drama f ▢ the news

b **V** p.158 **Vocabulary Bank** Television

c What kinds of programmes do you usually watch? What do you never watch?

2 PRONUNCIATION /w/, /v/, and /b/

a ▶ 5.4 Look at the sound pictures. What are the words and sounds? Listen and repeat.

we	TV	be
switch	volume	broadcast
weather	over	problem

b ▶ 5.5 Listen to the pairs of words. Can you hear the difference? Practise saying the words.

1 a boat   b vote
2 a B   b V
3 a very   b berry
4 a bin   b win
5 a wool   b bull
6 a why   b buy
7 a vet   b wet
8 a wine   b vine

c ▶ 5.6 Listen and circle the word you hear.

d Practise saying the sentences.

We want to buy a bigger TV.
I never watch live sport.
Can we turn over to channel five?
The film won't be over before eleven.

3 LISTENING & SPEAKING

a Look at the two photos of people watching TV. In pairs, **A** describe photo 1, and **B** describe photo 2. Then discuss how they show the way in which watching TV has changed.

b   Read a questionnaire about 21st century TV habits. Complete the definitions with the highlighted words and phrases.

Watching TV the 21st century way

1 How do you watch TV programmes, on a television or on another **device**?
2 Do you **'two-screen'** while watching TV? What kinds of things do you do?
3 Do you normally watch live TV or **catch-up**?
4 Have you ever **binge watched** a TV series? How many episodes did you watch in one go?
5 Do you use a **streaming** service like Netflix? What do you like about it?
6 How often do you watch YouTube, or online **channels** like Apple? What kinds of things do you watch?
7 Do you ever interact with TV shows by voting for **contestants**?

_____ (verb, slang) watch a TV programme or series on one device while using another at the same time, e.g. to tweet about the programme or check information

_____ (noun) a television station

_____ (verb, idiom) watch several episodes of a TV series one after the other

_____ (noun) a method of sending or receiving data over a computer network

device (noun) a piece of equipment that has been designed to do a particular job

_____ (noun) a person who takes part in a game, quiz, or competition

_____ (noun) a service that allows you to watch television programmes after the time when they were originally broadcast

c ◆ 5.7 Listen to different people answering questions 1–7 in **b**. Match them to the programme or kind of programme they mention.

d Listen again. How do the people answer the questions in **b**?

e Answer the questionnaire in **b** with a partner.

4 GRAMMAR present perfect simple

a Look at some extracts from the listening in **3**. What are the missing words?
1 When something _____ happened on the news, I might watch it live.
2 Yesterday, I was watching *MasterChef* and I _____ some small cake tins.
3 I haven't done it _____ a long time.
4 For example, a few months _____, I watched all the episodes of *Brideshead Revisited*.
5 I've _____ watched someone preparing a fish dish.
6 I have _____ several times for contestants, when they've done a really good dance.
7 Once, I _____ addicted to a TV show.

b ◆ 5.8 Listen and check. For each sentence, say why either the present perfect or past simple is used.

c **G** p.140 Grammar Bank 5A

d Change the **bold** words to make the statements true for you. Then compare with a partner.
• I've watched about **20** hours of TV since this time last week.
• Today, I've used **three** devices to watch or listen to programmes.
• I've downloaded ***Blue Planet***, but I haven't watched it yet.
• I haven't watched **the news** for a long time.
• I've never enjoyed watching **live sport**.

(*I've watched about ten hours of TV, I think. And you?*)

47

5 READING

a Do you ever watch films or TV series in another language with subtitles? Why (not)?

b Look at the images from eight TV drama series which have been successful all over the world. With a partner, try to match them to the countries they are from.

▇ Argentina ▇ Brazil ▇ Denmark ▇ France (x2)
▇ Italy ▇ Spain ▇ Sweden / Denmark

A FORBRYDELSEN (THE KILLING)

B SÉ QUIÉN ERES (I KNOW WHO YOU ARE)

C LES REVENANTS (THE RETURNED)

D SUBURRA (BLOOD ON ROME)

E ENGRENAGES (SPIRAL)

F BRON|||BROEN (THE BRIDGE)

G EL MARGINAL (EL MARGINAL)

H DUPLA IDENTIDADE (MERCILESS)

c **Communication** TV dramas **A** p.108 **B** p.112 Check your answers to **b** and tell each other about the series.

d Have you seen any of the series in **b**? If yes, which did you most enjoy?

e Read the first paragraph of the article on p.49. Choose the best title from the three below.

> Turn it off! It isn't in English…

> Why is the UK in love with foreign TV series?

> What's the problem with British TV?

f Now read the whole article. Choose a, b, or c.

1 Foreign-language dramas nowadays are considered ____.
   a an unusual taste
   b normal because everyone watches them
   c only suitable for educated people

2 *The Killing* was the first foreign series which ____.
   a became really popular
   b the BBC showed
   c Denmark exported

3 One reason for the popularity of foreign-language dramas is that ____.
   a it's much easier to watch them than it used to be
   b everybody is talking about them
   c UK and American series aren't as good as they used to be

4 Programmes with subtitles make the viewers ____.
   a do other things while they watch
   b want to tweet about them
   c pay more attention to what they are watching

5 Walter Iuzzolino is in favour of foreign-language TV because ____.
   a it encourages people to learn foreign languages
   b it allows people to experience life in other countries
   c it encourages people to visit the countries the series are set in

A few years ago, if you'd mentioned to a British friend or colleague that you were addicted to a Danish drama series, people would have thought you were a bit strange. But in the UK today, subtitled foreign-language dramas aren't just in fashion, they're completely mainstream.

It all began when the BBC bought the French crime drama *Spiral*, though it was Denmark's *The Killing* that was the tipping point. 'I remember hearing people talking about it on the bus,' admits Sue Deeks, Head of Programming at the BBC. 'It was clearly growing and growing in popularity, but the extent of it took everyone by surprise.' *The Killing* was followed by *The Bridge*, in which a crime is committed on the bridge between Denmark and Sweden, which regularly topped a million viewers. The British were hooked.

One of the reasons for the success of foreign TV is that it is more accessible than it used to be, thanks to catch-up and online services. And if you haven't watched the latest foreign series that everybody is talking about, you can binge watch the episodes that you've missed, and tweet about how much you love *The Returned*.

There may be something else in foreign TV's new popularity, too. In a world in which we're frequently distracted from our TV viewing by Twitter and WhatsApp, subtitles force us to focus. 'When you read subtitles, you have to be glued to the screen,' says Deeks. 'That concentration gives a particular intensity to the viewing experience. You just can't multitask when you're watching a foreign-language drama.'

'When you read subtitles, you have to be glued to the screen'

And while foreign-language dramas are often remade for the Anglo-American market – for example, *The Bridge* became *The Tunnel* – the originals still dominate, because they transport us to a different culture. As Walter Iuzzolino, who has set up a new streaming service dedicated to foreign-language TV, says, 'You develop a love for the distant world, because while you're watching, you're in the country. If you see something amazing set in Argentina, then Argentina itself, the houses, the people, what they wear, what their voices sound like, the language, is one of the biggest appeals. There is a huge pleasure in that.'

Adapted from The Independent

Glossary
tipping point the point at which an idea suddenly spreads quickly among a large number of people, as a result of a number of small changes over a period of time before that

g Do you agree with Walter Iuzzolino that watching TV series from other countries helps you 'develop a love for the distant world'?

6 SPEAKING

a Write the names of TV series or films in as many boxes as you can.

a TV series you've just finished watching

- What kind of series was it?
- Where was it set?
- What was it about?
- Who were the main characters?
- Did you enjoy it?
- Do you know if it's going to continue?

a film you've seen more than three times

- How many times have you seen it?
- Why do you like it so much?
- Do you think you'll ever watch it again?

a TV series that lots of people you know have seen, but you haven't

- Why haven't you seen it?
- Do you think you're going to? Why (not)?
- What do your friends think of it?

the TV series you've watched the most seasons of

- How many seasons have you watched?
- Are there going to be any more or has it finished?
- Which season did you think was the best?
- Did you get tired of it towards the end?

b Work in small groups. Talk about the boxes where you have written the name of a TV series or film, answering the questions.

> **Expressing enthusiasm**
> I think it's absolutely brilliant!
> I'm completely hooked!
> It's the best thing ever.
> I adore the main character.
> I can't wait for the next season.

Go online to review the lesson

49

5B A quiet life?

> How long have you been living in the country?
>
> For two years. We moved here when we retired.

G present perfect continuous **V** the country **P** vowel sounds, sentence rhythm

1 READING & SPEAKING

a Read the introduction to an article about Italian villages. Answer the questions.

1 Why are some Italian villages becoming 'ghost towns'?
2 What do you think the 'new ways of surviving' could be?
3 Are there similar problems in small villages in your country?

b Read the first paragraph about Civita. Complete it with problems A–D.

A the earthquakes, landslides, and floods
B can only be reached by a footbridge
C has only ten year-round inhabitants
D that can reach Civita are scooters

c Now read the second paragraph. What was the mayor's brilliant idea? Complete the tourist information about Civita.

VISIT CIVITA DI BAGNOREGIO AND GO BACK TO THE MIDDLE AGES!

Entrance fee:
Monday–Saturday €____
Sunday and public holidays €____

You can also book a private _____ and you can buy refreshments.

---

d Now read about Santo Stefano. Answer the questions.

1 What problems did the village have at the end of the 20th century?
2 Who was Daniele Kihlgren and what was his idea?
3 How has his idea benefited the local people?
4 What is the situation in the village now?

e Answer the questions with a partner.

1 Which of the two villages would you most like to visit? Why?
2 Do you think either of the solutions in the article would work for a town or village in your country?
3 Do you agree that these solutions are a good idea? What could be the disadvantages? Can you think of any other ways to help towns or villages survive?

A new life for dying towns

Italy is famous for its picturesque small towns and villages, many of them originating from medieval times, but a recent report suggests that almost 2,500 risk becoming abandoned ghost towns. It all started with the post-war economic decline of rural Italian communities, when many inhabitants of these small towns and villages emigrated to cities. As more and more young people left, birth rates fell, and the villages began to empty. But recently, some of these villages have discovered new ways of surviving.

Civita is a tiny village about 120 kilometres north of Rome. It was founded by the Etruscans more than 2,500 years ago. The main piazza has a bell tower and a 13th-century church, the narrow streets have beautiful stone houses on either side, and there are ruins of Renaissance palaces. However, Civita ¹___ which connects it to another small town, Bagnoregio. The only vehicles ²___, and a couple of tractors, which are used to transport building materials, or to bring supplies for the small number of restaurants and bars. Civita ³___, although in the summer, this rises to 100. It became known as 'the dying town', because of ⁴___ that have been threatening its survival since the 17th century, and it seemed destined to become a ghost town.

But in 2013, a brilliant idea from the local mayor saved it from certain death. His idea was to charge people an entrance fee to visit the village. Visitors now have to pay €3 Monday to Saturday and €5 on Sundays or public holidays. For a few euros more, they can get a private tour of the village, or a sandwich and a glass of wine. As they walk through its main entrance – a huge stone gateway – any irritation at having to pay quickly evaporates, as visitors are taken back to the Middle Ages. In only five years, the number of tourists has grown from 40,000 to 850,000 per year. As the mayor says, 'Today Civita is not only alive, but it's keeping the entire area alive, too.'

Another approach has worked for the tiny medieval village of **Santo Stefano di Sessanio**, 145 kilometres east of Rome. At the end of the 20th century, the village was in ruins, with only 70 inhabitants. But in 1999, Swedish-Italian millionaire Daniele Kihlgren drove through the village on a solo motorbike tour, and decided to do something about this sad situation. He started by buying one house and quickly followed that with another ten. He then made a deal with local government officials to preserve Santo Stefano and not allow any new buildings. In return, he would restore it to its original state and give the village a chance to live again by making the houses into hotel rooms.

Five years later, the village was opened to visitors and became the first 'Albergo Diffuso', which means a hotel which is in fact a whole village with rooms in different buildings. 32 of the restored houses are now hotel rooms. Kihlgren buys everything from local people in and around the village, from the food for the restaurants to the accessories in the guest rooms. As a result, local crafts and the local economy have been revived. In spite of a recent earthquake, the village is now thriving, and Kihlgren has since bought several more villages, which he plans to restore in the same way. Staying in Santo Stefano is like stepping back in time. Walking back in an intense silence from a cosy restaurant to the warmth of your own private, medieval house has a comforting and calming effect. Where once there were empty buildings and locked doors, now fireplaces burn again and soft light pours through the small windows of the centuries-old houses. Santo Stefano di Sessanio is alive again.

2 VOCABULARY the country

a Look at the photo. What kind of place do you think it is? Where do you think it might be?

b **5.10** Listen to a woman talking about her life there. Check your answers to **a**.

c Listen again and answer the questions.
1 What did she like about the village when she lived there?
2 What didn't she like as much?
3 Where does she live now?
4 What does she miss about life in the village?

d **5.11** Listen and complete four extracts from the listening. Do you know what the missing words mean?
1 There's a large _____ nearby…
2 …the _____ are covered with pine trees
3 People worked in the _____.
4 …we had our own _____ and generator

e **V** p.159 **Vocabulary Bank** The country

f What's the countryside like near where you live?

3 PRONUNCIATION vowel sounds

a Look at the pairs of words below. Are the vowel sounds the same or different? Write **S** or **D**.

1	leaf	wheat	5	pick	cliff
2	bush	mud	6	rock	stone
3	plant	farm	7	lamb	grass
4	grow	cow	8	sheep	field

b **5.15** Listen and check. Practise saying the words.

51

FROM THE CITY TO THE COUNTRY
AND SOMETIMES BACK AGAIN

Not everyone in the UK who moves to the country ends up staying there. In fact, for the first time in years, as many people are moving back to cities as are moving out to the country.

LIZ JONES

I was just divorced, and bored with my easy, if super-busy, London life. I wanted to live somewhere quieter, simpler, more beautiful, so I sold my house and bought a big farmhouse with 50 acres of land. I'll look after horses, I thought. I'll get a dog. I'll grow all my own food. It will be idyllic and friends will come to stay and tell me how lucky I am to live here.

BOB AYERS

My wife, Jean, and I had lived in London for years, and we both worked right in the city centre. I was a police inspector and Jean was a police dog handler. We enjoyed our jobs, but it was pretty stressful, dealing with accidents, drugs, shootings, and so on. We'd often talked about moving out of London, and we'd had holidays in the country, so we thought we knew what living in the country would be like. Ten years ago, we bought a house in a village in Dorset, with a huge garden.

4 LISTENING & SPEAKING

a Read the title and introduction to the article. Why do you think people move from the city to the country? Why do some people move back?

b Read about Liz Jones and Bob Ayers. Why did they both move to the country?

c ► 5.16 You're going to listen to Liz and Bob talking about what life was really like in the country. First, listen and complete some extracts. Who do you think stayed, and who do you think moved back to the city?

Liz
1 you have to drive miles to find a _____
2 they look at you as if you were from _____
3 another thing I _____ was the shooting
4 an amazing _____ and a pair of nesting herons
5 I sat outside underneath millions of _____

Bob
6 my wife always wanted to have a _____ or a _____
7 so we started with four _____
8 it gets incredibly _____
9 it can get physically very _____
10 there were some local _____ who didn't really like newcomers

d ► 5.17 Now listen to them talking about their experiences. Check your answer to the question in c.

> **Glossary**
> **free-range hens** hens which live outdoors and can move freely
> **battery farms** farms which keep hens indoors in small cages

e Listen again. Mark the sentences **L** (Liz), **B** (Bob), or **Bo** (Both).

Who...?
1 ☐ had problems with the house when he / she moved in
2 ☐ found prices much higher in the country
3 ☐ got a new job
4 ☐ bought more land
5 ☐ didn't behave like the local people expected
6 ☐ kept animals
7 ☐ had problems with the weather
8 ☐ gave work to the local people

f Why do you think one of them succeeded in their new life and the other failed?

g **Communication** City or country? p.106 Ask and answer questions with a partner.

5 GRAMMAR present perfect continuous

a Look at the photos and speech bubbles. (Circle) the correct verb form.

I'm fixing / I've been fixing the tractor at the moment. Can I call you back?

Take those boots off, they're covered in mud!

Sorry, but I'm working / I've been working in the fields all day.

b Compare with a partner. Explain why you chose each verb form.

c **G** p.141 Grammar Bank 5B

6 PRONUNCIATION & SPEAKING sentence rhythm

a ◉ 5.19 Listen and complete the sentences with verbs in the present perfect continuous. Use contractions if possible.
1 I _____ hard this week.
2 I _____ well lately.
3 My neighbours _____ a lot of noise recently.
4 I _____ about getting a new phone.
5 I _____ with my family a lot recently.
6 I _____ much TV lately.
7 I _____ very stressed for the last few weeks.
8 I _____ a lot of exercise this month.
9 I _____ a lot recently.
10 I _____ a lot of time on social media.

b Listen again and repeat. Copy the rhythm.

c Work with a partner. For each sentence in **a**, say if it is true for you or not, and give reasons.

1 is true for me. I've been working really hard this week because I have exams soon.

d Now think of two things you have or haven't been doing this week or recently. Work in pairs, **A** and **B**. **A** tell **B** what you've been doing. **B** show interest by asking for more details. Then swap roles.

I've been eating out a lot recently.
Oh really? Why?
Because some friends of mine are visiting, so we've been going out together.

7 WRITING

W p.119 Writing An informal email
Write an email about things you've been doing recently.

Go online to review the lesson   53

EPISODE **3** **Practical English** Time to tell the police

making a police report

1 ▶ A WORRIED PHONE CALL

a ◉ 5.20 Watch or listen to Jenny talking to Rob on the phone. In the end, what does Rob say she should do?

b Watch or listen again. Answer the questions.
1 Is Jenny sure the man in the news is the man she met on the plane? Why (not)?
2 What time were Jenny and Henry planning to have dinner?
3 What time is it now? Why is Rob worried about this?
4 How does Jenny describe the house?
5 What doesn't she think she'll be able to do?

If you were Jenny, would you stay in Henry's house alone?

2 ▶ MAKING A POLICE REPORT

a ◉ 5.21 Watch or listen to Jenny and Luke at the police station. What information does the police officer ask for about Henry? How do Jenny and Luke describe him?

b Watch or listen again. Complete the **You hear** phrases in the conversation.

c ◉ 5.22 Watch or listen and repeat some of Jenny's **You say** phrases. Copy the rhythm and intonation.

d In groups of three, practise the conversation in **b**.

e ⓒ **Communication** Reporting a missing person **A** p.108 **B** p.113. Role-play two conversations.

You hear	You say
…You also said that your father-in-law – Henry Walker – hasn't returned home yet. How long has he been ¹_____?	He was supposed to be home three hours ago.
OK. It's a bit early to report him missing but I'll ²_____ a statement. So, your name's Jenny Zielinski.	That's right.
And you're staying at The Grange, Marsh Lane, Long Crendon.	Yes.
OK. Can you ³_____ Mr Walker?	He's 62, I think. He's average height and build. He has grey hair and glasses. I don't know what colour his eyes are. *They're brown. Here is a photo of him.*
When did you ⁴_____ see him?	This morning. Around ten.
Where were you?	At his house in Long Crendon.
And do you remember what he was ⁵_____?	Oh, just a brown jacket, a dark green shirt, and jeans.
Do you remember anything ⁶_____ about the last time you saw him?	Yes, actually. We were going to go to Oxford, but Henry's two front tyres had been punctured.
Really? So you left for Oxford and he stayed to fix the car?	Yes.
Do you know what his ⁷_____ were for the rest of the day?	No.

54

You hear	You say
Can you give me some idea of his normal 8_____?	Not really… Well, he's an academic. He teaches at the university a few days a week, but he often works from home. He goes on a lot of long walks, but never this late.
And Jenny, do you 9_____ seeing anything unusual when you got back to the house this afternoon?	Well, there was my suitcase. The airport had returned my lost luggage and the lock was broken.
Is there anything 10_____?	There were some books on the floor. Really? That's weird. Henry's normally really tidy.
OK. Try not to 11_____, we'll look into this. In the meantime, perhaps you should stay with Luke, and if you think of anything else, or he turns up, give me a call.	

3 ▶ A THREATENING MESSAGE

a **5.23** Watch or listen to Jenny and Luke talking the next morning. What's the good news? What's the bad news?

b Watch or listen again. Circle the correct answer.
1 Jenny feels *safer* / *less safe* in Luke's house.
2 The username on the laptop *is* / *isn't* Jenny's.
3 When Luke opens a file, he finds *a photo* / *a formula*.
4 Jenny receives *a text message* / *a video message* from Henry.
5 Henry says the people who are holding him want her *laptop* / *suitcase*.
6 Henry shows them *today's* / *yesterday's* newspaper.
7 He asks Jenny and Luke *to go* / *not to go* to the police again.
8 He asks them *to give Rob a message* / *not to say anything to Rob*.

What do you think has happened to Henry? Why?
What do you think Jenny and Luke should do?

c Look at the **Social English** phrases. Can you remember any of the missing words?

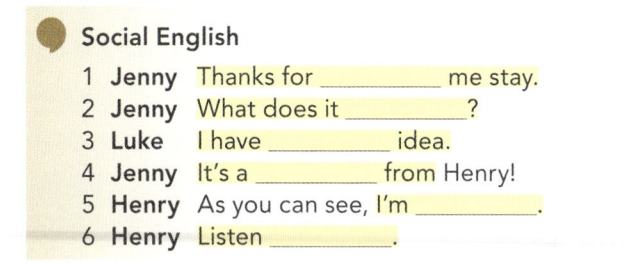

> **Social English**
> 1 Jenny   Thanks for _____ me stay.
> 2 Jenny   What does it _____?
> 3 Luke   I have _____ idea.
> 4 Jenny   It's a _____ from Henry!
> 5 Henry   As you can see, I'm _____.
> 6 Henry   Listen _____.

d **5.24** Watch or listen and complete the phrases. Then watch or listen again and repeat.

e Complete conversations A–F with **Social English** phrases 1–6. Then practise them with a partner.

A	Are you feeling OK?	Yes, don't worry,
B	Have a safe journey! It was really lovely to see you!	Yes it was great.
C	OK, we're going to do a dictation. I'm going to repeat each sentence twice.	Will you say them slowly?
D	Your phone just made a noise.	Yes. my sister. She's coming round this evening.
E	Do you know where my dad's gone?	Sorry,
F	I don't understand this message.	I don't understand it either.

CAN YOU…?
▢ describe someone's appearance and routine
▢ report a problem to the police
▢ thank someone for helping you

Go online to watch the video, review the lesson, and check your progress

6A What the waiter really thinks

Do we need to leave a tip?

Yes, we ought to leave about 12%.

G obligation, necessity, prohibition, advice **V** at a restaurant **P** word pairs with *and*

1 VOCABULARY at a restaurant

a Look at these phrases. Who says them? Mark them **C** (customer) or **W** (waiter).
1 Are you ready to order?
2 Would you like the dessert menu?
3 I'll have the lasagne, please.
4 Enjoy your meal!
5 Can we have the bill, please?
6 Today's specials are on the board over there.
7 How would you like your steak?
8 Can I have the wine list, please?
9 Is service included?
10 I'm sorry, but this fish isn't cooked.

b **V** p.160 **Vocabulary Bank** At a restaurant

c Work with a partner. What's the difference between each pair of words or phrases?
1 a cup / a glass
2 a plate / a saucer
3 a jug / a mug
4 a tablecloth / a napkin
5 a plate / a dish
6 a meal / a course
7 lay the table / clear the table
8 take an order / order food

2 PRONUNCIATION word pairs with *and*

a Look at the photo. What do you think the 'n' stands for? Why do you think it's written like that?

b 🔊 6.3 Listen and repeat the phrases.
fish and chips   cup and saucer
oil and vinegar   knife and fork
salt and pepper

> 🔍 **Word pair order**
> With many pairs, we always say them in a certain order, e.g. we say *oil and vinegar* **NOT** ~~vinegar and oil~~.

c What two kinds of food and drink can you see in the photos?

d 🔊 6.4 Listen and check.

3 READING

a Look at the title of the article on p.57. Do people in your country usually complain in restaurants if things aren't right, or do they suffer in silence? Have you ever 'lost your cool' in a restaurant? What happened?

b Read the article once. Who do you think the writer sympathizes with most, restaurant staff or customers?

c Read the article again and complete it with headings A–H.
A **Put yourself in their shoes**
B **There's bad cooking...and there's different cooking**
C **Ask to speak to the manager**
D **'Oh no, not TripAdvisor!'**
E **Respect people's expertise**
F **Be clear about what's wrong and what you want**
G **Don't wait to complain**
H **The menu is there for a reason**

d Look at the highlighted words in the article. What do you think *over-* and *under-* mean when they are used before another word?

e Which of the pieces of advice in the article do you think is the most useful?

56

How to complain in restaurants...
without losing your cool

People often lose their temper when they try to complain about bad food or service. So how do you do it effectively?

1

Seventy-five per cent of all problems in restaurants are caused by bad organization, bad training, or employing the wrong staff. The waiters are often innocent victims, so they are not the right person to complain to.

2

Have a reasonable idea in your head of how you want the complaint dealt with (i.e. the dish re-cooked, removed from the bill, etc.). Make your case politely, but clearly; don't start your sentence with 'Sorry…'. What are you apologizing for?

3

A waiter's job isn't easy. You need to recognize the difference between when they are being genuinely rude or lazy, and when they are simply overworked. Booking systems crash. A big group of people who haven't booked suddenly arrives. Staff get ill. Look around you. Are you waiting for your drinks because the staff are chatting by the till, or are they rushing around because the restaurant is clearly understaffed?

4

Never tell restaurant staff how you think a dish should be cooked or how a drink should be served. If you want something done in a specific way, ask for it. Good restaurants will do it. You don't need to prove how much you know about food and wine by talking about your holiday in Italy or your best friend who has a vineyard. Please also bear in mind that you probably don't know everything. They are the professionals. You aren't.

5

The fact that a dish has not been made 'how you do it at home' is not a good reason to complain. The same applies to portion size, unless you can see that the table next to you got twice as much as you. But too much salt, important ingredients missing, undercooked fish, cold or burnt food: these are all good reasons for complaining.

6

You want a dish served without one of its ingredients? Within reason, that's fine. You want your steak cooked until it's like shoe leather? It's OK to ask for that. However, if you want spaghetti bolognese and it isn't on the menu, that's too bad. Similarly, you can't expect the staff to run to the nearest supermarket to get you some white bread because you don't like the chef's wholemeal loaf.

7

Don't threaten to write a bad review on a restaurant review site if you are unhappy with the food or service. If your complaint hasn't been satisfactorily resolved on the night, email the restaurant. You will be amazed how receptive restaurants can be.

8

Don't continue drinking your vinegary wine or eating your overcooked steak until you are halfway through and then complain. Similarly, there's no point in telling the waitress who is clearing the table that there wasn't enough sauce. Speak up while the mistake can be corrected.

Adapted from The Guardian

4 LISTENING & SPEAKING

a **6.5** You're going to listen to three people talking about bad experiences in restaurants. First, listen to some extracts and write down the food you hear.

b **6.6** Now listen to the three stories. Make notes in the chart.

c Answer the questions with a partner.
1 Think of some places where you've eaten out. Have you ever had really bad service? What happened?
2 Have you ever seen a customer who behaved badly? Have you ever worked as a waiter?
3 When you go to a restaurant, which do you think is more important, the service or the food? Why? What other aspects of a restaurant are important to you when you go out?

	1	2	3
Was the speaker a waiter or a customer?			
Where did the incident happen?			
What is the speaker complaining about?			
What happened in the end?			

5 GRAMMAR obligation, necessity, prohibition, advice

a Do you normally leave a tip in restaurants? How much do you leave?

b Read an article about tipping. Is the situation in your country similar to any of the countries mentioned? Do you agree with the waiter's advice in the last paragraph?

Tipping in restaurants – a waiter's guide

Knowing how to tip in restaurants can be a nightmare, especially on holiday. A waiter tells you what to do…

Is there anywhere where people never tip?

In Japan. You mustn't do it there. The Japanese think that tipping someone means treating them like a servant. The price is the price.

Where should you tip?

Everywhere else. As a waiter, I find it hard to imagine anyone being upset with extra cash. You should never feel embarrassed to leave a tip on the table. In fact, in countries where you don't have to tip, it's even more appreciated.

Do you need to tip if service is already included?

In countries like France and Australia, service is always included in the prices. The service charge is often shared with the kitchen staff as well – which is a good thing, helping everyone to earn a bit more. When you have to pay a service charge, of course, you needn't add an extra tip unless you really want to. If you do tip, check that the money is going to the waiter and not to the restaurant owner, and if in doubt, leave cash.

How much should you tip?

The standard service charge is 12.5% of the bill in Britain, so if your bill doesn't include service, you should tip about 10% (the USA and Canada are another story – there's no upper limit!). But – and this is important – if you're leaving a good tip, don't make a big thing about it and expect the waiter to look at you adoringly. Do it discreetly and enjoy the feel-good factor instead.

When shouldn't you tip?

The only circumstances when I think you shouldn't tip are when the service is really really bad, for example, if you ask for things that never arrive, or if staff are extremely unfriendly. But remember that what many people think of as 'slow service' is often more the kitchen's fault than the waiter's.

Adapted from The Guardian

c Match the highlighted phrases to their meaning. What other verbs could you use for 1, 4, and 5?

1 It's an obligation / necessity.
   _____

2 It isn't an obligation / necessity.
   _____   _____

3 Don't do it! It's prohibited / dangerous / wrong.
   _____

4 It's a good idea.
   _____

5 It isn't a good idea.
   _____

d ⓖ p.142 Grammar Bank 6A

e In pairs, circle the correct answer.

1 *You shouldn't / You ought to* speak rudely to waiters.
2 *You mustn't / You don't have to* order food containing nuts if you have a serious nut allergy.
3 *You ought to / You oughtn't to* send something back just because you don't like it.
4 *You have to / You needn't* book a table in advance at really popular restaurants.
5 *You don't need to / You shouldn't* order things which aren't on the menu.
6 *You mustn't / You don't have to* finish everything on your plate.
7 *You needn't / You should* leave a tip if the service was mediocre.

58

6 LISTENING

a ▶ 6.11 You're going to listen to an interview with Sally, an American, about tipping in US restaurants. First, listen to two short extracts. What American English words does she use for the following nouns?

tip   bill   waiter or waitress
note (= money)

b ▶ 6.12 Now listen to the interview. In which situations does Sally say you <u>don't</u> have to tip in the USA?

c Listen again. Complete the information with a number.
1 Many waiters earn $____ to ____ per hour.
2 The minimum wage in the USA is around $____ per hour.
3 A normal tip is ____ to ____% of the bill.
4 If the service is excellent, you should pay ____%.
5 If the service isn't good, you should pay ____%.
6 In a bar, you should tip $____ for each drink you order.

d Was there anything that surprised you about the US tipping system? Do you think it's fair? Why (not)?

7 SPEAKING

a Look at the photos. What jobs do they show? What services do these people provide?

b In pairs, answer the questions about your country.
1 Do people usually tip for the services in the photos? If yes, about how much? If no, do you think they should?
2 Is it usual to tip anybody else who provides a service, for example, refuse collectors or postmen / women at Christmas or for other special occasions?
3 Have you ever felt embarrassed about tipping or not tipping someone? Why (not)?

8 WRITING

W p.120 Writing A restaurant review
Write a website review of a restaurant you've been to recently.

To tip or not to tip?

Go online to review the lesson

59

6B Do it yourself

G can, could, and be able to **V** DIY and repairs, paraphrasing **P** consonant clusters

> Could you help me put up some shelves?

> Sorry, I can't. I've never been able to do DIY.

1 READING

a Look at the photos of everyday things. Which do you think you might be able to use…?

- instead of shaving cream
- to get rid of smells
- to keep insects away
- to make towels soft
- to make your hair shiny

b Read the blog. What are the 'extraordinary' uses for the things in **a**? Were you right?

c Read the blog again. As you read, focus on the highlighted verbs and read the sentences they appear in carefully. Try to guess what the verbs mean.

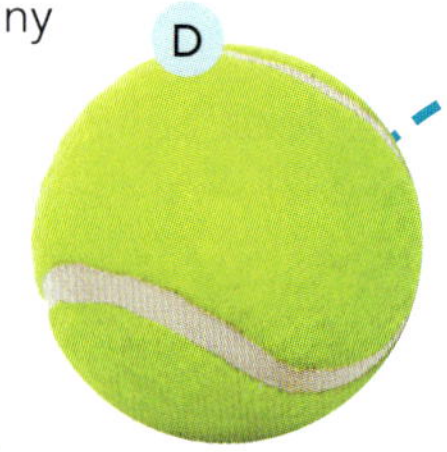

Marina's extraordinary uses for ordinary things

Your house is full of everyday items that can be used for things you would never have expected. I promise all these ideas work – I've tried them!

1 Do you have a problem with insects? Don't like spiders in your house? Citrus or lemon oil is a traditional repellent for insects of all kinds – and the oil is in the peel. Take large pieces of peel and place them along window sills and cracks outside your house, to stop spiders, ants, and other unwelcome guests from coming in. Cats also really dislike the strong smell of lemons, so you can use lemon peel or lemon juice to keep them away from specific areas in your house or garden. However, despite what you may have heard, lemon oil doesn't have any effect on mosquitoes, sadly, so it won't protect you from their bites.

2 Even after you've washed them, plastic food containers often end up with a rather unpleasant smell from the food you kept in them. Newspaper can absorb all sorts of moisture and smells. Just crumple a piece of newspaper and put it inside your food container, then seal the container and leave it overnight. In the morning, throw away the newspaper and enjoy your clean container. You can also use the same method to deal with smelly trainers. Just stuff them with newspaper overnight and they'll be smell-free the next day.

3 Towels are always soft and lovely when they're new, but they soon become a bit rough. You could buy fabric conditioner to help to restore that softness, but you can also use a tennis ball. Just put the ball in the dryer with your towels or sheets. Because of the movement of the ball against the material, they will feel really soft when you take them out. Make sure you use a new tennis ball, though, or you risk ruining your lovely clean laundry.

4 Eggs are rich in proteins that are very similar to those found in our hair, so they make a great conditioner. Try beating an egg with a bit of olive oil, and apply it to your hair. (Use a couple of eggs if your hair is really dry.) If you want to smell less like an omelette and more like you've just come back from the hairdresser's, add a couple of drops of scented oil. Leave on for about 20 minutes and then rinse with warm water. Your hair will be shiny and extra smooth. But be careful not to use really hot water or you might cook the eggs!

5 Many people know that you can use olive oil to stop doors from making a noise, or to make machines work more smoothly. But you might be surprised to learn that it is also a great alternative to shaving cream. Just rub it on your skin and shave normally. Olive oil can also help with dry skin, so you can use it to moisturize your face or legs after you finish shaving.

d Now match the verbs in **c** to the definitions below.
1. _____ to wash sth with clean water only, not using soap
2. _____ to move a cloth or your hand backwards and forwards on sth while pressing hard
3. _____ to take in liquid from sth
4. _____ to put or spread sth such as paint, cream, etc. onto a surface
5. _____ to close a container tightly or fill a crack, especially so that air, liquid, etc. cannot get in or out
6. _____ to put sth in a particular position
7. _____ to make paper into a ball
8. _____ to bring sth back to a former condition
9. _____ to prevent sb / sth from going somewhere
10. _____ to fill a space or container tightly with sth

e Do you think you might try any of the tips in the blog? Which one(s)? Can you think of any other 'extraordinary' uses for the things in the photos in **a**?

2 GRAMMAR can, could, and be able to

a Complete some more tips with the correct form of *can* or *be able to*.
1. If you cover your children's drawings with hairspray, you'll _____ keep them for years.
2. You _____ rescue soups or stews which are too salty by putting pieces of apple or potato in them.
3. If you haven't _____ remove a water mark on wooden furniture, make a paste with salt and water and rub the mark with it.
4. If you want your candles to last longer, you _____ try putting them in the freezer for two hours before lighting them.
5. If you _____ find any silver polish at home, rub your silver jewellery with toothpaste.

b **G** p.143 Grammar Bank 6B

c Talk to a partner. Make sentences with phrases 1–5 and the ideas in the boxes, or your own ideas.
1. I think everybody **should be able to**…
2. I hate **not being able to**…
3. I've never **been able to**…
4. I'd love **to be able to**…
5. I hope I'**ll be able to**…in a few years' time.

Abilities	Possibilities / Permission
cook a two-course meal	spend more time with your family
change a wheel on a car	travel more
deal with computer problems	use your phone in class
drive do DIY dance well	work less
give first aid	vote at the age of 16

I think everybody should be able to drive.

I don't agree. If you live in a big city, you don't need to be able to drive – you can use public transport.

3 SPEAKING & WRITING

a What would you suggest in these situations? Compare your ideas with a partner.

WHAT **COULD** YOU DO?

- you've spilt red wine on your white shirt
- one of the screws in your glasses keeps coming out
- you have a pen mark on your jeans
- the heel breaks on one of your shoes
- there's a power cut and you have a freezer full of food
- you've dropped your phone in the toilet
- the zip on your suitcase breaks at the airport
- your car is nearly out of petrol and the nearest petrol station is 20 km away
- one of your shoelaces breaks while you're out

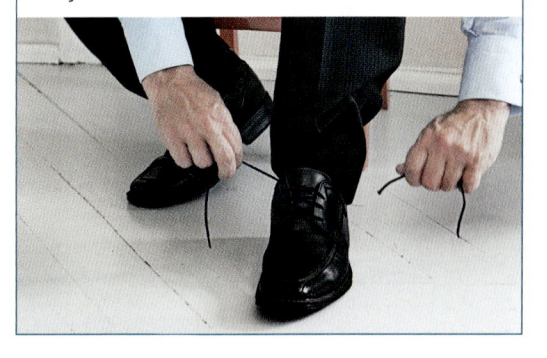

🔎 **Responding to other people's suggestions**
That's a good / brilliant idea!
Are you sure that would work?
I suppose that could work.
I think / don't think that would work.

b Choose the best solution you discussed in **a** and write a short paragraph about it for a blog. Describe the problem and give instructions for solving it.

61

4 VOCABULARY DIY and repairs, paraphrasing

a Look at the photo of the shop. What kinds of things does it sell? Do you ever go to shops like this?

string *screws* *a light bulb* *a screwdriver*

b **6.15** Listen to somebody asking about things in a DIY store. Which two of the four objects above does he want to buy?

c Listen again and complete the conversation. Then practise it with a partner.

> A Excuse me.
> B Yes, can I help you?
> A Yes, please. I'm ¹_____ for some… Sorry, I don't know the ²_____. They're the ³_____ that you put into wood. I want to make some shelves.
> B You mean screws?
> A Ah, yes, that's it. And I need one more thing. My ⁴_____ doesn't ⁵_____. I need a new, er…
> B Light bulb?
> A Yes, thank you.
> B You'll find them both over there, behind the gardening things.

d **Communication** What's it called? **A** p.109 **B** p.112 Explain what you want to buy to a partner.

e **V** p.161 **Vocabulary Bank** DIY and repairs

5 PRONUNCIATION consonant clusters

> **Consonant clusters**
> Some words have three (or even four) consonant sounds together, and these can be difficult to pronounce. These are common:
> 1 in words beginning with *scr*, *spr*, or *str*, e.g. **scr**ipt, **spr**ing, **str**uggle
> 2 in the middle of a word, e.g. su**ngl**asses, de**scr**ibe
> 3 when you add an *-s* to a word ending in two consonant sounds, e.g. pou**nds**.

a **6.19** Listen and repeat the groups of words.
 1 screw screwdriver scream screen string stress stream straight
 2 paintbrush toothbrush electrician handle
 3 needles shelves lamps bulbs

b Practise saying the sentences.
 1 I need some screws and a screwdriver.
 2 Go straight down the next street.
 3 Two electric toothbrushes, please.
 4 That's strange – this string's not very strong.
 5 Put some new bulbs in the lamps.

6 LISTENING & SPEAKING

a Have you ever been to IKEA or similar stores that sell self-assembly (or flat-pack) furniture? Did you buy anything there? What?

b Look at the cartoon with the article below. What problem does it show?

c Read about IKEA. What information in the article…?
 1 shows that IKEA is very popular outside Sweden
 2 shows that there are also problems with IKEA

It looks so easy at first…

The Swedish furniture store Ikea has transformed homes around the world with its cheap, modern, Scandinavian style. Since it started in 1943, IKEA has also changed the way we live: one in ten Europeans now sleeps in an IKEA bed, and its catalogue is in more homes than any other publication, including the Bible and the complete works of Shakespeare. But along with the pleasure of inexpensive furniture is the pain, for example, the frustrating one-way system used to navigate the stores, or some of the strange names given to the products. Most of all, there's the problem of getting the furniture home and trying to put it together.

d 🔊 6.20 Listen to three people describing an experience with flat-pack furniture. What did they buy? Were they happy with it in the end?

e Listen again. Which speaker…? There is one item you do not need.
   A ☐ didn't have all the parts he / she needed
   B ☐ assembled the furniture in the wrong place
   C ☐ had problems understanding what to do
   D ☐ had to take the furniture apart, move it, and reassemble it
   E ☐ had to return the item to the store
   F ☐ had to take the furniture apart and reassemble it without the missing pieces
   G ☐ had to get help to assemble the furniture

f 🔊 6.21 Listen to some extracts from the listening and write the missing words. What do you think they mean?
   1 After hours and hours, and a lot of _____, I finally managed to put it together.
   2 So I had to _____ it to _____, move all the bits into the bedroom…
   3 I'm quite _____, quite practical, so I thought, 'No problem'…
   4 I realized I'd put the door handle on the _____ _____ round.
   5 So now at least it has four legs, but it's rather _____ …

g Talk to a partner. Have you ever had problems putting something together (e.g. furniture), setting something up (e.g. a new router), or mending something that was broken? What happened? Use the questions below to help you.

Describing a process
↳ When and where did you do it?
↳ Did anyone help you?
↳ How long did it take?
↳ What problems did you have?
↳ How successful were you in the end?

7 ▶ VIDEO LISTENING

a You're going to watch a documentary about the history of flat-pack furniture. Before you watch, with a partner, guess the answers to 1–6.
   1 The first flat-pack furniture was invented by a man from ____.
      a Sweden   b the USA   c Japan
   2 He originally invented it in order to make his furniture ____.
      a quicker to make   b cheaper to sell   c easier to transport
   3 He patented the idea in the ____.
      a 1930s   b 1950s   c 1970s
   4 IKEA started selling flat-pack furniture ____ years later.
      a 5   b 10   c 15
   5 Today most people have a flat-pack ____.
      a bookcase   b kitchen   c bed
   6 In general, ____ people are able to assemble flat-pack furniture.
      a very few   b not many   c most

b Watch the documentary once and check your answers to a.

c Watch again and answer the questions.
   1 What two problems does the presenter say that people talk about?
   2 What kind of furniture did Sauder's company originally make?
   3 What did two travelling salesmen do with one of Sauder's coffee tables?
   4 What was Gillis Lundgren having a problem with?
   5 How did he solve the problem?
   6 What reasons are given for the success of flat-pack furniture?
   7 What problem does the presenter have at the end with his bookcase?

Go online to watch the video and review the lesson

5&6 Revise and Check

GRAMMAR

Circle a, b, or c.

1 **A** What's this programme?
   B I don't know. I've ____ turned it on.
   a already   b just   c yet
2 We've never been to Madrid, but ____ to Barcelona last year.
   a we went   b we've been
   c we've gone
3 **A** Shall I make some photocopies?
   B No, it's OK – ____ them.
   a I already did   b I already have done
   c I've already done
4 She's worked here ____.
   a for two months   b two months ago
   c since two months
5 Where have you been? ____ here since 7.00!
   a I'm waiting   b I've been waiting
   c I've waited
6 How long ____ to your family?
   a is this farm belonging
   b has this farm been belonging
   c has this farm belonged
7 The fields are wet. ____ recently.
   a It's raining a lot   b It rains a lot
   c It's been raining a lot
8 You ____ come shopping if you don't have time.
   a mustn't   b don't have to
   c needn't to
9 I didn't have any screws, so I ____ use nails instead.
   a had to   b must to   c must
10 You ____ pay me back till next week.
   a needn't   b don't need
   c don't have
11 She thinks I ____ sell my car.
   a need   b ought   c should
12 When we're on holiday, ____ go swimming every day.
   a we'll can   b we'll be able to
   c we'll be able
13 She ____ to come to the party.
   a might not can   b might not be able
   c might not
14 The exam was hard, but I ____ pass.
   a was able to   b could   c could to
15 He ____ be from Paris – he doesn't speak French.
   a could   b can   c can't

VOCABULARY

a Circle the word that is different.
   1 sheep   cow   barn   hen
   2 sitcom   documentary   episode   reality show
   3 rope   drill   hammer   screwdriver
   4 knife   fork   tray   spoon
   5 mug   cup   glass   saucer

b Complete the words.
   1 Can you **t**_____ the TV up? I can't hear it.
   2 I find some **s**_____ operas really addictive.
   3 Have you seen the weather **f**_____ for tomorrow?
   4 I'm not very interested in **c**_____ affairs programmes.
   5 I'm watching the **b**_____ set of *Breaking Bad* at the moment.

c Write words for the definitions.
   1 trees grow these in spring and lose them in autumn _____
   2 a small, narrow river _____
   3 an area of low land between hills or mountains _____
   4 to take fruit from the plant where they are growing _____
   5 a young sheep _____

d Circle the correct word.
   1 I'm not tall enough – do you have a *hammer / ladder*?
   2 I can't see anything. Pass me the *torch / penknife*.
   3 Do you have a needle and *string / thread*?
   4 I've lost one of the *nails / screws* from my glasses.
   5 We need to *set up / put up* our new computer.

e Complete the phrases with a verb.
   1 _____ for the bill   4 _____ a button back on
   2 _____ a tip   5 _____ a light bulb
   3 _____ an order

PRONUNCIATION

a Practise the words and sounds.

   Vowel sounds   Consonant sounds

   computer   bull   up   nose   vase   bag   girl   leg   yacht

b 🅿 p.166–7 **Sound Bank** Say more words for each sound.

c What sound in **a** do the pink letters have in these words?
   1 dr**a**ma   2 v**a**lley   3 w**oo**d   4 **k**nife   5 b**u**cket

d Underline the stressed syllable.
   1 pro|gramme   3 vi|ne|gar   5 screw|dri|ver
   2 do|cu|men|tary   4 re|co|mmend

CAN YOU understand this text?

a   Read the article once. Choose the best option to complete the title.

1   *do it myself*
2   *watch a video*
3   *call my dad*

I won't call a professional. I'll _____.

A few months ago, I ¹_____ to open the petrol tank of my car. When I googled, 'How to open stuck Volvo petrol tank', the first result was a video clip by a man called Robert, in Arkansas, USA. Robert demonstrated exactly how to get into the car and undo the tank from the inside. The video wasn't great, but it worked.

Every task you can think of now has a step-by-step video guide on the internet. Siobhan Freegard, who set up the online video platform Channel Mum, explains why video guides are so popular. 'I was in a café chatting about ²_____ to a young mother. We both took out our phones, and I went to the BBC food website to find one. But she searched on YouTube. For her, a video was easier than reading.'

Some of the online videos are rubbish. However, you can find some very useful ones. I've now successfully fixed a cupboard door, mended some tiles, and unblocked the sink. I am not ³_____. A survey by an insurance company found that for DIY advice, 50% of people go to YouTube first. Lisa Carney and her husband recently moved to a new house, and couldn't find reliable professionals, so she went online and found a site called DIY Doctor. Before long, she and her husband were doing the jobs ⁴_____. 'When I see a video of someone doing a job,' she says, 'I realize I don't always need to hire a specialist.'

People also turn to the internet because professionals are not available. William Hall moved house just after Christmas and on New Year's Eve he discovered that he had a blocked drain. He knew he wouldn't find anyone to come out that night, ⁵_____ he watched a DIY Doctor video, which explained exactly what to do. 'It was hard work,' said William, 'but it was so satisfying when I finally unblocked it.'

Some online videos have astonishing viewing figures. Chez Rossi runs a YouTube channel called Ultimate Handyman, most of which is ⁶_____ in his garage. Some of his videos have been watched more than a million times. Rossi earns a couple of thousand pounds a month from adverts and he even gets recognized in the street. 'I try to make my videos idiot-proof,' he says. So next time you don't know ⁷_____ to do something around the house, don't call someone. There'll be a video that explains it all.

Adapted from The Times

Glossary
drain a pipe that takes away dirty water or other liquid waste

b   Read the article again and complete the gaps with the best word or phrase.

1   wasn't able / didn't want / didn't use
2   receipts / results / recipes
3   lonely / alone / only
4   himself / themselves / herself
5   because / so / although
6   kept / seen / filmed
7   what / how / when

▶ CAN YOU understand these people?

◉ **6.22** Watch or listen and choose a, b, or c.

1 Rafael   2 Melanie   3 Royce   4 Julia   5 Lynn

1   Rafael sometimes watches ____.
    a   foreign TV shows
    b   TV in bed
    c   more than three hours TV a day
2   Melanie prefers the city to the country because ____.
    a   it's where she's always lived
    b   she hates it when it's too quiet
    c   it's more lively
3   Royce gets annoyed when waiters ____.
    a   overcharge him
    b   ignore him
    c   are rude to him
4   Julia doesn't always know how much to tip ____.
    a   waiters
    b   hairdressers
    c   taxi drivers
5   Lynn redecorated her bedroom ____.
    a   on her own
    b   three years ago
    c   last weekend

CAN YOU say this in English?

Tick (✓) the box if you can do these things.

Can you...?

1   ☐ talk about TV series you've watched and how many episodes you've seen in one go
2   ☐ say three things you've been doing recently
3   ☐ talk about things you should or shouldn't do when you're eating out
4   ☐ talk about things you are or aren't able to fix in your home

Go online to watch the video, review Files 5 & 6, and check your progress

7A Take your cash

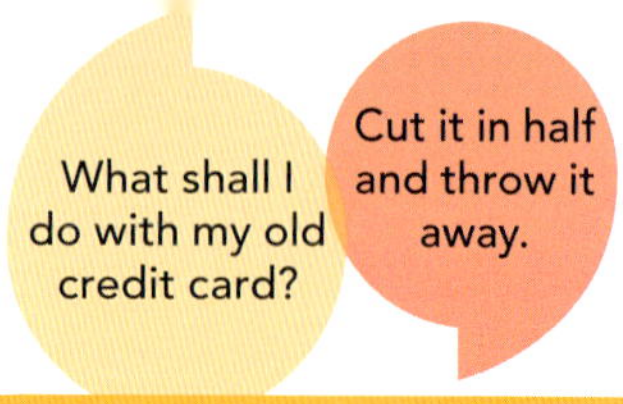

G phrasal verbs | V cash machines; phrasal verbs | P linking

What shall I do with my old credit card? — Cut it in half and throw it away.

1 VOCABULARY cash machines

a Look at the message on the screen below. What are the missing words? How do you feel when you see this message? What do you do?

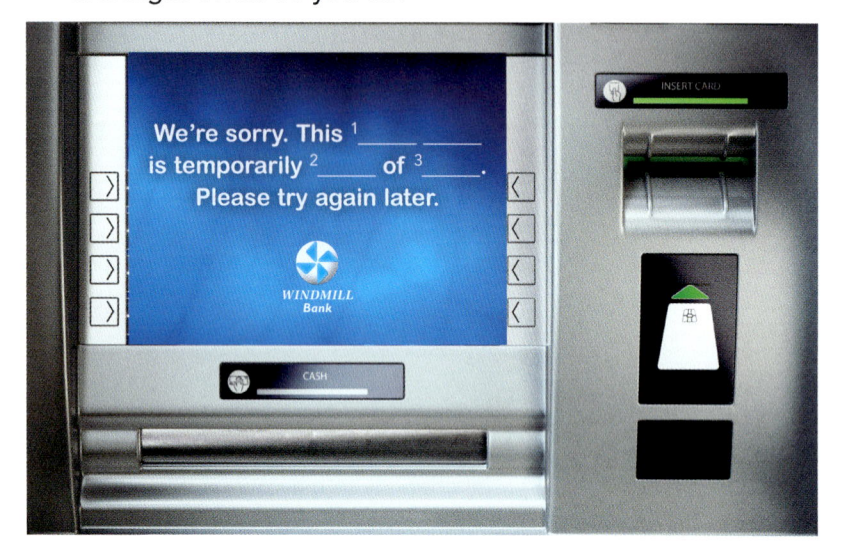

We're sorry. This ¹_____ _____ is temporarily ²_____ of ³_____. Please try again later.

WINDMILL Bank

b Read the text and answer the questions.
1 Why did John Shepherd-Barron come up with the idea of a cash machine?
2 Why do we usually have a four-digit PIN and not a six-digit one?
3 How much money could you take out of the first cash machines?
4 What things does the text say you can do at a cash machine nowadays? Can you think of any other things?

c Look at screen instructions 1–9 telling you how to take money out of a cash machine. Match each screen to its meaning.

A Choose 'Withdraw cash' from the main menu.
B Decide if you want a receipt, and press YES or NO.
C Choose the language you want.
D Take your card out of the machine.
E Choose or key in the amount of money you want to take out. Then press ENTER.
F Put your card into the machine.
G Key in your four-digit PIN. Then press ENTER.
H Choose the bank account you want to use.
I Take your money out of the machine within 30 seconds.

d 🔊 7.1 Listen and check.

e Match the formal words from the screens to their synonyms.

1 insert   a key in
2 enter   b choose
3 select   c put in
4 withdraw d take out
5 remove   e take money out of a bank account

Welcome to your ATM

Over fifty years ago, on 27th June 1967, the world's first ATM (Automated Teller Machine) was opened at a branch of Barclays Bank in north London. Today, we think nothing of stepping up to a hole in the wall when we need cash, but until the late 1960s, banks were only open until 3.30 p.m. John Shepherd-Barron, Managing Director of a banknote manufacturer, found his bank was closed when he needed some money. In the bath later that evening, he came up with the idea of something similar to a chocolate bar vending machine, with cash replacing the chocolate. Within days, Barclays agreed to create the first cash machines. Shepherd-Barron, a former soldier, suggested a six-figure personal identification number, based on his army number. But his wife Caroline said she could only remember four digits, so he settled on the four-digit PIN we use today. The first cashpoint only allowed the customers to take out £10 at a time, in £1 notes. Nowadays, you can do many other things at an ATM, for example, print a bank statement, or top up your phone, and new machines will even allow customers to print digital photos.

Adapted from the Barclays Bank website

How to use an ATM to withdraw cash

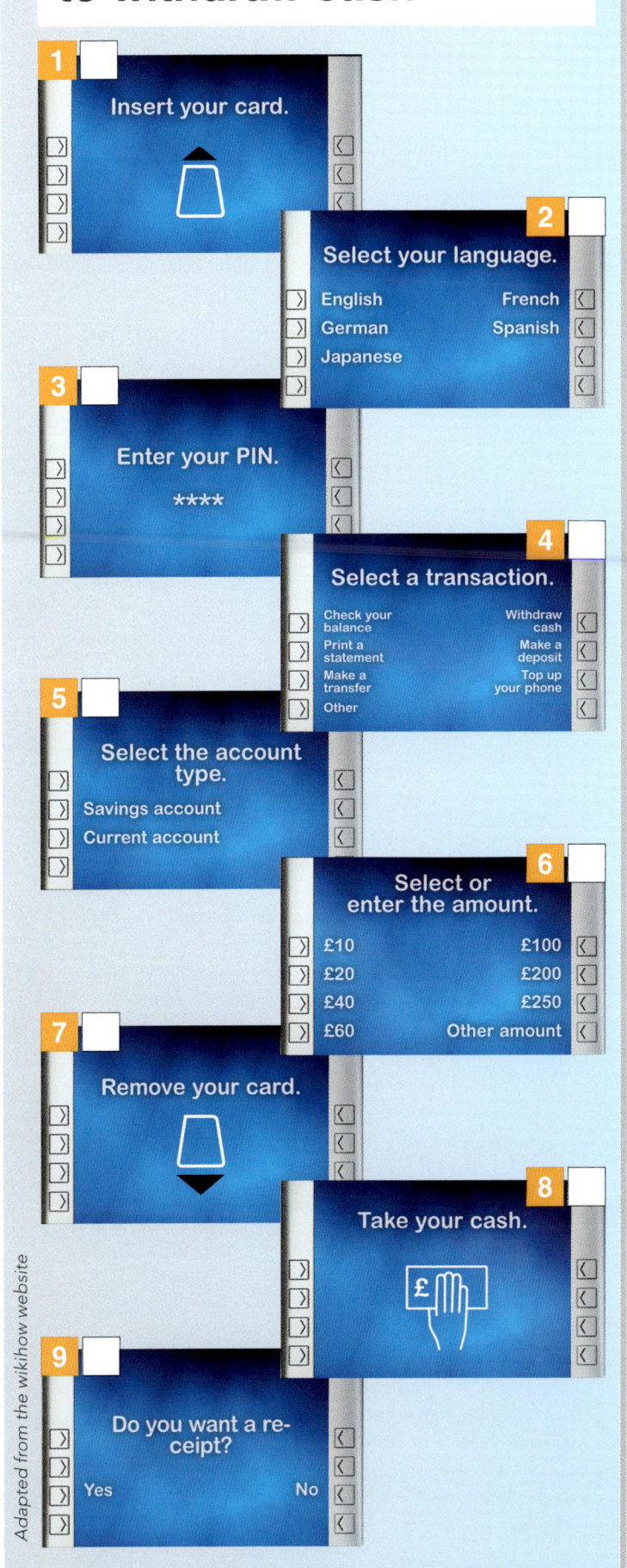

1. Insert your card.
2. Select your language.
   - English
   - German
   - Japanese
   - French
   - Spanish
3. Enter your PIN.
   ****
4. Select a transaction.
   - Check your balance
   - Print a statement
   - Make a transfer
   - Other
   - Withdraw cash
   - Make a deposit
   - Top up your phone
5. Select the account type.
   - Savings account
   - Current account
6. Select or enter the amount.
   - £10
   - £20
   - £40
   - £60
   - £100
   - £200
   - £250
   - Other amount
7. Remove your card.
8. Take your cash.
9. Do you want a receipt?
   - Yes
   - No

Adapted from the wikihow website

2 LISTENING & SPEAKING

a 🔊 7.2 Listen to two true news stories about ATMs and look at the pictures. What did each machine give out? Did both the stories have a happy ending?

b Listen again and answer the questions about each story.

Story 1
1. What happened when people heard about the machine?
2. How many people used the machine and for how long?
3. What kind of people were they?
4. Why did some people become aggressive?
5. What did the police do?
6. What did the bank say?

Story 2
1. What was the man doing when he locked himself in?
2. What did he leave in his van?
3. Why was this a problem?
4. How did he try to get help?
5. What did customers think at first?
6. What did the police do?

c Look at two extracts from the stories. Why do you think the villager and the man 'asked not to be named'?

Story 1: *'One villager, who asked not to be named, said that some people had used five or six bank cards and had got £300 free with each card.'*

Story 2: *'A man, who asked not to be named, had locked himself in.'*

d Talk to a partner.
1. How often do you use cash machines? What do you use them for?
2. Have you ever had a problem with a cash machine? What happened? What did you do?
3. If a cash machine gave you more money than you asked for, what would you do?

3 VOCABULARY & GRAMMAR phrasal verbs

a Circle the phrasal verb which you can't use with the **bold** noun.

1 give away	settle down	take out	**some money**
2 close down	switch off	turn up	**the TV**
3 look for	try on	look round	**a sweater**
4 throw away	set up	take out	**some rubbish**
5 grow up	put together	take apart	**a bookcase**

b **V** p.162 **Vocabulary Bank** Phrasal verbs

c Read the sentences in groups 1–4 and tick (✓) the one(s) where the word order is correct.

1 He gave away his money.   He gave it away.
   He gave his money away.   He gave away it.

2 We asked for the bill.   We asked for it.
   We asked the bill for.   We asked it for.

3 She got up early.   She early got up.
   She got early up.

4 I'm looking forward to my holiday.
   I'm looking forward my holiday to.
   I'm looking forward to it.
   I'm looking forward it to.

d **G** p.144 **Grammar Bank 7A**

4 PRONUNCIATION linking

> 🔍 **Linking**
>
> Remember that when a word ends with a consonant and the next word begins with a vowel, the words are linked together and pronounced like one word.
>
> If the final consonant is w, a /w/ sound is pronounced between the two words, e.g. *throw it* is pronounced /θrəʊwɪt/.

a Match 1–6 to a–f.

1 ___ The machine says 'Insert your card'.   a Take it out.
2 ___ Your shoes are really dirty.   b Throw it away.
3 ___ Waiter, I can't finish this steak.   c Put it in.
4 ___ This chicken's past its sell-by date.   d Take it away.
5 ___ The rubbish is beginning to smell.   e Look it up.
6 ___ It's probably on Wikipedia.   f Take them off.

b 🔊 7.9 Listen and check.

c 🔊 7.10 Listen and repeat a–f, linking the words.

d Work with a partner. **A** cover a–f. **B** say a sentence from 1–6. **A** say a response from a–f from memory. Then swap roles.

e 🔊 7.11 Listen to the sentences. Make a second sentence with a phrasal verb from the list and a pronoun (*it*, *me*, or *them*).

fill in   pay back   pick up   put away
switch off   try on   turn down   turn up

1 🔊 *You owe me money.* (Pay me back.

5 SPEAKING

Answer the questions with a partner. Give background information, and details or examples where you can.

I lent some money to my brother a few months ago because…

- Have you ever lent money to someone? Did they **pay** you **back**?
- Have you ever tried to do something and **given up**? What was it? Why did you give up?
- Do you think it's possible today for couples to **live on** one salary? Why (not)?
- When you started school (or university), did you find it difficult to **fit in**?
- What would you do if a friend borrowed your tablet, but it didn't work when he or she **gave** it **back**?
- If someone offered to **take** you **out** for a meal to a restaurant of your choice, where would you go?
- Have you ever left something on a bus or train, or in a taxi? Did you ever **get** it **back**?
- Who do you **take after** most in your family? In what way?
- Is there a new hobby or sport you'd really like to **take up**? Will you ever do it?
- When you get a missed call, do you **call back** immediately, later, or not at all?
- When was the last time you **gave** something **away**? Who to? Why?

68

6 READING

a Look at six ways of spending money. Which three do you think would make you happiest? Compare with a partner.
- going on a luxurious holiday
- buying a birthday present for a friend
- giving a donation to charity
- paying off your credit card bill
- buying yourself some new clothes
- giving a few coins to a homeless person

b Read a short article about the relationship between money and happiness. According to research, which three things in **a** will make you happiest? Why?

Can money buy you happiness?

According to research, it seems that it can. But what makes us really happy is not buying ourselves the latest iPhone, it's spending our money on other people. In a study of the link between money and happiness, researchers from Zurich University divided 50 people into two groups. The first group was asked to plan how to spend 25 Swiss francs a week on gifts or outings for other people, and the second group was asked to plan how to spend the same amount of money on themselves. The people in the first group increased their happiness more than the group who planned to buy themselves treats. Spending on ourselves, it turns out, doesn't make us nearly as happy as giving to other people. Other studies in which people have been given envelopes of money to spend show that those who spent some of it on a gift, or gave some to charity, felt happier than those who spent it on something for themselves or on a bill they needed to pay. A study of young children found that even toddlers felt happier giving rather than getting treats. And the best news is that you don't have to give a lot of money away to feel the benefits.

Adapted from The Guardian

Glossary
treat (noun) sth very pleasant and enjoyable

c Now read an article about Grayden Reece-Smith. Why did he decide not to work for a charity? Do you think it was a sensible choice?

He gives away his salary to save the world

Working for a big financial company in London on a six-figure salary, you might expect Grayden Reece-Smith to [1]____, going on expensive holidays or driving a sports car around south London, where he lives. In fact, the 28-year-old lives a very different existence from his colleagues. He [2]____ – a figure that he calculated he could comfortably live on.

Over the past five years, Reece-Smith has handed over more than £250,000 to organizations such as International Care Ministries, which [3]____, and the Against Malaria Foundation. He is part of a growing number of young professionals described as 'effective altruists'. Effective altruists typically donate regularly to a charity which they think will have a significant impact. Some [4]____ to make more money, which can then be given away.

Reece-Smith considered working in the charity sector after graduating from university, but calculated that he could make a bigger difference by donating a large part of his salary. He had [5]____ at a school in Tanzania, but then realized that earning and giving would be more effective. 'The cost of my flights there could have paid the salaries of two teachers for an entire year,' he says. Instead, he could 'stay at home, living a nice life and still [6]____.'

He is not frugal – last year he went to Cuba on holiday, and [7]____. But his lifestyle isn't as luxurious as some of the people he works with. 'I tend not to buy supermarket-branded food products, but I don't [8]____. Other people on my salary might have a bigger house. Some of my colleagues have four-bedroom houses, but we only bought what we needed – a two-bedroom flat. £42,000 is more than enough to live on and still save,' he says.

Adapted from The Guardian

d Read the article again and complete it with **verb phrases A–H**.
A change careers
B gives away everything he earns over £42,000
C have an extravagant lifestyle
D helps poor families in the Philippines
E make a huge difference in the world
F own a car
G spent several thousand pounds on a new sofa
H volunteered as a teacher

e 🅒 **Communication** Giving it away **A** p.110 **B** p.113 Read about two more people who give money away and tell your partner about them.

f Which of the three stories did you find the most inspiring? Have you ever helped to raise money for a good cause? What was it for? Did raising the money make you happy?

Go online to review the lesson

7B Shall we go out or stay in?

> Do you enjoy going to clubs?
>
> No. I prefer spending time with my friends at home.

G verb patterns **V** live entertainment **P** homographs

1 VOCABULARY live entertainment

a Talk to a partner.
1 How often do you go to live events, e.g. concerts, the theatre, sporting events, etc.?
2 What was the last live event you went to?
3 Where are the best places to go for live entertainment in your (nearest) town / city?

b ◉ 7.12 Listen to conversations 1–3. Match them to the events below. Are the people talking before, during, or after the event?

☐ a concert ☐ a play ☐ a sporting event

c Look at the list of words related to live entertainment and listen again. Who says each word, speaker 1, 2, or 3?

| ☐ box office | ☐ crowd | ☐ half-time | ☐ interval | ☐ matinee |
| ☐ performance | ☐ stadium | ☐ stage | ☐ stalls / circle |

d Write the words from **c** in the correct column. Then add these words to the chart.

arena   audience   curtain   extra time   fans   final whistle
opponent   plot   programme   row   scene   score
spectators   tickets

Sporting event	Play, musical, or concert	Both

e ◉ 7.13 Listen and check. Then listen and repeat the words in each column.

2 PRONUNCIATION homographs

a ◉ 7.14 Listen and repeat the sentences. What do the highlighted words mean in each sentence? Which two pairs of words are pronounced differently?

1 a We went to a **live** concert last weekend.
  b We **live** next to the concert hall.
2 a We're massive **fans** of Ed Sheeran.
  b The air conditioning has broken, so we've bought two electric **fans**.
3 a We sat in the back **row**, so we couldn't hear very well.
  b After the concert, we had a terrible **row**.
4 a We had really good seats for the play – we were right next to the **stage**.
  b My son is at a **stage** of life where all he's interested in is his phone.

b Read the information box. What kind of homograph is each pair of words in **a**?

🔍 **Homographs**

1 Some words in English are spelled and pronounced exactly the same, but have different meanings, e.g. *stalls* (a place where people sit in the theatre, tables where people sell things in a market), *park* (a green area in a town, to leave your car somewhere).

2 A few words are spelled the same, but pronounced differently and have different meanings, e.g. *bow* /baʊ/ (to put your head down, e.g. at the end of a concert or play when people are clapping), but *bow* /bəʊ/ (a weapon that you use to shoot an arrow).

c   Match the pairs of meanings to the words from the list.

   bear   close   lie   minute   second   wind

   1 a (verb) the opposite of open, b (adj) a synonym for near
   2 a (noun) a 60th part of a minute, b the ordinal number from two
   3 a (noun) air that moves quickly, b (verb) to turn a knob or handle round several times to make something work, e.g. a watch or toy
   4 a (adj) tiny, very small, b (noun) a 60th part of an hour
   5 a (verb) accept and deal with sth unpleasant, b (noun) a heavy wild animal with thick fur and sharp claws
   6 a (verb) say sth which is not true, b (verb) put yourself in a horizontal position, e.g. in bed

d   7.15 Listen and check. In which three pairs of words is the pronunciation different?

3 LISTENING

a   Do you prefer going to see a concert or a sporting event live or watching it on TV? Why? Think about the following things.

   atmosphere   comfort   noise   people
   performance   safety   weather

b   7.16 You're going to listen to three people talking about a live event they went to which they didn't enjoy. Listen to the beginning of each story. What event did each person go to? Where did it take place?

c   7.17 With a partner, think of all the possible reasons why each person in b might not have enjoyed the event. Then listen to the rest of the stories. What went wrong? Did you predict any of the reasons correctly?

d   7.18 Now listen to the three stories again and tick (✓) two people for each question.

Who…?	Andy	Cathy	Clive
1 went in the evening			
2 had good seats			
3 went to an outdoor event			
4 went with a family member			
5 waited for a long time for something to happen			

e   Which of the three experiences do you think was the most frustrating? Why?

4 SPEAKING & WRITING

a   You're going to tell a partner about a live event you went to (a concert, play, sporting event, or other). Read the prompts and think about what you're going to say.

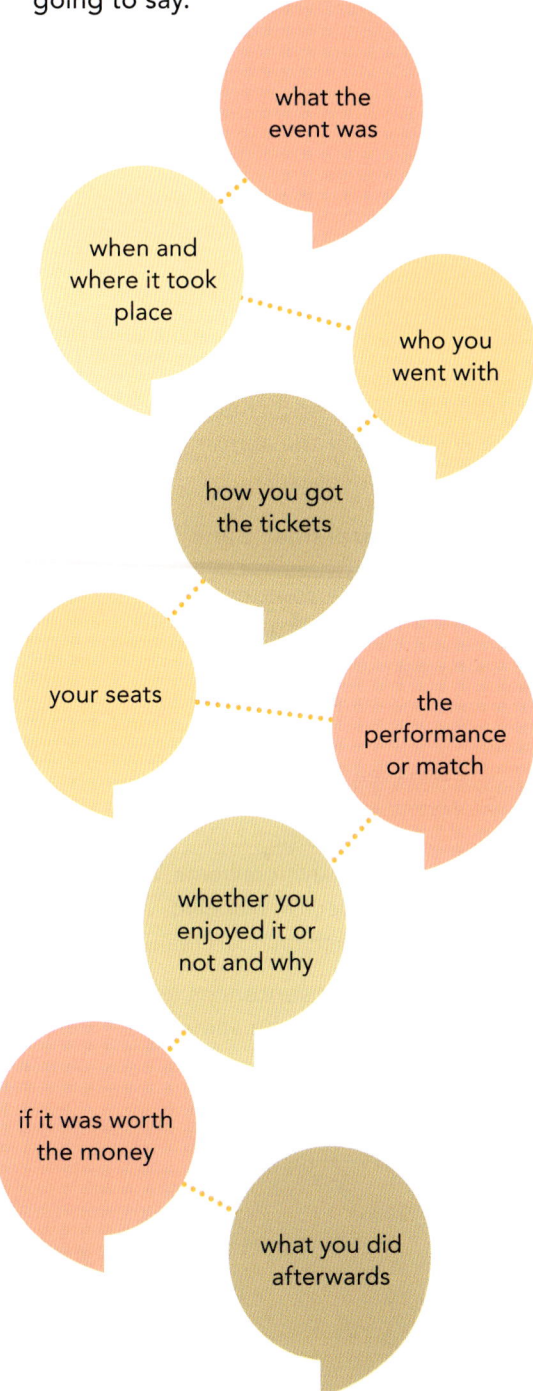

- what the event was
- when and where it took place
- who you went with
- how you got the tickets
- your seats
- the performance or match
- whether you enjoyed it or not and why
- if it was worth the money
- what you did afterwards

b   Now work in pairs. Tell each other about the event you went to. Would you like to have gone to your partner's event?

c   Write a description of the event you talked about in a, or another event. Use the prompts in a to help you.

71

5 GRAMMAR verb patterns

a Complete the sentences with the correct form of the verbs in brackets (infinitive, *to* + infinitive, or verb + *-ing*).
1. If a friend asked me _____ to a classical music concert, I think I'd _____ no. (go, say)
2. I love _____ films in 3D – they're much better than ordinary ones. (watch)
3. My parents didn't use to let me _____ out late during the week when I was young. They wanted me _____ my evenings _____. (stay, spend, study)
4. I hate _____ to clubs. I don't like _____ in places where there are lots of people and noise. (go, be)
5. I never feel like _____ out on New Year's Eve. I prefer _____ in. (go, stay)

b ◀)) 7.19 Listen and check. Then with a partner, say if the sentences in **a** are true for you or not, and why.

c **G** p.145 **Grammar Bank 7B**

d Complete the sentences with a verb phrase so that they are true for you.
1. I'd like to be able to afford…
2. At weekends, I often spend a long time…
3. When I was young, my parents made me…
4. I don't really like housework, but I don't mind…
5. When I leave the house in the morning, I sometimes forget…
6. When I'm away from home, I really miss…
7. Next summer, I'm planning…
8. When I'm with friends, I really enjoy…

e Compare your sentences with a partner. Are any of them the same?

6 READING

a Match the five games from the box to the type of game they are. Have you ever played any of them?

Candy Crush	board game
Dungeons and Dragons	brain-training game
Poker	card game
Scrabble	role-playing game
Sudoku	video game

b ◀)) 7.23 Listen and check.

c Read the first part of an article about board games. What is unusual about the Thirsty Meeples café? Where does its name come from?

A different kind of social network

It's a bright Thursday morning in Oxford and the Thirsty Meeples café is a buzz of activity. As I, my wife, and two sons sit at a sunny window table, the assistant, Gareth, introduces himself and recommends some games. First,
05 he suggests **Forbidden Desert**. 'You have crash-landed in a desert,' explains Gareth. 'You have to find all the pieces of a flying ship in order to escape.' Next, he suggests **Small World**, in which wizards, giants, and humans with special powers battle for land in a world that's too small for them all. Last, he
10 recommends **Citadels**, a game where you compete to become the King's Master Builder by building a medieval city. We choose Citadels. As we play, next to us Eveline, a 30-year-old Dutch university teacher, is playing **Ticket to Ride** with her Belgian husband, Roger – they are racing against each other to
15 build railway tracks across Europe. Two teenagers play **Sushi Go!**, a card game where they have to create sushi dishes. What has drawn all these different people here, from serious gamers to families? Eveline thinks she has the answer. She looks around at the other customers and at the library of games on
20 the shelves. 'I would say it's the original social network.'

Thirsty Meeples's name comes from the combination of 'meeples', the pieces that board gamers play with, and wanting a drink. It is one of a growing number of board game shops and cafés popping up all over the UK, inspired by their growing
25 popularity in the USA.

d Read the first part again and look at the photos of the games. In which game, A–E, do players have to…?
1. ☐ try to get an important job
2. ☐ make a transport network across a continent
3. ☐ fight others to get more living space
4. ☐ make something to eat
5. ☐ get out of somewhere after an accident

e   Now read the second part of the article. What are the three main reasons why board games have become so popular?

Peter Wooding, a former punk rocker, opened a board game shop called Orc's Nest in Covent Garden, London, in 1987. For the first few years, the shop hardly made any money at all, but over 30 years later, it is thriving.

Wooding says that one of the reasons for its success is that the games and players are very different from 30 years ago. Today, they are young professional couples, who like the idea of playing a game with friends and having a few drinks, rather than going out to the pub. Another reason is that there are also far more women playing games. Wooding says the game **Pandemic**, where players must collaborate to control global diseases, and whose main character is a female scientist, has had a huge influence. 'Much wider appeal,' says Wooding. 'More friendly.' Pandemic is an example of the newer, less aggressive games, with themes like farming or landscape building. One such game, **Catan**, in which players have to buy and sell natural resources to build roads and new cities, has sold more than 22 million copies in 30 languages.

The growth of the video games industry has, perhaps surprisingly, also been one of the biggest factors in the new popularity of board games, largely because they have made playing games such a normal thing for adults to do. Everyone has at least one game on their phone, and more people are open to the idea of playing a game than ever before. Social media has also provided an easy way for people to recommend new games to each other.

You connect with people across the table. It's a very human thing.
Matt Leacock, creator of Pandemic

At Thirsty Meeples in Oxford, I talk to owners John and Zuzi Morgan. What's Zuzi's explanation for the trend? 'There's so much technology,' she says. 'Everybody's busy and you want to bring people back together in a way that's not just staring at screens. It's a natural thing in people. We are supposed to be together and communicating with each other in the real world.'

Adapted from The Guardian

f   Read the second part again. With a partner, explain in your own words what these phrases mean.
1 it is thriving *l.30*
2 young professional couples *l.34*
3 rather than going out to the pub *l.36*
4 much wider appeal *l.42*
5 one of the biggest factors *l.51*
6 not just staring at screens *l.63*
7 in the real world *l.66*

g   Which games in the article would you most like to try? Can you suggest any other good games?

7 SPEAKING

a   What do you like doing with friends in your free time? Tick (✓) or cross (✗) the activities and add one more option in each list.

If you go out
- eating at a favourite restaurant
- going to see the latest film at the cinema
- watching a live sports event
- going to a concert, play, or show
- chatting in a café or bar
- going to a club
- _____

If you stay in
- playing board games or video games
- watching a film or a box set together
- cooking and having a meal together
- getting a takeaway
- watching sport on TV
- listening to music and chatting
- _____

b   Compare your list in small groups. Say why you like / don't like doing each of the activities.

c   Think about the last time you spent an evening with friends. What did you do? Compare with a partner.

Go online to review the lesson

EPISODE 4

Practical English Is it a clue?

talking about house rules

1 ▶ ROB GETS INVOLVED

a 🔊 **7.24** Watch or listen to Jenny, Luke, and Rob talking about Henry's disappearance. What are two possible clues they notice in the video?

b Watch or listen again. Mark the sentences **T** (true) or **F** (false). Correct the **F** sentences.
 1 Rob thinks they should ask the police for help.
 2 Rob and Luke agree that they shouldn't give the laptop to the criminals.
 3 Rob noticed something strange about how his father looked.
 4 The phrase that really surprises Rob is 'his old dad'.
 5 He doesn't know how to interpret the clue.
 6 Rob has booked a flight to the UK.
 7 Jenny is going to go back to Henry's house.

What do you think the clues might mean? Who do you think Simon is?

2 ▶ TALKING ABOUT HOUSE RULES

a 🔊 **7.25** Watch or listen to Luke telling Jenny about the rules in his house. Complete **Rules for guests**. Why does he ask her to move her car?

Rules for guests

1 This is a no-_____ house.
2 Don't cook _____ or leave _____ products in the fridge.
3 If you need to use the internet, the _____ for the wi-fi is *lukeandsimonrule*.
4 If you use the washing machine, please use the _____-_____ detergents in the cupboard.
5 Please help us save energy – don't use a _____ water programme.
6 There isn't a _____. Hang your clothes on the _____ _____ instead.

b Read the conversation between Luke and Jenny. Can you remember any of the missing words? Watch or listen again and check.

Luke It's a great location, and the rent is cheap, but Simon can be a bit difficult.
Jenny Oh, right.
Luke He's got a few rules. After all, it is his house.
Jenny That's fine.
Luke To start with, it's a no-smoking house.
Jenny Great.
Luke And he's a strict vegetarian so ¹_____ _____ cook meat or leave meat products in the fridge.
Jenny Uh huh.
Luke He just feels really strongly about not eating ²_____.
Jenny That's not a ³_____.
Luke What about you? Is there ⁴_____ you need?
Jenny There is one thing – could I ⁵_____ my phone to your wi-fi?
Luke ⁶_____. The ⁷_____ is *lukeandsimonrule*, all lower case, all one word.
Jenny Got it.
Luke Anything ⁸_____?
Jenny Yeah. I have some clothes I need to wash. Is it ⁹_____ if I use your washing machine?
Luke Of ¹⁰_____ you can. But Simon prefers us to use the eco-friendly detergents. There's some in the cupboard.

74

Jenny Cool.
Luke Oh, and you ¹¹_____ use a hot water programme. He's very keen on saving energy.
Jenny OK, and ¹²_____ you _____ if I use your dryer too?
Luke ¹³_____, we don't have one, but you can hang it out on the washing line.
Jenny Great. Is there ¹⁴_____ else I ¹⁵_____ know?
Luke No, I don't think ¹⁶_____ – oh! You should probably move your car.
Jenny I guess Simon doesn't like cars either.
Luke Well no, but it's not that. We know the kidnappers have been watching us, right? They might see it and recognize us.
Jenny You're right. I'll move it right away.
Luke Look, I'll come with you and we can get a coffee. There's a nice café round the corner.
Jenny Thanks, Luke.

c 🔊 7.26 Watch or listen and repeat the highlighted phrases. Copy the rhythm and intonation.

d Practise the conversation in **b** with a partner.

e **C Communication** Renting a room **A** p.109 **B** p.114. Role-play two conversations.

3 ▶ TAKING A RISK

a 🔊 7.27 Watch or listen to Jenny and Luke discussing the situation with Rob. Where are they going to go tonight? Why?

b Watch or listen again and answer the questions.
1 Who is more optimistic at the beginning, Jenny or Luke?
2 Has Rob managed to get a flight to London? Why (not)?
3 What does Rob think the words 'old man' might refer to?
4 What does he think Luke and Jenny need to do?
5 How are they going to get to the house?
6 Why does Luke know the back way well?

What do you think will happen when they go to the house?

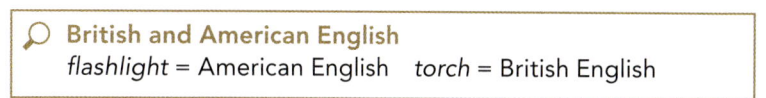

> **British and American English**
> *flashlight* = American English   *torch* = British English

c Look at the **Social English** phrases. Can you remember any of the missing words?

> **Social English**
> 1 **Jenny** It's all _____ a mess.
> 2 **Jenny** I hope _____. I just don't know.
> 3 **Jenny** Any _____?
> 4 **Rob** I know, but I'll _____ trying.
> 5 **Rob** I've been thinking about Dad's message. That 'old man' _____.
> 6 **Jenny** Did you _____ that?

d 🔊 7.28 Watch or listen and complete the phrases. Then watch or listen again and repeat.

e Complete conversations A–F with **Social English** phrases 1–6. Then practise them with a partner.

A	What do you want to talk to Jim about?	'family argument' We need to agree what to do.
B	That was my sister on the phone.	How's it going with the new boyfriend?
C	So what's his address?	241 Willow Road, Flat 3, SW7 2TM. No, can you give me the postcode again, please?
D	Why don't we go for a walk? It's lovely day.	Yes, let's do that.
E	I don't think I'll ever be able to play this music. It's just too difficult.	You have to In the end you'll succeed.
F	Do you think you'll pass your driving test?	I've had loads of lessons and I've been practising a lot, too.

CAN YOU…?
- ask about the rules in a house
- explain the rules in a house
- suggest and agree on a plan of action

Go online to watch the video, review the lesson, and check your progress

8A Treat yourself

> I love your nails! Where did you have them done?
>
> At that nail bar near my office.

G have something done **V** looking after yourself **P** sentence stress

1 GRAMMAR have something done

a Look at the photos. Who…?

1 ☐ is **cutting** his hair
2 ☐ is **having** his hair **cut**
3 ☐ is **doing** her nails
4 ☐ is **having** her nails **done**
5 ☐ are **painting** their flat
6 ☐ are **having** their flat **painted**
7 ☐ is **taking** a photo
8 ☐ is **having** her photo **taken**

b **G** p.146 Grammar Bank 8A

c Cover the sentences in **a** and say what's happening in each photo.

2 PRONUNCIATION & SPEAKING sentence stress

a 🔊 8.2 Listen and repeat the sentences. Copy the rhythm. Then say if any of them are true for you.
1 I **had** my **hair cut last week**.
2 I usually **have** my **food shopping delivered**.
3 I **ought** to **have** my **eyes tested**.
4 I'm **going** to **have** my **flat repainted soon**.
5 I **hate having** my **photo taken**.

b Ask and answer the questions with a partner. Give more information where you can.

Do you ever…? How often?	Have you ever…?
have your hair dyed	had clothes made for you
have your clothes dry-cleaned	had your bedroom redecorated
have your passport or ID card renewed	
have your car washed	had your photo taken by a professional photographer
have prints made of your digital photos	had your fortune told
have takeaway food delivered	

3 VOCABULARY & LISTENING looking after yourself

a Have you ever had any of these hairstyles? Would you like to have any of them?

b **V** p.163 Vocabulary Bank Looking after yourself Do Part 1.

c You're going to listen to an interview with Dino Karveli, a hairdresser. First, in pairs, read the interview questions and guess the missing words.

DINO KARVELI

DINO KARVELI is a hairdresser in London. His parents are Greek, and he came to live in London in 1990. He has been working as a hairdresser since 1993.

- **Q** What made you ¹_____ hairdressing?
- **Q** What sort of ²_____ did you do?
- **Q** What sort of things do you ³_____ or ⁴_____ doing in hairdressing?
- **Q** What do you think are important ⁵_____ for a hairdresser?
- **Q** Are ⁶_____ clients very different from ⁷_____?
- **Q** What do you do if a client doesn't like the ⁸_____?
- **Q** Have you ever had a really bad ⁹_____?
- **Q** Is it true that hairdressers always want to ¹⁰_____ off more hair than their clients want?
- **Q** If you completely ¹¹_____ with what a client wanted, would you still do it?
- **Q** Do you have any ¹²_____ for having good hair?

d 8.4 Listen and check.

e 8.5 Now listen to the whole interview. Mark the sentences **T** (true) or **F** (false). Correct the **F** sentences.
1 Dino's father was a barber in Greece.
2 When he came to the UK, he trained with Vidal Sassoon for two years.
3 He does a wide variety of hair treatments.
4 He thinks it's important for hairdressers to be good listeners.
5 He thinks men get just as stressed about their hair as women.
6 It's difficult to fix a mistake in hair colour.
7 A woman once got very upset with him because he cut her hair very short.
8 Hairdressers often think a client's hair needs to be cut more.
9 Dino would never say no to a client's request.
10 He thinks to have good hair, you need to go to a good hairdresser.

f Do you usually go to the same hairdresser? Do you think he / she would agree with what Dino says? Do you think it's true that women care more about their hair than men?

4 SPEAKING

a What do you think the phrase 'to have a bad hair day' means? Have you had one recently?

b Ask and answer the questions with a partner.

Which hairstyles are very popular at the moment for a) men, b) women?

How long have you had your current hairstyle or colour? What was your hair like before?

What's the best or worst haircut you've ever had?

Is there a hairstyle you would never have?

Do you know anyone (friends, family, celebrities) who has really great or really terrible hair? What's it like?

Do you think having a good hairstyle is important? Why (not)?

5 VOCABULARY looking after yourself

a Look at the advert for a spa and gym. Would you like to go there? Do you have any similar places near where you live?

Mind & Body
WELLBEING CENTRE

Our 1,200 m² Wellbeing Centre offers you everything you need to recharge your mind and body.

- The spa area has a large pool, a hammam, and massage rooms offering a variety of treatments for the body, facials, and manicures and pedicures. The whole area is beautifully illuminated, with relaxing music, aromas, and gentle lighting.
- The gym has the most advanced fitness equipment and a spacious aerobics studio. Yoga, t'ai chi, and Pilates classes are also offered, either individually or in groups.
- The lounge and bar area offers a healthy assortment of all-organic snacks and juices.

b **V** p.163 **Vocabulary Bank** Looking after yourself Do Parts 2 and 3.

c If you went to the Wellbeing Centre in **a** for a day, what would you choose to do and why?

6 READING & LISTENING

SPA TREATMENTS – WOMEN LOVE THEM. CAN MEN ENJOY THEM TOO?

The Sunday Times decided to find out. Two of their journalists, Joanna Duckworth and Stephen Bleach, went to spend a day at a health spa and try out the treatments. These are some of the treatments they had:

KANEBO KAI ZEN FACIAL
Deep intensive cleaning with face and neck massage. 1 hr 40 minutes.

BANANA, PAPAYA, AND STRAWBERRY BODY POLISH
Leaves your skin feeling smooth and hydrated. Includes head massage. 40 minutes.

ELEMIS FOOT TREATMENT
Pedicure and foot massage. 55 minutes.

Adapted from The Sunday Times

a Read the introduction to the article. Why did the journalists go to the spa? Which treatments do you think a) Joanna, b) Stephen will like best?

b Read about the facial. Why did Stephen score the treatment only 4/10? Why did Joanna give it 9/10?

c 🔊 8.8 You're going to listen to Stephen and Joanna talking after two more treatments. First, listen to some extracts and write the missing words. Which comments are positive and which are negative?

1 It was hot and _____, and incredibly _____.
2 And the head massage was _____.
3 _____ _____ the time and money.
4 A real _____.

THE FACIAL

STEPHEN

Laura, the therapist, started by suggesting five different products for me to use every morning, and five more at night. I was shocked – it normally only takes me a minute to wash my face in soap and water in the morning. The actual treatment took nearly two hours. Laura used 12 different creams and things on my skin and I was very bored indeed. Afterwards, I had to admit my face felt quite different: it was much smoother and quite shiny. But I'm not sure I liked it. I don't think smooth and shiny is a good look for me.

My score: 4/10. Quite nice, but it went on forever.

JOANNA

The therapist told me that the treatment would last nearly two hours. Total bliss! But I knew Stephen would be bored, and we weren't having lunch until after the session, so he wouldn't be able to relax. He's terrible when he's hungry. I had more processes (exfoliation, cleansing, masks, massages, more masks, more massages) than I ever thought possible for a facial, and I enjoyed every second.

My score: 9/10. My skin felt fantastic, really healthy, and afterwards, I was completely relaxed.

d 🔊 **8.9** Now listen to them talking and complete the chart.

		Stephen	Joanna
The body polish	Score out of 10		
	Reasons		
The foot treatment	Score out of 10		
	Reasons		

e Did you predict correctly in **a** which treatments Joanna and Stephen would like best? Which of the three treatments do you think you would enjoy the most?

f Do you know anyone who has health and beauty treatments regularly? How important do you think it is to look after a) your face and skin, b) your hair, c) your hands and feet?

7 SPEAKING

a Look at the categories below. In pairs, add more ways of looking after yourself to each category. Then try to agree on the three things that you think are the most important.

- keeping fit
- being healthy
- boosting your brainpower

walking, e.g. to work

using sunscreen

reading (books / newspapers, etc.)

I think it's really important to walk a little bit every day.
Yes, but going to the gym regularly is better exercise.

b Read the ideas below about encouraging healthy eating in schools. Which ideas do you think would work best?
- Offer all children a healthy breakfast at school.
- Make all pupils and teachers eat school lunches together.
- Produce a free recipe book of easy meals to encourage parents not to buy ready-meals.
- Set up classes to teach children how to cook cheap, healthy meals.
- Ban machines selling sweets, crisps, or soft drinks in schools.
- Provide free, healthy snacks such as fresh fruit or cereal bars.
- Stop fast food restaurants opening near schools.

c You're going to create and present a campaign to help young people to eat healthily. In groups of three, plan your campaign:

1. Choose **three** main proposals for the campaign. Use some of the ideas in **b**, or your own ideas.
2. Think of a name for your campaign. Decide why your campaign is important.
3. Think of reasons why people should support your campaign.

d In your groups, decide what each person is going to say. Then practise presenting to each other. Use the language from the **Presenting a campaign** box.

> 🔍 **Presenting a campaign**
> Our campaign is called…
> We think this campaign is vital because…
> Recent research suggests that…
> Our plan has three main proposals. Firstly…, Secondly…, Lastly…
> We think you should support our campaign because…

e Present your campaign to the class, and listen to the other groups. Have a class vote to choose the best campaign.

Our campaign is called 'Cook at school'. We think this campaign is vital because nowadays, many young people and their parents don't know how to cook real food…

🔄 Go online to review the lesson

8B Sites and sights

G the passive | V wars and battles, historic buildings | P silent consonants

Where was the Duke of Wellington buried?

In St Paul's cathedral – his tomb is in the crypt.

1 GRAMMAR the passive

a   Read the History Quiz questions and check you understand them. Then do the quiz in small groups.

History Quiz

1   Napoleon was defeated in the battle of Waterloo. Where is Waterloo?
    a Belgium   b France   c England

2   Whose fleet was attacked in Pearl Harbor in 1941?
    a the British fleet   b the Japanese fleet   c the American fleet

3   Which city, which had been divided by a wall for 28 years, was reunified in 1989?
    a Belfast   b Berlin   c Sarajevo

4   Which city has a church which was started in 1882 and is still being built?
    a Barcelona   b Florence   c Paris

5   Which city, which according to legend fought a famous war against Greece, has never been located for certain?
    a Atlantis   b Timbuktu   c Troy

6   Which pre-Columbian city was built by the Mayans between 750 and 900 AD?
    a Machu Picchu   b Chichen Itza   c Tenochtitlan

7   Which American president was assassinated while he was being driven through Dallas in 1963?
    a Gerald Ford   b John F Kennedy   c Richard Nixon

8   Which city had to be evacuated in 1986 after a catastrophic nuclear accident?
    a Chernobyl   b Fukushima   c Pripyat

b   ◉ 8.10 Listen and check.

c   Underline all the examples of the passive in the quiz questions. What form of the passive are they?

d   G p.147 Grammar Bank 8B

e   In pairs, write three questions for a History Quiz about your country. Ask the class your questions.

2 READING & VOCABULARY
wars and battles

a   Look at the photos and label 1–5 with words from the list. What do you think is happening?

archer   arrow   bow   helmet   shield

b   Read the information on p.81 from a website about the Battle of Hastings. Were you right about what was happening in the photos in **a**? Then match 1–5 on the map to the places from the list.

| Battle | Bayeux | Hastings |
| Norway | Stamford Bridge | |

80

| VISIT | ABOUT US | SUPPORT US | LEARN | SHOP | JOIN |

THE BATTLE THAT CHANGED ENGLAND'S HISTORY

Every year, on 14th October, a famous battle is re-enacted on the exact site where the original battle took place. Over 600 people dress up in period costumes and bring the story of an 11th century battle to life. The Battle of Hastings, which was fought in 1066, is one of the best-known events of English history, when William of Normandy defeated the army of King Harold of England. This marked the end of the Anglo-Saxon era and the beginning of Norman rule.

1066 was a turbulent year for England. King Harold had succeeded his brother-in-law, Edward, as King of England, but he was being attacked by others who wanted to rule the country – the King of Norway, and Duke William of Normandy (in what is now France). The Norwegians invaded in the north, and were defeated by the English army at the battle of Stamford Bridge on 25th September, but soon after, the Normans landed in Sussex on the south coast, and made their camp near the small seaside town of Hastings.

The English army immediately travelled south. On 13th October, after covering 275 miles, they arrived exhausted near Hastings, and on the morning of 14th, the two armies met in a field about 7 miles north-west of the town. Each army had between 5,000 and 7,000 men. They had similar armour and weapons, but William had over 2,000 cavalry, whereas the English fought on foot. William also had archers with powerful bows.

The battle lasted all day. The English soldiers used their shields to protect themselves against the Normans' arrows, but gradually the Normans gained control, and in the last attack, King Harold was killed. The English lost the battle, and on Christmas Day, William of Normandy was crowned King of England. He later became known as William the Conqueror.

In 1071, King William built an abbey on the site where the battle had taken place, as a memorial to all those who had died. Although no relics of the battle have ever been found there, we have very strong evidence that it took place, because an enormous tapestry was made – nearly 70 metres long – showing the story of the battle. This tapestry, which was completed in about 1077, is known as the Bayeux tapestry, and it has been kept in France for nearly 1,000 years. It can be visited in a museum in the town of Bayeux, Normandy.

William's abbey was called Battle Abbey, and the town that grew up nearby was also called Battle. The whole of the town would once have been part of the battlefield; for example, Harold's soldiers almost certainly retreated up what is currently Battle high street. Although the abbey was destroyed by King Henry VIII in the 16th century, the ruins and the battlefield remain one of the most atmospheric historical sites in Britain today.

Adapted from the English Heritage website

c Read the information again. Number the events in chronological order.

☐ Battle Abbey was built.
☐ Battle Abbey was destroyed.
1 Harold became King of England.
☐ King Harold was killed.
☐ The Bayeux tapestry was finished.
☐ The Battle of Hastings was fought between the English and the Normans.
☐ The Normans landed in Sussex.
☐ The town of Battle was named after the battle that took place there.
☐ The Norwegians attacked the north of England.
☐ William became King of England.

d Look at the highlighted verbs related to wars and battles. Which one is irregular? What is the infinitive? Guess their meaning from the context.

3 SPEAKING

a Talk to a partner.

1 Have you ever visited a famous historical site? Where? When? What happened there?
2 In your country, are there any famous historical events that are re-enacted? Have you ever watched or taken part in one?

b **Communication** Local history **A** p.110 **B** p.114
Role-play being a tourist and ask your partner about the history of your local area.

81

4 VOCABULARY & PRONUNCIATION
historic buildings; silent consonants

a Complete the names of five historic British buildings with a word from the list.

Abbey   Castle   Cathedral   Palace   Tower

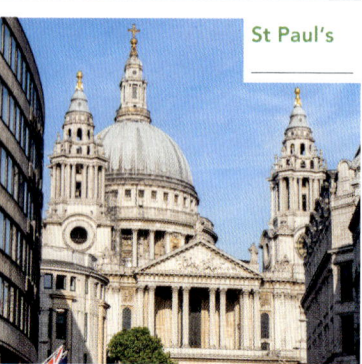

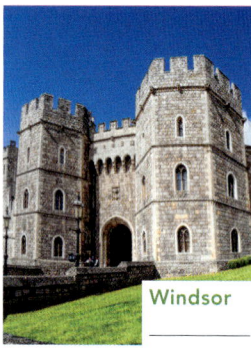

Buckingham ____
St Paul's ____
Westminster ____
Windsor ____
The ____ of London

b ▶ 8.12 Listen and check. Which are the two oldest buildings?

c Read the definitions for parts of a building. Then look at all the photos on p.82–3. Which things can you see?

aisle /aɪl/ a side passage between rows of seats in a church or theatre
column /ˈkɒləm/ a tall, solid, vertical post, usually round and made of stone
crypt /krɪpt/ a room under the floor of a church, used especially in the past for burying people
dome /dəʊm/ a round roof with a circular base
gallery /ˈɡæləri/ a raised platform along the inner wall of a building
nave /neɪv/ the long central part of a church where most of the seats are
tomb /tuːm/ a large grave, especially one built of stone above or below the ground

d Which consonants are not pronounced in these words? Cross them out.

aisle   castle   column   tomb

e ▶ 8.13 Listen and write five sentences which include common words with silent consonants. Be careful with your spelling!

5 LISTENING

a Read about St Paul's Cathedral in London and look at the photos. What famous event took place here in 1981? Do you know anything else about the cathedral?

Welcome to St PAUL'S CATHEDRAL

When you come to St Paul's, we hope to give you a visit you will remember. With your sightseeing ticket, you can walk in the footsteps of royalty on the Cathedral floor, climb the dome to try the unique acoustics of the Whispering Gallery, go even higher to enjoy some of the most spectacular views over London, or head down to the crypt where our nation's heroes are buried. Guided tours available on request.

Adapted from the St Paul's Cathedral website

b ▶ 8.14 Listen to extracts from a guided tour of St Paul's Cathedral. Follow the route and number the places the guide talks about 1–6.

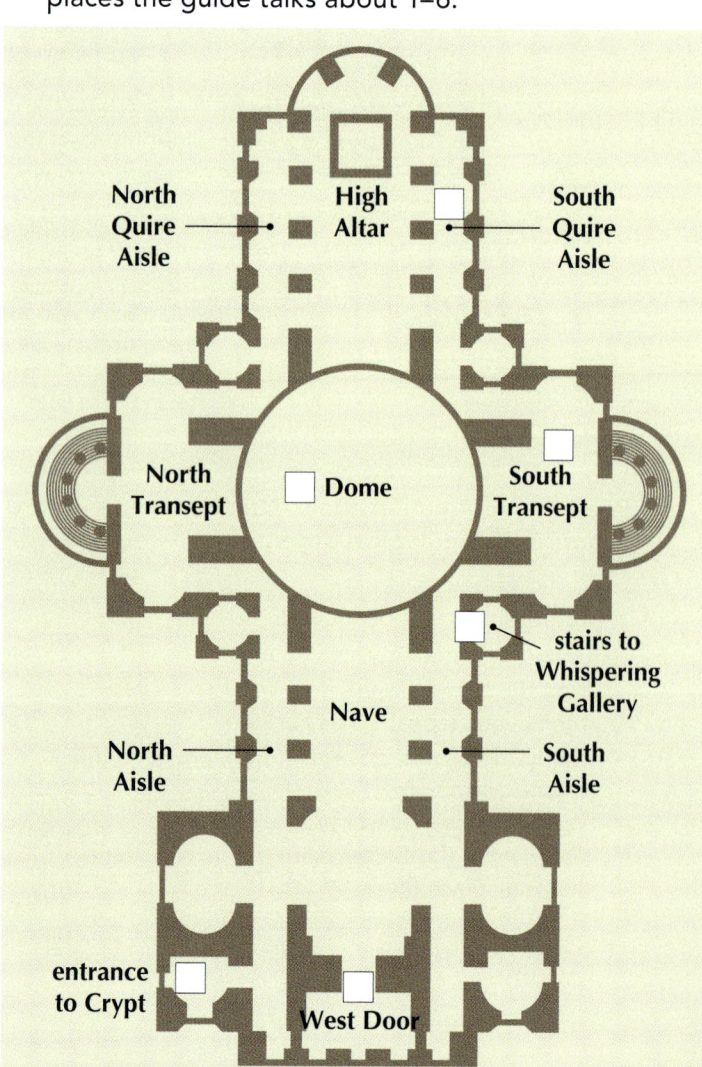

6 SPEAKING & WRITING

a Tell a partner about a famous building you've visited. Use the questions to help you and add your own ideas. Include any interesting details or anecdotes that you can remember.

> **A FAMOUS BUILDING**
> - Where is it?
> - When was it built?
> - What was it used for originally?
> - What is it used for now?
> - What did you learn about it while you were there?
> - How long did you spend there?
> - How much did you have to pay to visit it?
> - Would you recommend visiting it?

b **W p.121 Writing** Describing a building Write a description for a tourism website of a building in your town or country.

c ◉ 8.15 Now listen to the first part of the tour and complete the notes.

The West Door and the Nave
- The previous church burned down in [1]_____, in the Great [2]_____ of [3]_____.
- The new [4]_____ was designed by Sir [5]_____ Wren.
- The doors are [6]_____ metres tall and are only opened when, e.g. the [7]_____ visits.
- The Nave is a good place to see the [8]_____ _____ of the cathedral.

d ◉ 8.16 Now listen to the rest of the guided tour. Pause after each area and take notes. What does the guide say about these people and things?

The Dome
- the cross
- the height of the Dome
- something that was true until the 1960s

The South Transept
- Horatio Nelson

The South Quire Aisle
- the statue of John Donne

The Whispering Gallery
- the number of steps you have to climb
- the reason the gallery gets its name

The Crypt
- the famous people in the tombs
- the Latin words on Wren's tomb

e Would you like to do the tour of St Paul's Cathedral? Are there any other historic buildings in London that you would like to visit?

7 ▶ VIDEO LISTENING

a Watch a documentary about the Globe Theatre. Who was Sam Wanamaker? Why did he decide to rebuild the Globe Theatre?

b Watch again. Mark the sentences **T** (true) or **F** (false). Correct the **F** sentences.

1 The first Globe Theatre was built by the Lord Chamberlain's Men in 1599.
2 The first theatre burned down in 1630.
3 It was rebuilt, but the second theatre also burned down.
4 Sam Wanamaker was not allowed to act in the USA.
5 He wanted to rebuild the Globe in Shakespeare's birthplace, Stratford-upon-Avon.
6 Everyone encouraged him to go ahead with his plan to reconstruct the Globe.
7 He died in the same year as the Globe opened.
8 The indoor theatre is named after Sam Wanamaker.

c Watch some extracts from the documentary. Then, with a partner, say what the **bold** words mean.

1 And it has a **thatched roof**...
2 He was shocked when all he found was a dirty old **plaque**.
3 There are 857 seats in the stalls, and 700 people can stand in the **pit**...
4 All the lighting is provided by **candlelight**.

d Have you ever seen a Shakespeare play? Where did you see it? Was it in your language or in English? Did you enjoy it?

Go online to watch the video and review the lesson

7 & 8 Revise and Check

GRAMMAR

a Circle a, b, or c.

1 I didn't know the answer, so I ____ online.
   a looked up it   b looked it up
   c looked up
2 Tim's upset – he ____ last night.
   a broke up with Anna
   b broke with Anna up
   c broke Anna up
3 He really doesn't get ____.
   a on with his family   b on his family
   c on his family with
4 My new shoes don't fit. I need to ____.
   a take back   b take back them
   c take them back
5 They decided ____ to a concert.
   a to go   b go   c going
6 You should ____ more careful.
   a to be   b be   c being
7 Please don't keep ____ that noise.
   a to make   b make   c making
8 He wanted ____ him.
   a me help   b me to help   c that I help
9 My mother never used to let me ____ late.
   a to stay out   b stay out
   c staying out

b Complete the second sentence so that it means the same as the first.

1 I'm going to pay someone to take my photo.
   I'm going to have _____ _____.
2 The hairdresser cut my hair last week.
   I had _____ _____ _____ last week.
3 I'd like someone to paint my flat.
   I'd like to have _____ _____ _____.
4 They built the cathedral in 1443.
   The cathedral _____ _____ in 1443.
5 The government should pay nurses more.
   Nurses _____ _____ _____ more.
6 I don't like it when people tell me what to do.
   I don't like _____ _____ what to do.

VOCABULARY

a Complete the phrasal verbs. Use the correct form of the verb where necessary.

1 I tried to _____ out some cash, but the ATM was out of order.
2 She _____ away all her old clothes to the charity shop.
3 I lent him some money, but he never _____ me back.
4 Since our son was born, we've been _____ on one salary.
5 I'll _____ away next week. Can we postpone the meeting?
6 I'm just going out – I'll be _____ in 15 minutes.
7 The man took her bag and then ran _____.
8 She takes _____ her father – they're both very selfish.
9 I always feel nervous when the plane is taking _____.
10 I'm going to take _____ yoga – everybody says it's good for you.

b Write words for the definitions.

1 the place where theatre tickets are sold _____ _____
2 a short period of time separating parts of a play or concert _____
3 the events that form the story of a novel, play, or film _____
4 an afternoon performance of a play _____
5 the person that you are playing against in a game _____

c Complete the words.

1 She's had her hair d_____ red.
2 My nails look terrible – I need a m_____.
3 My mum used to put my hair in two pl_____ when I was little.
4 A m_____ is a very good way to relax.
5 It's important to do s_____ after you've been running.
6 Queen Elizabeth II lives in Buckingham P_____.
7 The d_____ on top of the cathedral is really beautiful.
8 During the cathedral tour, we went down into the cr_____.
9 Lenin's t_____ is in Red Square in Moscow.
10 King Harold was d_____ in the Battle of Hastings in 1066.

PRONUNCIATION

a Practise the words and sounds.

Vowel sounds   Consonant sounds

phone   owl   clock   boot   house   witch   monkey   thumb   mother

b p.166–7 Sound Bank Say more words for each sound.

c What sound in a do the pink letters have in these words?
   1 crowd   2 whistle   3 yoga   4 cathedral   5 tomb

d Underline the stressed syllable.
   1 per|for|mance   2 au|di|ence   3 ae|ro|bics   4 ped|i|cure   5 co|lumn

84

CAN YOU understand this text?

a Read the extract from a website. Would you like to visit the Roman Baths? Why (not)?

VISIT BATH

THINGS TO DO > ROMAN BATHS

The spa city of Bath is situated on natural hot springs, and the water has played an important role throughout the city's history. The Roman Baths were constructed around 70 AD as a grand bathing and socializing centre. The Baths are now in the centre of the city, and are one of the best preserved Roman ruins in the world.

The Great Bath, which lies below street level, is situated at the centre of the building, and here you can walk on the ancient paths, as the Romans did 2,000 years ago. 1,170,000 litres of hot water, reaching 46°C, still fill the baths every day. The Romans believed that this was the mystical work of the gods, but we now know that the water, which comes out of the ground at the King's Spring, fell as rainwater around 10,000 BC. There are statues around the terrace, from where you can look down on the Great Bath, and see the tower of Bath Abbey above you. You can visit the Roman heated rooms and changing rooms, as well as the other smaller bathing pools which were filled with warm and cold water.

With an audio guide, you can listen to the fascinating commentary as you slowly walk around the site. These are available in 12 different languages. A special English-speaking audio guide is also available, narrated by the travel writer Bill Bryson, who gives his thoughts and observations on all things Roman. As well as walking around the ruins, you can explore the interactive museum, where you will find out about the lives of the people of Aquae Sulis, the Roman name for Bath.

Afterwards, try the spa water in the Pump Room, which is included in the admission price. The spa water contains 43 minerals and is believed to be very good for you. This is a unique opportunity to get a real taste (literally!) of Roman Bath. Then go for afternoon tea in the Pump Room restaurant, where you'll be accompanied by classical music from the Pump Room Trio.

During July and August, the Roman Baths are open until 10.00 p.m. You can explore them by moonlight, and by the light of torches placed around the site, which creates a magical atmosphere.

Adapted from the Visit Bath website

Glossary
spring a place where water comes up naturally from under the ground

b Read the extract again. Find the names for the descriptions below.

1 _____ a place where you can taste the spa water
2 _____ the Roman name for the city of Bath
3 _____ part of the building decorated with statues
4 _____ the largest bathing pool in the building
5 _____ / _____ the two months when you can visit the Baths at night
6 _____ a church near the Baths
7 _____ the narrator of the audio guide
8 _____ the place where the hot water rises out of the ground

▶ CAN YOU understand these people?

🔊 8.17 Watch or listen and choose a, b or c.

1 Diarmuid   2 Victoria   3 Keith   4 Carolina   5 Erin

1 Diarmuid would only go to a bank if ____.
  a he was having problems with online banking
  b he wanted to borrow money
  c he needed to transfer money
2 Victoria doesn't watch the LA Dodgers much because ____.
  a they're not very good this year
  b she doesn't live there any more
  c they're in a new Series
3 Cluedo is a board game that ____.
  a Keith prefers to Monopoly
  b Keith didn't use to like as a child
  c is similar to Monopoly
4 Carolina ____.
  a goes to the hairdresser's every week
  b only ever has her hair cut
  c once had her hair dyed super blonde
5 Erin and her husband ____.
  a hadn't planned to visit the Colosseum
  b couldn't find the Galileo museum
  c enjoyed both the Colosseum and the Galileo museum

CAN YOU say this in English?

Tick (✓) the box if you can do these things.

Can you…?
1 ☐ explain how to take money out of a cash machine
2 ☐ talk about what you enjoy doing when you go out or stay in
3 ☐ talk about things you can have done at the hairdresser or a beauty salon, and which ones you sometimes do yourself
4 ☐ describe a famous building you know, including its history

Go online to watch the video, review Files 7 & 8, and check your progress

9A Total recall

I asked her to phone you.
She said she had forgotten my number.

G reported speech **V** word building **P** word stress

1 SPEAKING

a How easy or difficult do you find it to remember things? Do the questionnaire. Then compare with a partner. Give examples. Who do you think has the better memory?

I've got a good memory... or have I?

Tick (✓) each statement below that is true for you.

1 ☐ I find it difficult to remember where I've put things.
2 ☐ I usually remember faces, but I often forget people's names, even immediately after I've been introduced to them.
3 ☐ There are some English words that I find really difficult to remember, however hard I try.
4 ☐ I only remember people's birthdays because Facebook reminds me.
5 ☐ I often forget my passwords, so I usually use the same one for everything.
6 ☐ I find it difficult to remember things in my calendar – dates and things I've planned to do.
7 ☐ I have problems remembering my PINs and passwords and I often have to reset them.
8 ☐ I can never remember anyone's phone number because my phone does it for me.

> 🔍 **Giving examples**
> I often forget where I've put things **like / such as** my phone and my car keys.
> I have problems remembering my passwords, **for example / for instance**, when I'm shopping online.

b Which of the things in the questionnaire in **a** causes you the biggest problem?

2 READING

a Look at this credit card number for 30 seconds. Then close your book and write the numbers in the correct order. How many digits could you remember?

9674 5038 2142 6937

b You're going to read an extract from a book called *How to Develop a Brilliant Memory Week by Week* by Dominic O'Brien. First, look at the ten objects in the photo. With a partner, try to write the word for as many as you can.

c Read the extract once and check your answers to **b**. In pairs, decide if you prefer any different objects for the numbers 0–9.

d Read the extract again and complete each paragraph with one of the phrases below.

A a story involving a chain of 20 linked number shapes
B think of an image similar to the shape of the number itself
C memorize a sequence of up to 2,000 digits within one hour
D the number picture to the thing you want to remember

e Look at the three highlighted verbs, which are all connected to the verb *remember*. Match them to their meaning.

1 _____ help sb to remember something
2 _____ remember sth from the past
3 _____ learn sth by heart

f Now do the task in the last paragraph of the extract. Then use the Number-Shape System and the Link Method to memorize the credit card number in **a**. Could you do it better than the first time?

g Do you think the author's method is a good one? Do you know any other good ways of remembering things like PINs and passwords?

h You're now going to do an activity called **Build Words into a Picture**, and use images to learn new vocabulary. Your teacher will tell you what to do.

How to remember numbers

We are surrounded by numbers – PINs, codes for credit card security, online accounts, or entry codes to buildings – and we are expected to memorize them all. Wouldn't it be great if we could remember these numbers instantly, whenever we needed them? I am not brilliant at remembering numbers, but I have trained my memory. Now I can [1]____. How is this possible?

I use a method called the Number-Shape System. This is a great way to store any sequence of digits, such as PINs, calendar dates, telephone numbers, and much longer ones as well. First, for numbers 0-9, [2]____. For example, '0' could be a ball, '1' could be a pencil, and so on. My suggestions for numbers 2-9 are: 2 a swan, 3 handcuffs, 4 a sailing boat, 5 a seahorse, 6 an elephant's trunk, 7 a boomerang, 8 an egg timer, and 9 a balloon on a string. You can use these ideas, or choose images of your own, for example, number 8 could also be a snowman.

Now you can start using the pictures. Connect [3]____. So, to remind you that you have to catch a number 67 bus, imagine an elephant ('elephant trunk' = number 6) standing at the bus stop throwing a boomerang ('boomerang' = number 7); an unlikely scene, but certainly one you won't forget. Or if you want to remember that oxygen has the atomic number 8, imagine a snowman wearing an oxygen mask. Now, suddenly, numbers come to life and are instantly more memorable. This is called the Link Method. It works by linking one object to the next by creating an imaginary connection between the two items.

> You're going to try to memorize the following 20-digit number.
>
> **7 9 0 4 6 2 1 3 5 8 5 9 9 4 0 1 3 2 7 6**
>
> First, using the Number-Shape System, convert each number into its equivalent shape (use either your own number shapes or mine). Then connect them together using the Link Method. So to start, imagine throwing a boomerang at a balloon on a string. Continue by connecting the balloon on a string to a ball, and so on. You should now have created [4]____, starting with a boomerang and ending with an elephant's trunk. Now try to write down the sequence of numbers. Score one point for each digit you can recall before making a mistake. *Maximum points: 20.*

Adapted from The Times

3 GRAMMAR reported speech

a 🔊 9.1 Listen to two true stories. Why were Sarah and Kim annoyed?

b Can you remember who said what? Write **S** (Sarah), **R** (Rick), **K** (Kim), **C** (Caro), or **M** (Mum). Then listen again and check.

1 Sarah's story
- 'Have you seen my car keys?'
- 'I can't find them.'
- 'You've moved them.'
- 'Have you looked in your coat pocket?'
- 'They're not there.'

2 Kim's story
- 'I want to do something to help.'
- 'I'll bring a birthday cake.'
- 'Where's the cake?'
- 'I completely forgot about it.'
- 'It's no problem.'

c Complete the sentences from **b** in reported speech with one word.

1. Rick asked me _____ I had seen his car keys.
2. He told me that he _____ find them.
3. He said I _____ moved them.
4. I _____ him if he had looked in his coat pocket.
5. He _____ me they weren't there.
6. My sister _____ that she wanted to do something to help.
7. She said she _____ bring a birthday cake.
8. After lunch, I asked her where the cake _____.
9. She said _____ had completely forgotten about it.
10. Mum said that it _____ no problem.

d 🄶 p.148 **Grammar Bank 9A**

e Work in pairs. Write down **three** questions to ask your partner. Then ask your questions and try to remember your partner's answers. Don't write them down!

What did you have for breakfast this morning?
I had coffee and toast.

f Now test your memory. Tell a new partner what you asked your previous partner, and what he or she said.

I asked Luisa what she'd had for breakfast this morning. She told me she'd had coffee and toast.

4 LISTENING

a With a partner, look at the days and dates below. Can you remember where you were? What did you do? Try to remember as many details as you can.

yesterday morning
last Saturday evening
your last birthday
31st December last year
1st July 2010

b 🔊 9.5 Listen to the first part of a radio programme about Jill Price, a woman with an extraordinary memory. Answer the questions.

1 Complete the name of Jill's condition: **H**ighly **S**uperior A_____ M_____.
2 How old was Jill when the condition started?
3 How does she feel about her condition?

Glossary
The *Challenger* explosion On 28th January 1986, the US space shuttle *Challenger* broke in two 73 seconds into its flight, killing all seven crew members.

c Listen again and answer the questions.

1 What day of the week was each of these dates? What did Jill do on each day?
   24th January 1986
   29th August 1980
   10th January 1981
2 What is Jill's first memory? How old was she at the time?
3 What two things happened on 1st July 1974?

d 🔊 9.6 Now listen to the second part of the programme. Make notes to answer the questions.

1 How did Dr McGaugh test Jill's memory?
2 What does she remember happening on 16th August 1977 and 14th October 1977?
3 How was Dr McGaugh able to confirm that Jill's memories were accurate?
4 According to Dr McGaugh's research, what are the most memorable experiences?
5 What kinds of things is Jill good at remembering?
6 What kinds of things can't she remember?
7 How many people are there with HSAM?
8 What does Jill say are the two big problems with her condition?
9 What's the title of her autobiography?
10 Why hasn't her brother read it?

Glossary
Elvis Presley and Bing Crosby two famous American singers

e Would you want a memory like Jill's? Why (not)?

Jill Price

5 VOCABULARY & PRONUNCIATION
word building; word stress

a Look at some words from Jill Price's story. Complete the chart with nouns, adjectives, and adverbs formed from these words.

Noun	Adjective	Adverb
1 memory		
2		confidently
3	emotional	
4	important	
5	accurate	
6		personally

b 🔊 9.7 Listen and check. Under<u>line</u> the stressed syllables in all the words. Practise saying them.

c Complete some common collocations with a noun, adjective, or adverb from the chart in **a**.
1 I'm reading a new book about _____ **intelligence**.
2 The witness gave a very _____ **description** of the suspect.
3 _____, **I think** you're making a big mistake.
4 The wedding last summer was **a** _____ **occasion**.
5 In half an hour, the press office is going to make **an** _____ **announcement**.
6 **I can** _____ **say that** the business is doing well.

d Can you remember these words? They have all come up in this lesson.
1 the adjective from **atom**
2 the noun from **enter**
3 the negative adjective from **likely**
4 the noun from **secure**
5 the noun from **connect**
6 the adjective from **autobiography**
7 the adverb from **easy**
8 the noun from **able**
9 the negative adjective from **pleasant**

6 SPEAKING

a Choose two of the topics below and think about what you're going to say. Add details and give examples.

- someone you know who has an incredibly good or bad **memory**
- a **memorable** moment from your school days
- something you were made to **memorize** as a child and found difficult
- an **unforgettable** birthday or Christmas
- something from your past that you wish you could **remember** better
- a time when you **forgot** an important date or appointment

b Work in groups of three or four. Talk about your topics, and listen and respond to the other people in the group.

> I'm going to tell you about my brother, who has an incredibly good memory…

c From memory, tell the rest of the class about something someone in your group told you.

9B Here comes the bride

G third conditional and other uses of the past perfect **V** weddings **P** sentence stress

Why didn't he tell her the truth?
It wouldn't have made any difference if he'd told her.

1 READING & LISTENING

a You're going to read a short story by William Somerset Maugham. Read the information about him below. Do you think it was right or wrong of him to write about people he met? Why (not)?

William Somerset Maugham
(1874–1965)

William Somerset Maugham (/ˈsʌməset ˈmɔːm/) was a well-known English novelist and short story writer whose stories were often set in China, Singapore, Burma (now Myanmar), Malaya (now Malaysia), and other East Asian countries. Maugham wrote at a time when many of these places were colonies of Great Britain. The language of his stories reflects the social and political context of the time; country and city names have since been changed and some ways of referring to people would not be considered appropriate today. Many of the people in Maugham's stories were real, and they were often upset to recognize themselves in his books.

b 🔊 9.8 Read and listen to Part 1 of *Mabel*. Answer the questions with a partner.
1 Who were George and Mabel?
2 Why couldn't they get married for seven years?
3 What do you think *his nerve failed him* in line 13 means? Why did it happen?
4 What was George's dilemma?
5 What did he decide to do?

What do you think of George's behaviour?
What do you think will happen next?

c 🔊 9.9 Find the following places on the map. How do you think you say them in English? Listen and check.

Bangkok	Cheng-tu	Chungking
Hong Kong	Manila	Saigon	Shanghai
Singapore	the Yangtze River	Yokohama

d 🔊 9.10 Now listen to Part 2. Mark George's route on the map.

Mabel
Part 1

George was working in Burma for the British colonial government. He and Mabel became engaged when he was back in England. When he returned to Burma, it was arranged that she
05 would join him there in six months. But one difficulty came up after another. Mabel's father died, the war came, then George was sent to a district which was unsuitable for a white woman. In the end,
10 it was seven years before she was able to start. He made all the arrangements for the marriage, which was going to take place on the day of her arrival, and went down to Rangoon to meet her. Then, suddenly, without warning, his nerve failed him. He had not seen Mabel for seven years. He had forgotten what she was like. She was
15 a total stranger. He felt a terrible feeling in his stomach. He couldn't go through with it. He must tell Mabel that he was very sorry, but he couldn't, he really couldn't marry her. But how could a man tell a girl a thing like that when she had been engaged to him for seven years and had come 6,000 miles to marry him? He didn't have the nerve for
20 that either. There was a boat just about to sail for Singapore; he wrote a letter to Mabel, and without any luggage, just in the clothes he was wearing, he boarded the boat. The letter Mabel received said:

Dearest Mabel,
I have been suddenly called away on business and do not know when
25 *I will be back. I think it would be much wiser if you returned to England. My plans are very uncertain.*
Your loving George.

Glossary
the war the First World War, which started in 1914
Rangoon the old name for Yangon, the largest port in Myanmar (Burma)

e Listen again and complete Mabel's four telegrams.

TELEGRAM

1. Quite _____. _____ _____.
   Love Mabel

2. _____ _____.

3. So _____ I _____ you at _____.
   Love Mabel

4. _____ _____.
   Love Mabel

How do you think George felt when he got the last telegram? What do you think he will do now?

f Read Part 3 (don't listen yet). Continue drawing George's journey on the map. Then complete the gaps with an adverb or adverbial phrase from the list.

after that   already   at last   never   one morning   only

Part 3

No, no, she wasn't going to catch him so easily. He had ¹ *already* made his plans. He could catch the last ship along the Yangtze river to Chungking. ² _____, no one could get there until the following spring. He arrived at Chungking, but he was desperate now. He was not going to take any risks. There was a place called Cheng-tu, the capital of Szechuan, and it was 400 miles away. It could ³ _____ be reached by road, and the area was full of thieves. A man would be safe there.

George set out. He sighed with relief when he saw the walls of the lonely Chinese city. He could rest ⁴ _____. Mabel would ⁵ _____ find him there. The British consul was a friend of his and he stayed with him in his luxurious house.

The weeks passed lazily one after the other. ⁶ _____, George and the consul were in the courtyard when there was a loud knock at the door.

g ◉9.11 Listen and check. What do you think *he sighed with relief* in line 10 means?

h ◉9.12 How do you think the story ends? Listen to Part 4 and check.

i Discuss the questions with a partner.
   1 How do you feel about what Mabel did in the story? Do you have more sympathy for Mabel or for George?
   2 Do you think Mabel and George had a happy marriage? Why (not)?

2 GRAMMAR third conditional and other uses of the past perfect

a Look at three extracts from *Mabel*. Which highlighted phrase…?
   1 ☐ says how things could have been different in the past
   2 ☐ describes something that happened earlier in the past
   3 ☐ reports what someone said or asked in the past

   a He went straight to the club and asked *if he had received any telegrams*.
   b Then, suddenly, without warning, his nerve failed him. *He had not seen Mabel for seven years.*
   c *It would have been terrible if I hadn't been able to marry you after all.*

b G p.149 Grammar Bank 9B

3 PRONUNCIATION sentence stress

a ◉9.15 Listen to five sentences. Write the stressed words in the pink rectangles.

   1 When ___ read ___ email, ___ understood ___ left.
   2 ___ ___ ___ , ___ ___ .
   3 ___ ___ , ___ ___ .
   4 ___ ___ .
   5 ___ ___ .

b Look at the stressed words and try to remember what the unstressed words are. Write in the unstressed words.

c Listen again and check. Then listen and repeat the sentences.

d Complete the sentences with a verb phrase in the past perfect. Then take turns to say your sentence to your partner. Are they the same?
   1 I would have been very annoyed if you had…
   2 I was really surprised when I saw him because…
   3 I was furious with my mum when she told me…

4 LISTENING

a Read the introduction to an article and look at the photos. What two words do you think are missing from the title? With a partner, decide for each couple who you think proposed to who, and how they did it.

'Will you _____ _____?' 'No, I won't.'

Look up 'failed marriage proposal' on YouTube and you will find hundreds of videos of people proposing marriage and being rejected. What these videos don't offer is a chance to ask the people involved what the experience actually feels like. I wanted to find out, so I found two people who either turned down a proposal, or whose proposal was turned down, and asked them to tell me all about it. (Names have been changed!)

b 9.16 Listen to Alex and Emma talking about what happened. Are the two couples both together now?

c 9.17 Listen again to Alex's story. Then complete the sentences with a partner.
1 Alex didn't want to…
2 Chloe began to talk about…
3 On 29th February, Chloe invited Alex to…
4 Chloe gave Alex…
5 The letters spelled…
6 Alex started putting the letters on the bracelet in…
7 Chloe got upset and explained that on 29th February, women…
8 Alex didn't see her…

d 9.18 Now listen again to Emma's story. Explain why the following things were important.
1 ten years
2 two years
3 the cathedral
4 a bottle of champagne and a bunch of flowers
5 a necklace
6 a crowd of tourists
7 white and shocked
8 walking to the station

e What do you think about the way Alex and Emma behaved? Do you feel sorry for Chloe and Tom?

5 VOCABULARY weddings

a Look at the wedding photo opposite. Match people A–E to the words below.
- the bride
- the (bride)groom
- the best man
- a bridesmaid
- a pageboy

b Read the magazine article about wedding costs and complete it with the words from the list.

best man   bridesmaids   couples   engaged
guests   invitations   married   reception

c Now read the list of wedding expenses and in pairs, try to match the prices to the cost of each thing.

350   640   1,160   1,300   2,500
4,500   5,500   8,500

Venue (for the ceremony and the reception)	£_____
Five bridesmaids' dresses	£_____
Food	£_____
Flowers	£_____
Rings	£_____
Groom's suit	£_____
Wedding dress, veil & shoes	£_____
Honeymoon	£_____

d 9.19 Listen and check. Do you think couples nowadays spend too much money on their wedding?

e Talk to a partner about weddings where you live.
- Who are the main people?
- Where is the wedding ceremony usually held?
- What kinds of things do people wear?
- Is there usually a reception? Where?
- What kind of food and drink is typical?
- Do people make speeches?
- What else happens?

This is how much a wedding really costs!

After we got ¹_____ and started seriously planning our wedding, I read ALL the wedding magazines, and they all tell you that the average cost of a UK wedding is now £25,000. After the event, I can tell you that unless you are having the ²_____ in your garden, and are only inviting ten ³_____, this is just not true.

We didn't have an enormous wedding. We got ⁴_____ in a country house in Surrey, and invited about 100 people, which I think is the average, judging by every other wedding I've been to. We saved money where we could. We were very lucky because friends designed the ⁵_____, and did the music and photography for free. My sister made the cake, and my parents paid for the drinks. We bought the dresses for the ⁶_____ and the suit for the ⁷_____ ready-made from a department store.

Still, we ended up spending over £30,000, and if we hadn't had very kind and helpful friends, it would've been more like £35,000. Just to give other ⁸_____ a little bit of guidance, I'm sharing some of our biggest expenses with you so it'll hopefully be a bit less of a shock when you get the bills!

Adapted from Marie Claire

6 SPEAKING

a Look at some controversial statements about weddings. Decide whether you agree or disagree. Think of reasons why and examples to support your opinion.

1. It should be the woman who proposes to the man because it's usually the woman who wants to get married.
2. It's better to marry for money or security than to marry for love.
3. It's completely unacceptable to ask for money as a wedding present.
4. Parents choose better partners for their children than the children choose for themselves.
5. You shouldn't invite people you don't like to your wedding, even if they are relatives.
6. Brides enjoy their wedding day more than bridegrooms.

b In small groups, discuss each statement. Take turns to explain your reasons and give examples. Respond to what other students say. Use the language from the **Agreeing and disagreeing** box.

> **Agreeing**
> I agree with you 100%.
> I couldn't agree with you more.
> That's so true.
> You're absolutely right.
>
> **Disagreeing**
> I see your point, but…
> That's not always true.
> I don't think you're right.
> Let's agree to disagree.
> I completely disagree.
> No way!

7 WRITING

W p.122 **Writing** A story Write a story describing a memorable event.

EPISODE 5

Practical English Finding Henry

giving directions in a building

1 ▶ WHAT THE CLUE MEANS

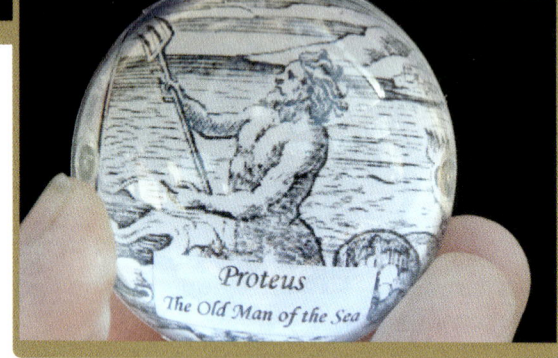

a ◉ 9.20 Watch or listen to Jenny and Luke looking in Henry's study. What does 'old man' refer to? Where do they think Henry is?

b Watch or listen again. Complete the sentences with **Jenny**, **Luke**, or **Rob**.
1 _____ has checked all the paintings.
2 _____ thinks maybe the old man thing wasn't a message.
3 _____ suggests looking on top of the bookcase.
4 _____ finds the two paperweights.
5 _____ discovers that Proteus is a company in Oxford.
6 _____ phones the Police Inspector.
7 _____ downloads the plans of the Proteus building.
8 _____ is going to guide the police officers.

What do you think they are going to find in the building?

2 ▶ GIVING DIRECTIONS IN A BUILDING

a ◉ 9.21 Look at the plan of the building. Watch or listen. Mark the rest of the police officers' route. Where do they end up, A, B, or C?

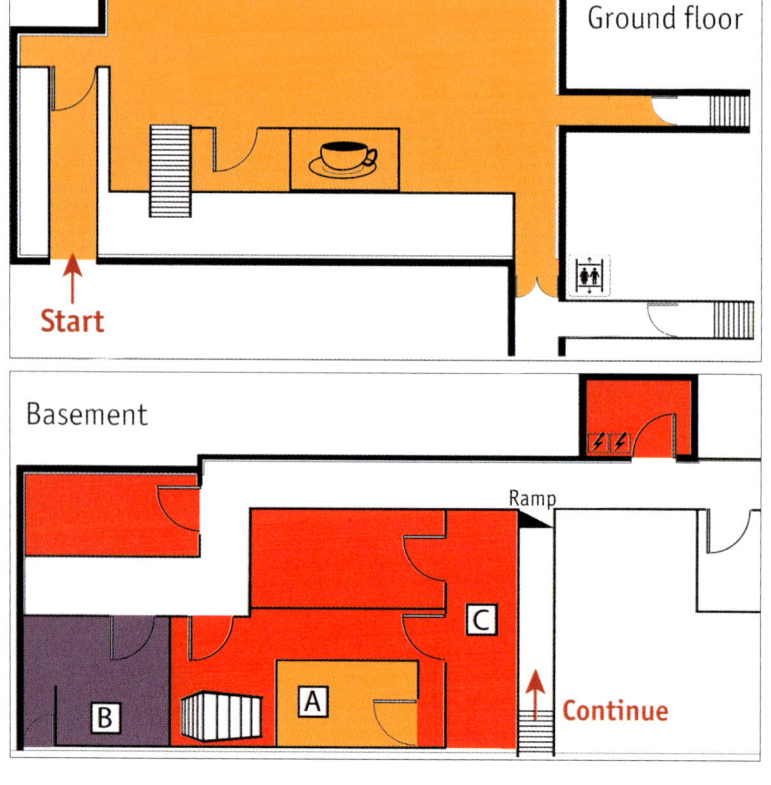

b Read the conversation between Luke and Tom on p.95. Can you remember any of the missing words? Watch or listen again and check.

c ●)) 9.22 Watch or listen and repeat the highlighted sentences. Copy the rhythm and intonation.

Luke OK, go to the end of the corridor, go ¹_____ the door, and turn ²_____.
Tom We're in a large open area.
Luke That's right. Now, go ³_____ ahead. You should see some stairs on your right. Go ⁴_____ the stairs and a coffee bar. Turn right. ⁵_____ on and you should see a set of double doors.
Tom Should we go through?
Luke Yes. Now, you should see some stairs on your ⁶_____.
Tom Yeah, I see them.
Luke Right. Go ⁷_____ the stairs, continue straight on, and walk down the ramp.
Tom We're at the end of the ramp. Which ⁸_____ now?
Luke ⁹_____ right and carry on straight ¹⁰_____ the corridor. Go past a maintenance room and two fuse boxes, and try the next door on your right.
Tom The door's locked. Is there ¹¹_____ way?
Luke Hold on. OK. Turn ¹²_____ and go ¹³_____ down the corridor.
Tom Should we go back up the ramp?
Luke No. Go straight to the end of the corridor and turn left.
Tom We're here. There are two doors. Which ¹⁴_____ should we take?
Luke ¹⁵_____ the one on your left.
Tom It's open!
Luke What can you see?
Tom There are three big safes and cages full of documents. Are you sure this is the ¹⁶_____ way?
Luke Yes, you're in the store room. Can you hear a generator?
Tom Yes! It's coming from the end of the corridor.
Luke Head ¹⁷_____ it. But watch out for guards!
Tom There's a door here and a narrow corridor to the right. What should we do?
Luke I don't know!
Tom Wait. I can hear voices. There are people in there.
Police Inspector That must be the room.
Tom OK. We're going in.

d 👥 In pairs, practise giving directions in a building.
   A Choose a place on the plan but don't tell B. A give B directions to the place.
   B Check with A that you are going the right way, and anything else you don't understand. Then swap roles.

3 ▶ A HAPPY ENDING?

a ●)) 9.23 What do you think the police officers found? What do you think happens to all the characters? Watch or listen. Were your predictions correct?

b Watch or listen again. Mark the sentences **T** (true) or **F** (false). Correct the **F** sentences.
   1 The news report says that Andrew Page is getting better.
   2 Selina and Grant managed to escape.
   3 Rob thinks the clue was very difficult.
   4 Henry is very grateful for all their help.
   5 They go out for a meal to celebrate.
   6 Rob thinks it is still worth coming to the UK.
   7 Jenny wants to stay longer in the UK.

c Look at the **Social English** phrases. Can you remember any of the missing words?

> 💬 **Social English**
> 1 **Henry** I must _____, I was beginning to lose hope.
> 2 **Henry** Goodness _____ what would have happened if you hadn't found me in time.
> 3 **Henry** Could you _____ the glasses, Luke?
> 4 **Rob** It's _____ to have you back, Dad.
> 5 **Henry** I just _____ you were here, Rob.
> 6 **Jenny** I can't _____ to get back to the peace and quiet of New York!

d ●)) 9.24 Watch or listen and complete the phrases. Then watch or listen again and repeat.

e Complete conversations A–F with **Social English** phrases 1–6. Then practise them with a partner.

A	Shall we have some wine?	Great idea. ▢ please, Jon?
B	Has your nephew lost his job?	Yes. ▢ if he'll ever find another one.
C	Could you help me with my homework?	I'll try, but ▢ I'm not very good at maths!
D	It's so good to be home.	▢. I've really missed you.
E	Can you meet me at the airport?	Sure. ▢ to see you again!
F	So, is the hotel really amazing?	It's wonderful. ▢.

CAN YOU...?
▢ give directions inside a building
▢ check that you understand the directions
▢ express relief and gratitude

🔎 **Go online** to watch the video, review the lesson, and check your progress

95

10A The land of the free?

> Do you like living in New York?
>
> I love it. Everyone is so friendly.

G be, do, and have: auxiliary and main verbs **V** British and American English **P** stress on be, do, and have

1 GRAMMAR be, do, and have: auxiliary and main verbs

a Do the quiz with a partner.

How much do you know about the USA?

Are these statements true (T) or false (F)?

1. The USA **has** more billionaires than any other country.
2. In American English, the words *colour* and *centre* **are** spelled the same as in British English.
3. Over 90% of Americans **don't** own a passport.
4. American men **do** an average of 15 minutes of housework each day.
5. The world's first skyscraper **was** in New York.
6. In 1950, only 22% of adult Americans **were** single; now the figure **is** about 50%.
7. English **has** always **been** the official language of the USA.
8. Texas used **to be** part of Mexico – it **didn't** join the USA until the mid-19th century.
9. The USA once **had** the world's biggest economy, but it **was** overtaken by China in 2014.
10. In the USA, football **is** known as *soccer*. This is the name which the sport **had** originally **been** called at British public schools in the 1860s.

b 🔊 10.1 Listen and check. Correct the false statements.

c Look at the **bold** verbs in **a**. With a partner, circle the ones which are **auxiliary** verbs.

d **G** p.150 Grammar Bank 10A

2 PRONUNCIATION stress on be, do, and have

a 🔊 10.5 Listen and repeat the sentences. Underline the highlighted words if they are stressed.

1. The capital of the USA is Washington, DC.
2. When are your friends arriving?
3. The world's tallest skyscraper isn't in New York.
4. Anne does Pilates twice a week.
5. Where does your sister live?
6. My brother doesn't like dogs.
7. I have a house in New Jersey.
8. How long have you known your best friend?
9. We haven't seen our cousins for ages.

b Listen again. What vowel sound do *are*, *does*, and *have* have when they are unstressed?

c Circle the correct word to complete the rules.

> 🔍 When are *be*, *do*, and *have* stressed?
> **be**
> 1 is usually *stressed / unstressed* in positive sentences or in questions.
> 2 is *stressed / unstressed* in negative sentences.
> **do** and **have**
> 3 are *stressed / unstressed* when they are main verbs.
> 4 are usually *stressed / unstressed* when they are positive auxiliary verbs or in questions.
> 5 are *stressed / unstressed* when they are negative auxiliary verbs.

d **C Communication** More facts about the USA? **A** p.110 **B** p.114 Say sentences to your partner, who must decide if they are true or false.

3 LISTENING

a 🔊 10.6 Listen to six people who live in New York talking about life there. Match the speakers to the things they talk about. Which speakers are negative?

☐ bureaucracy ☐ gun culture
☐ helpfulness ☐ multiculturalism
☐ opportunity ☐ sport

b Listen again and complete the notes for each speaker with examples that they give.

1 Yannis from Greece
- on the subway you see different _____ and hear different _____
- nobody is surprised if you have a _____

2 Cristina from Croatia
- the game is too _____ – didn't understand the _____
- the atmosphere is too _____

3 Louisa from the USA
- easy to:
  change your _____ _____
  renew your _____ _____

4 Laura from the USA
- in Germany, no one helped her with her _____ at the _____
- in the USA, people _____ _____ for you, and carry things up the stairs in the _____

5 Peter from the UK
- as an immigrant you can _____ _____ that you couldn't get back home
- likes the entrepreneurial _____

6 Sarah from the UK
- in Europe, people don't want to _____ _____ themselves
- it's up to the police to _____ _____ of people and make sure everyone is _____

c Is there anything they said that you already knew or thought about American culture? Is there anything that surprised you? Do you think people's opinions might be different in other parts of the USA?

4 SPEAKING

a Look at the cover and read the description of a recent book. What do you think 'Americanization' means? Do you agree that the world has been 'Americanized'?

> **Historian Peter Conrad** tells the story of American influence across the world since 1945. He describes America's unstoppable creativity: its great and bad art, its jeans and jazz, its cinema, fast food and fridges, its space travel and technologies that have all Americanized our world.

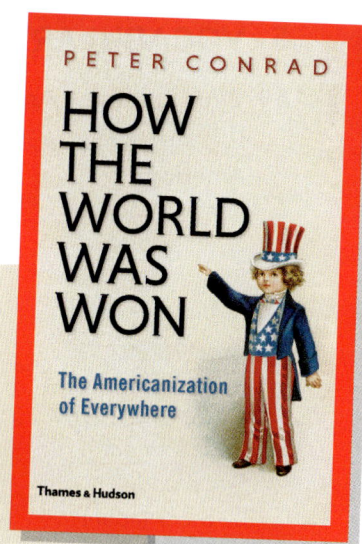

PETER CONRAD
HOW THE WORLD WAS WON
The Americanization of Everywhere
Thames & Hudson

b Look at the photos and talk to a partner. How important do you think these aspects of American culture are in your country?

> *Most films and TV series that we watch are American, so, yes, I think they're very important here...*

- films and TV series
- food and drink
- coffee shops
- chain stores
- technology
- language
- music
- sport

c Think of examples of the same kinds of things from your country. Which do you personally prefer: the American ones or the ones from your country? Which do you think people from your country generally prefer?

d What things about your country are you most proud of? Do you think any of them have had an influence in the world?

5 VOCABULARY British and American English

a What do these American English words mean? Write the British word.

American	British
1 cell phone	_____
2 restroom	_____
3 movie theater	_____
4 high school	_____
5 garbage	_____
6 sneakers	_____
7 elevator	_____
8 apartment	_____
9 zip code	_____
10 check (noun)	_____

b ◆ 10.7 Listen and check.

c Match some more British and American words.

British	American
1 ___ car park	a closet
2 ___ mean (adj)	b stand in line
3 ___ autumn	c faucet
4 ___ petrol	d fall
5 ___ queue (verb)	e parking lot
6 ___ garden	f gas
7 ___ wardrobe	g truck
8 ___ pavement	h stingy
9 ___ lorry	i sidewalk
10 ___ tap	j yard

d ◆ 10.8 Listen and check.

e The following words exist in both British and American English, but mean different things. Write **Br** or **Am** next to the photos or definitions.

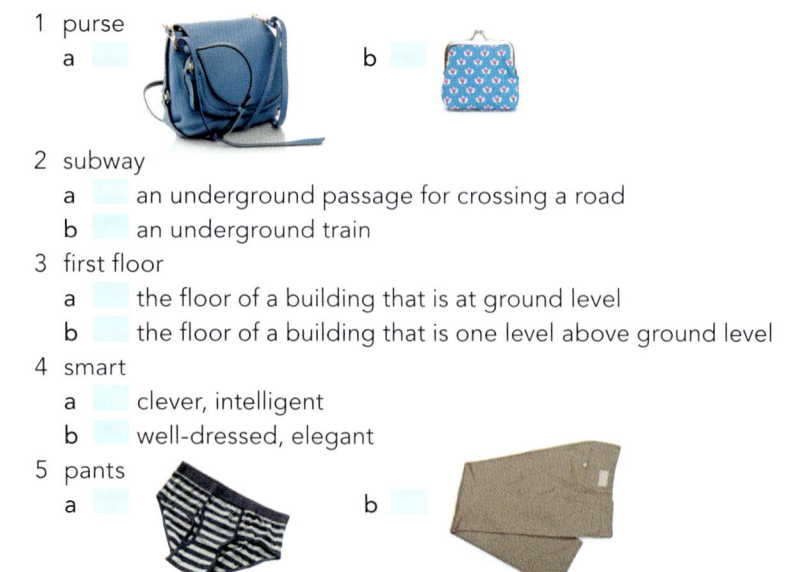

1 purse
  a ___
  b ___

2 subway
  a ___ an underground passage for crossing a road
  b ___ an underground train

3 first floor
  a ___ the floor of a building that is at ground level
  b ___ the floor of a building that is one level above ground level

4 smart
  a ___ clever, intelligent
  b ___ well-dressed, elegant

5 pants
  a ___
  b ___

f ◆ 10.9 Listen. Are the speakers British or American? What would they say if they were the other nationality?

6 READING

a Look at the title and the introduction to each blog on p.99. Which writer is British? Which is American?

b Read the blogs. Write the headings in the correct place. There is one heading you do not need.

A Being unfriendly
B Thinking we're stupid
C Not knowing how to spell words… or pronounce them
D Being a bit stingy
E Paying for health care
F Being too patriotic
G Being too nice
H Believing the stereotypes
I Rushing to clear the table

c Look at the highlighted words in the blogs and read the whole sentences. Decide whether they are adjectives, nouns, or verbs. Then match them to definitions 1–8.

1 _____ (adj esp. NAmE) fantastic, great
2 _____ (adj, informal) strange in a way that makes you feel frightened
3 _____ (adj) shy and quiet
4 _____ (adj) strange and difficult to explain
5 _____ (noun) a bird similar to a very large chicken
6 _____ (noun) something people say to express admiration, e.g. *He paid me a ~* – *he said I looked lovely.*
7 _____ (verb, informal) understand
8 _____ (verb) move your head up and down, e.g. to say yes or hello

d ◆ 10.10 Listen and check.

e Do you find any of these things about the Americans or the British annoying? Are there any customs in your country that might 'drive foreigners crazy'?

Six things Americans do that drive Brits crazy

By Ruth Margolis

American people are some of the friendliest you'll ever meet. But occasionally, they do things that we find a bit...eccentric.

1 **Saying 'I love your accent!'**
   Before I moved to the USA, I never imagined that my London accent made me sound intelligent. At first the compliments were nice, but then a New York mum asked me to teach her two-year-old how to talk like me. A bit too much, I thought.

2 _____
   In America, people in shops say things like 'Ma'am, you have been an awesome customer today', just because I bought some toilet paper. I do not want that.

3 _____
   American waiters love to please, but sometimes they're too helpful. Over-enthusiastic waiters take away your plate the second it's empty, even if no one else at the table has finished.

4 **Insisting that turkey is tasty**
   There's a good reason why Brits only eat this bird at Christmas. Turkey meat is dry and tasteless. But Americans put it in everything – burgers, meatballs, lasagna – everything!

5 _____
   We get it, you're proud to be an American. We Brits like our country too, but to your average Brit, hanging a giant flag from your house is a little bit creepy.

6 _____
   Having to remove 'u's from words like 'colour' and change 're' to 'er' in words like 'theatre' is a headache. And Americans, please note: saying 'erb' instead of 'herb' and pronouncing 'fillet' as 'fillay' (without the 't') is not clever or sophisticated. You are not French.

Six things Brits do that drive Americans crazy

By Maria Roth

Americans love the British. They're so charming and smart! But there are some things about them that we don't quite understand.

1 _____
   When strangers in stores and people on the street make eye contact, nod, or say, 'Hi!', it's OK to smile and say hello back. We won't bite!

2 **Overcooking vegetables**
   The authentic British way to prepare vegetables is to put them in boiling water for a fortnight. We Americans think this is weird and unpleasant.

3 _____
   Oh, we fat Americans with our big cars and flags! Too many Brits are convinced that this inaccurate picture of us is true, and we are not amused.

4 _____
   It seems that some Brits would rather not leave a 15 to 20 per cent tip for their waiter. They may not realize that waiters in the US are paid very low wages and depend on tips to survive.

5 **Not wanting to 'share'**
   Brits are famous for being reserved – they never complain or discuss their problems. But that's not the way we do things here. We're more open with our friends, and even with strangers, and when people don't share, we find it strange.

6 _____
   We get it, in British English, 'trousers' means pants and 'pants' are really underwear. And the letter 'z' is 'zee' to Americans, but 'zed' to Brits. We Americans just have a different way of speaking and writing. It doesn't mean we're stupid, and I promise we're not trying to offend you.

Adapted from the BBC America website

10B Please turn over your papers

> What's the hardest exam you've ever done?
>
> Probably my French speaking exam!

G revision of verb forms | V exams | P revision of sounds

1 VOCABULARY exams

a Look at the photo and describe what's happening.
- Who are the people in the photo? How old do you think they are?
- Where are they? What are they doing?
- How do you think they are feeling?
- Who else is probably in the room?

b Complete the mind map with the words and phrases from the list.

cheat (in)   do   essay   fail   multiple-choice   oral/speaking   pass
practical   retake   revise (for)   take   true or false   written

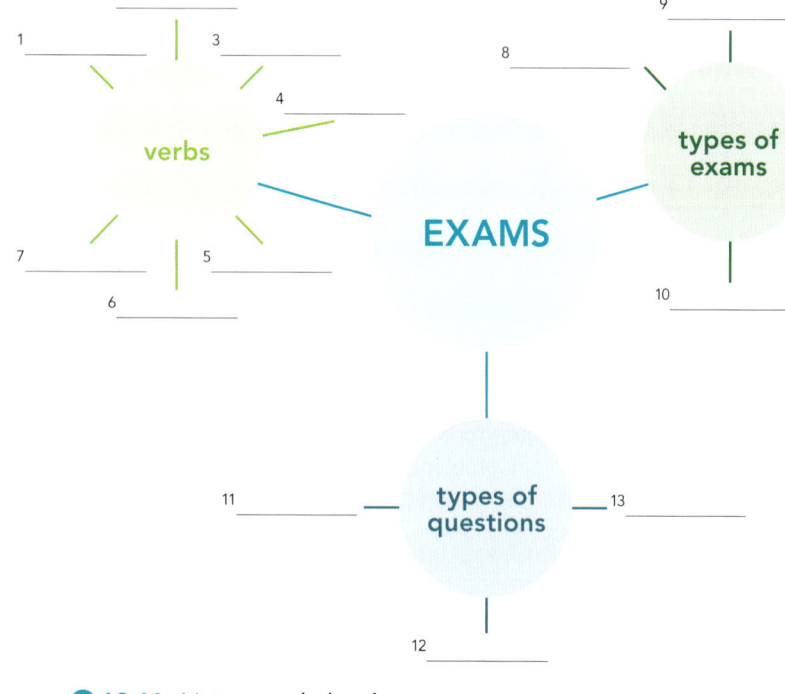

verbs: 1 ___ 2 ___ 3 ___ 4 ___ 5 ___ 6 ___ 7 ___

types of exams: 8 ___ 9 ___ 10 ___

EXAMS

types of questions: 11 ___ 12 ___ 13 ___

c ▶ 10.11 Listen and check.

d **Communication** Describing a photo A p.109 B p.111
Describe the photos and discuss the topic.

2 PRONUNCIATION revision of sounds

a Which word has a different sound? Say the three words aloud and then (circle) the one you think is different.

1	revis**es** / prepar**es** / giv**es**	6	**e**ssay / th**e**sis / degr**ee**
2	fail**ed** / stud**ied** / cheat**ed**	7	sch**oo**l / g**oo**d / childh**oo**d
3	m**a**rks / **a**nswer / ex**a**m	8	wr**i**tten / **i**dea / pract**i**se
4	w**or**k / **or**al / rep**or**t	9	g**u**ess / t**e**st / r**e**sult
5	wr**o**ng / pr**o**fessor / c**o**llege		

b ▶ 10.12 Listen and check.

c Look at the sentences. What sound does each of the pink letters have? Practise saying the sentences.
1 I went to a very g**oo**d sch**oo**l.
2 She **a**nswered all the ex**a**m questions.
3 My rep**or**t said that I'd w**or**ked hard.
4 I need to pract**i**se for the wr**i**tten exam.
5 He cheat**ed** in the exam, but he still fail**ed**.
6 There are some excellent pr**o**fessors at my c**o**llege.
7 I was really nervous when I got my t**e**st r**e**sults.

100

3 LISTENING & SPEAKING

a Tell a partner about the last time you took an exam or test. Did you pass or fail? Why?

b Read about exams in England. What is the exam system in your country?

Exams in England

Age 11 Most children go straight to a secondary school without taking an exam, but in some parts of the country, children can still take an exam called the 11+ if they want to go to a school which selects the most academic children.

Age 16 Students take exams called 'GCSEs' in 8–12 different subjects. Before 1988, students took similar exams, called 'O levels'.

Age 18 Students can take final exams called 'A levels' in 3 or 4 different subjects of their choice before leaving school. They need good results in these exams if they want to go to university.

c 🔊 10.13 Listen to Mark, Sophie, Diane, and Paul talking about their experiences with exams or tests. Who…?
  1 mentions an exam or test that they failed
  2 used to find exams stressful

> ⭐ **TIP: Multiple-choice listening**
> - Read the questions carefully before you listen.
> - After listening once, eliminate any answers that you are sure are wrong.
> - Make sure that <u>all</u> of the information is correct in the option you choose. Don't choose it just because it contains a word or phrase that you heard in the recording.

d Listen again. Choose a, b, or c.
1 Mark had problems with his history O level because…
  a he didn't have time to finish the questions.
  b he hadn't prepared the right questions.
  c he had drunk too much coffee the night before.
2 Sophie failed her driving test the first time because…
  a she didn't follow the examiner's instructions.
  b she didn't realize that what the examiner asked her to do was a trick.
  c she stopped somewhere where it wasn't safe.
3 Diane 'froze' in her French oral exam because she…
  a couldn't remember the right words.
  b had told the examiner a lie.
  c couldn't understand the examiner's questions.
4 Paul did badly in his GCSE chemistry…
  a because he'd done very little work for it.
  b because his memory failed.
  c although he thought he'd done well.

e Ask and answer the questions with a partner.

If you are still studying	If you are no longer studying
How do you usually prepare for a big exam…? a) during the previous weeks, b) the night before	How did you use to feel about taking exams? Can you remember any particularly bad ones?
What's the hardest exam you've taken recently? Why did you find it so hard? How did you do?	Did you use to revise a lot before exams? Did you revise right up to the last moment?
Have you ever done much better than you expected in an exam? What about one where everything went wrong? What happened?	Is there an exam that you're really proud of having passed?
	Do you think you will ever have to take any more exams in the future? Why (not)?

Do you think exams are a good way of testing how much people know? Why (not)?

4 WRITING

Ⓦ p.123 **Writing** An exam task Write an essay for an exam.

5 READING

a Is there a university entrance exam in your country? How difficult is it considered to be?

b Read the article about the *gaokao* (/gaʊkaʊ/), China's national university entrance exam. How does it compare with similar exams in your country?

A nation prepares for the dreaded *gaokao*

SHANGHAI, 5th June – Tomorrow, cities throughout China ¹will close roads near schools, prohibit the hooting of car horns, and even change some aeroplane flight paths, so that nine million students can concentrate on the *gaokao*, the three-day-long national university entrance exam.

University places are scarce in China, and most students ²are not going to have a chance if they do not do well in the *gaokao*, a name which means 'high exam' in Mandarin Chinese. The stakes are very high indeed: a place in a top university will almost always lead to a high-paid job after graduation. For millions of Chinese students, the exam is an important chance to improve their lives, and because most families ³have only one child, the pressure on candidates is intense.

We spoke to students who ⁴hadn't been out with their friends for many months, and who ⁵were studying all the time that they weren't sleeping. And while some cram, others cheat. Each year, candidates ⁶are caught with high-tech devices such as wireless earphones, as well as pens and watches with tiny scanners. James Bond would be proud.

Teachers' lives are difficult, too. One *gaokao* tutor ⁷explained her schedule: morning exercises start at 6.10 a.m., evening classes end at 10.00 p.m., students get only one day off a month – and teachers must spend that day marking practice exams.

To prepare for the exam, students memorize past exam papers and try to guess what questions ⁸will be asked this year. All candidates answer questions in Chinese, maths, and English, then choose two additional subjects: history, geography, physics, biology, chemistry, or political ideology. Some of the unusual essay questions that ⁹have appeared on past papers include:

- 'An Englishman dreams of living in Western China in another era. Write a story based on this.'
- 'Why chase mice when there are fish to eat?'
- 'Talk about water.'
- 'Why do we want to return to our childhood?'

The exam ¹⁰has been criticized for testing endurance rather than intelligence. Small reforms ¹¹were made to the exam a few years ago, but little has changed overall. More and more Chinese students ¹²have been moving overseas for university, or even secondary school, just to avoid the *gaokao*. The number of candidates who sit the exam has fallen dramatically in recent years, from 10.2 million in 2009, to 9 million this year.

However, at the same time, the *gaokao* ¹³is beginning to be more widely recognized abroad. The University of Sydney has said it will accept *gaokao* scores from Chinese students in place of its own entrance exam. China may not need to reform the *gaokao* after all – it will reform the rest of us.

Adapted from the *Financial Times*

> **TIP: True / False reading**
> - Quickly read the text for the main ideas, then read the statements carefully.
> - Re-read the text carefully and look for information that shows whether each statement is true or false.

c Read the article again. Mark the statements **T** (true) or **F** (false).
1 During the *gaokao*, nobody is allowed to drive in cities where the exam is being held.
2 Unless you do well in the *gaokao*, you probably won't get a place at university.
3 The exam gives young people the opportunity to do better in life.
4 Students preparing for the exam still have time for a social life.
5 Students always find different ways to cheat.
6 The *gaokao* was mentioned in a recent James Bond film.
7 *Gaokao* tutors only have one day a month when they don't have to work.
8 Science subjects are optional in the *gaokao*.
9 Some people don't like the exam because they don't think it shows how intelligent you are.
10 More Chinese students are taking the *gaokao* now than ever before.

d What do you think about the *gaokao*? What do you think is the best way to decide whether someone should get a place at university or not?

6 GRAMMAR revision of verb forms

a Look at highlighted verbs 1–13 in the article. With a partner, match them to the tenses and forms below.

☐ present simple (*I make…*)
☐ present continuous (*I'm making…*)
☐ present simple passive (*It is made…*)

☐ past simple (*I made…*)
☐ past continuous (*I was making…*)
☐ past simple passive (*It was made…*)
☐ past perfect simple (*I had made…*)

☐ future with *will* (*I will make…*)
☐ future with *be going to* (*I'm going to make…*)
☐ *will* passive (*It will be made…*)

☐ present perfect simple (*I've made…*)
☐ present perfect continuous (*I've been making…*)
☐ present perfect passive (*It's been made…*)

b **G** p.151 Grammar Bank 10B

7 ▶ VIDEO LISTENING

a Watch the documentary *Speaking exams – top tips for success*. Why is the speaking exam the most stressful? What is the very best way to prepare for the speaking exam?

b Watch again and complete each gap with 1–3 words.
1 You should arrive at least _____ beforehand, in order to feel _____.
2 Make _____ contact, smile, and _____ throughout the exam.
3 Look _____, respond to your partner's suggestions, and ask for their _____.
4 Always answer in _____ sentences and add more _____.
5 Don't _____ if you don't understand a question. Just ask the examiner to _____ it.
6 Don't memorize whole _____ or _____.
7 Don't just say _____ – try to explain it in a _____ way.

c Now watch an examiner giving you a task and discuss the picture below with a partner. Use some of the tips you heard in the documentary.

> **Go online** to watch the video and review the lesson

103

9 & 10 Revise and Check

GRAMMAR

a Circle a, b, or c.

1 They asked us how long ____.
   a did we live there
   b we'd lived there
   c had we lived there
2 She ____ she couldn't remember my name.
   a said   b told   c said me
3 He asked whether ____ British or American.
   a I was   b was I   c I am
4 We told them ____ make so much noise, but they didn't turn the music down.
   a not to   b don't   c that they didn't
5 I said that I ____ be late.
   a wouldn't to   b won't   c wouldn't

b Complete the sentences with the correct form of the verb in brackets.

1 He wouldn't have passed the exam if he _____ so hard. (not study)
2 If we'd had a smaller wedding, we _____ less money. (spend)
3 He _____ go to university if he'd had better exam results. (be able to)
4 I _____ much last weekend. (not do)
5 _____ you _____ your grandparents recently? (visit)
6 A I went on holiday to Turkey last month.
   B _____ you _____ there before? (be)
7 She _____ too hard lately – she looks exhausted. (work)
8 We got to the reception late and the speeches _____. (finish)
9 Work on the new bridge _____ by the end of next year. (complete)
10 I ran to the bank but it _____ already _____. (close)
11 Apple _____ more than 400 million tablets since 2010. (sell)
12 Why _____ you _____ biscuits? It's nearly lunchtime. (eat)
13 Alex _____ us his holiday photos when the boss came in! (show)
14 It's only 9.00 a.m. but she _____ already _____ at work for two hours. (be)
15 The film _____ in Japan in the 1960s. (make)

VOCABULARY

a Complete the sentences with the correct form of the word in brackets.

1 Her 60th birthday was a _____ occasion. (memory)
2 He told me very _____ that he was going to win. (confident)
3 Alan felt very _____ when he saw his newborn son. (emotion)
4 If you want to speak English well, both fluency and _____ are important. (accurate)
5 I don't like being asked _____ questions. (person)

b Write words for the definitions.

1 a woman on her wedding day _____
2 the holiday taken by a newly married couple _____
3 a male friend or relative who helps the groom _____
4 a formal social occasion to celebrate something _____
5 the people invited to the wedding _____

c Write **Br** or **Am**, and give the British or American alternative.

1 ____ movie theater _____   6 ____ toilet _____
2 ____ tap _____   7 ____ stand in line _____
3 ____ sneakers _____   8 ____ apartment _____
4 ____ lift _____   9 ____ pavement _____
5 ____ garbage _____   10 ____ petrol _____

d Complete the words.

1 Most of my friends passed the exam, but I **f**_____.
2 The questions were all **m**_____-choice.
3 In my English exam, I had to write an **e**_____ about the importance of recycling.
4 I passed my driving test the first time I **t**_____ it.
5 He **ch**_____ in the exam, so they gave him 0%.

PRONUNCIATION

a Practise the words and sounds.

Vowel sounds   **Consonant sounds**

b**oy**   **ear**   ch**air**   c**ar**   t**our**ist   **f**lower   si**ng**er   **p**arrot

b **P** p.166–7 Sound Bank Say more words for each sound.

c What sound in **a** do the pink letters have in these words?

1 autobiogra**phy**   2 lux**u**rious   3 t**oi**let   4 r**a**ther   5 w**ei**rd

d Underline the stressed syllable.

1 se|cu|ri|ty   3 pro|pose   5 prac|ti|cal
2 im|por|tant   4 brides|maid

104

CAN YOU understand this text?

a   Read the article once. Do you ever do any of these things when you're preparing for an exam?

How to learn without forgetting

To help yourself remember what you've learned, it is useful to use a wide range of study tips. Try these techniques – you will be surprised to see how easy it can be to remember things.

Make a study timetable Study when you are most awake. This may be at any time of day. You will ¹___ if you study a little each day (for 30 to 60 minutes at a time). Remember to include breaks in your schedule; take a short walk to help clear your mind.

Get enough sleep When you sleep, your brain ²___. If you don't have time for a sleep during the day, revise your notes at night before going to bed. Try to get between seven and nine hours' sleep each night.

Talk about what you are learning Saying words out loud and hearing them can be helpful – you could try reading your notes to your dog! Study with a friend, or try to teach the topic to a younger sibling. Teaching someone else makes you ³___.

Write things down that you need to memorize This process can help your brain recall it better. Take notes on what you've read. Make a mind map – a diagram which shows relationships between pieces of information – place the main idea in the centre and use connected branches to ⁴___. You can also make cards and write important facts on them.

Take practice tests This can be a good tool to find out what you know and which topics you still ⁵___. When you finish a test, revise the material you didn't know and try another in a few days.

Chew gum Some researchers believe that chewing gum ⁶___, which helps you concentrate better. If you chew a particular flavour of gum while studying, such as peppermint, you may be able to better remember information you studied if you chew the same gum during your test.

Use your sense of smell Smells are often associated with memories. Smell a perfume while studying. Then, smell the same perfume just before your exam. You may be able to better ⁷___.

Adapted from the wikihow website

b   Read the article again and complete it with verb phrases A–G.
  A   allows more oxygen into your brain
  B   add related information
  C   recall the information you studied
  D   converts facts from short-term memory to long-term memory
  E   retain information better
  F   think about the material more deeply
  G   need to study

▶ **CAN YOU** understand these people?

🔊 10.14 Watch or listen and choose a, b, or c.

1 Victoria   2 Jan   3 Keith   4 Royce   5 Diana

1 Victoria finds it difficult to remember ____.
   a people's names
   b names of plants
   c things she's eaten
2 Jan ____.
   a really enjoyed her first wedding
   b got married very recently
   c met her husband eight years ago
3 Keith thinks that ____ has had a very positive influence in the world.
   a British TV
   b American drama
   c the American dream
4 Royce thinks fast food is ____.
   a convenient
   b unhealthy
   c tasty
5 Diana had a bad experience in an exam because she ____.
   a was very nervous
   b couldn't think of anything to say for a short time
   c hates oral exams

CAN YOU say this in English?

Tick (✓) the box if you can do these things.

Can you…?
1 ☐ remember three things somebody said to you or asked you yesterday, and report them
2 ☐ describe a wedding you've been to, or talk about the kind of wedding you'd like to have
3 ☐ talk about the influence of American culture in your country, and say what you think about it
4 ☐ talk about an exam you took that went really well, or didn't go well at all

Go online to watch the video, review Files 9 & 10, and check your progress

Communication

1A MIDDLE NAMES QUIZ
Students A+B

Do the quiz with a partner.

Middle names quiz

Many celebrities are better known by their middle names rather than their first names. Do you know what these middle names are? How do you pronounce them?

1 Christopher **A**_____ Kutcher
2 Laura Jeanne **R**_____ Witherspoon
3 William **B**_____ Pitt
4 David **J**_____ Law
5 Hannah **D**_____ Fanning
6 Walter **B**_____ Willis
7 Thomas **S**_____ Connery
8 Robyn **R**_____ Fenty
9 James **H**_____ Laurie
10 Henry **W**_____ Beatty

5B CITY OR COUNTRY? Students A+B

Ask and answer questions with a partner.

Do you know anyone who…	
has moved from the city to the country? Did they stay? Why (not)?	has moved from the country to the city? Did they stay? Why (not)?
If you live in a large town or city…	**If you live in a village or small town in the country…**
Imagine you moved to a village or small town in the country. What do you think you would miss the most about the city?	Imagine you moved to a large town or city. What do you think you would miss the most about the country?
↓	↓
What do you think you would enjoy the most about the country?	What do you think you would enjoy the most about the city?
↓	↓
Do you ever go to the country? Why do you go? Do you enjoy yourself there? Why (not)?	Do you ever go to large cities? Why do you go? Do you enjoy yourself there? Why (not)?

1B THE COLOUR TEST Students A+B

Read about your chosen colour.

The colour test

● **grey** You are quiet and thoughtful and you prefer watching to doing. You don't have strong opinions and you are afraid of commitment. You usually prefer to let other people make the decisions.

● **black** You have strong ideas and you would like to be confident and ambitious, but you are a rather negative person and can be quite stubborn. You are afraid of trying new things and often say 'No'.

● **brown** You would love to be charming and attractive to others, but in fact you are rather insecure. You don't like change and you often worry about your health.

● **green** You like having nice possessions and you enjoy the good things in life. You are often successful in what you do, because you are quite persistent, and don't give up easily. However, you worry about making mistakes.

● **yellow** You are optimistic about life. You are a happy and positive person who enjoys hard work and likes getting results. You are also very sociable and enjoy being with other people.

● **red** You are passionate and energetic, and you live your life to the full. However, you are often too impulsive and sometimes make decisions without thinking enough. You focus a lot on your own happiness, and so sometimes you can seem rather selfish.

● **blue** You are a loyal and reliable person who likes to be in a stable relationship. You are also a sensitive person and your feelings can be easily hurt.

● **purple** You like excitement, but you are a bit immature and you can be moody. You are often restless and you dream of doing things which aren't likely to happen.

2A CAROLINE'S HOLIDAY PLANS
Student A

a   Ask and answer questions with **B** about Caroline's holiday. Use the information below and the correct form of the verb, present simple or present continuous.

What time does she leave London?

At eleven forty in the morning. What time does she arrive in Ibiza?

At five past three in the afternoon.

Thursday	
11.40 a.m.	leave London Gatwick, flight EZ 8629
3.05 p.m.	arrive in Ibiza
Friday	
_____	have yoga class
10.00 a.m.	go waterskiing with Emma (meet at rental shop)
Afternoon	go sightseeing in _____
Saturday	
8.30 a.m.	go on guided tour of the island
_____	have dinner at Bambuddha (table booked in Emma's name)
Sunday	
8.00 a.m.	go on boat trip to Formentera
6.00 p.m.	_____
Monday	
5.30 a.m.	get bus to airport
_____	leave Ibiza, flight EZ 8630
10.00 a.m.	arrive London Gatwick

b   Check your answers by comparing your notes.

3B SPOT THE DIFFERENCES Student A

Describe the picture to your partner. Your partner has a very similar picture. Find nine differences between the pictures.

In my picture, there's a…in the foreground.

There isn't one in my picture. There's a…

3A A REAL GROWN-UP? Student A

Carol Midgley   Like many other people of my age, I do plenty of things that aren't really adult at all. Like a teenager, I never remember to charge my phone. And I'm terrified of being in a bar or restaurant alone, even for a few minutes. Why? I'm not five years old! So am I an adult? The laws about age don't help you to find out. At 16, you can work full-time, get married, and join the army, but you can't drive or buy an alcoholic drink. So when did I first really <u>feel</u> grown-up? Maybe when I first went abroad for work, in my early twenties. I was alone in France, driving in the middle of the night with a map on my knees and no phone. That felt quite a grown-up thing to do. But the time when I really became an adult was when my baby fell and hurt her head. When I was lying by her hospital bed in the dark, feeling very afraid, asking the doctors and nurses about her progress, I had never felt more grown-up.

a   Read about Carol. Complete the sentences.
   Carol
   - does things that aren't very adult, for example…and…
   - thinks that the laws about being an adult are confusing because when you're 16…but…
   - first felt like an adult when…
   - became a real grown-up when…

b   Tell **B** about Carol. Use the prompts in **a**.

I read about Carol. She does things that aren't very adult, for example, she never…

c   Now listen to **B** tell you about Hugo.

d   Which of the two people do you think is more grown-up?

107

5A TV DRAMAS Student A

a Read about the TV series and check your answers to **5b**.

> **A** *Forbrydelsen – The Killing*
> A Danish detective drama.
> The series is set in Copenhagen, and follows detective Sara Lund. The first season is about the hunt for the killer of a schoolgirl. The series was also remade for American TV.

> **B** *Sé Quién Eres – I Know Who You Are*
> A Spanish crime drama.
> Juan Elías is a successful lawyer in Barcelona who loses his memory in a car crash. At the same time, his 23-year-old niece disappears and her blood is found in his car – but has he murdered her?

> **C** *Les Revenants – The Returned*
> A French mystery drama.
> This supernatural series is set in a small mountain town in France. People who have died begin reappearing, and try to continue their lives with family and friends as if nothing has happened. Then more people begin to die.

> **D** *Suburra – Blood on Rome*
> An Italian political drama.
> 'Suburra' was an area of ancient Rome and this is a story of corruption in the modern city. Based on real events, the plot involves the state, the Church, property developers, and organized crime.

b Read the texts again. Find the following information for each series, if it's available.
  – what kind of series it is
  – where it's set
  – what it's about
  – the name of the main character(s)

c Now work with **B** and take turns to tell each other about the series.

> *The Killing is a Danish detective drama. It's set in…*

PE3 REPORTING A MISSING PERSON
Student A

a You are going to report a missing person. Read your role and decide on the details.

> You are sharing a flat in London with a friend from your country. The address is 23 Barrow Street, London, W2 7EG.
>
> • *Decide which of your friends it is and where you last saw them.*
>   You saw each other in the morning.
>
> • *Decide what time and where you had planned to meet.*
>   You had arranged to have dinner together at home.
>   You got home at 5.00 p.m., but it is now 10.00 p.m. and he / she hasn't turned up, and isn't answering his / her phone.
>   You are worried and go to the police.
>
> • *Decide what your friend's normal routine is.*

b **B** is a police officer. He / She will ask you questions about your friend, and write a report. **B** will start.

c Swap roles. You are now a police officer. **B** is going to report a missing person. First, think about what questions you need to ask.

> **MISSING PERSON INFORMATION**
>
> **Reported by**   Name
>   Address
>   Phone
>
> **Missing person**
> Name
> Address
> Description
>   *(age and appearance)*
> Last seen
> Wearing
> Expected to see at   for
> Plans for rest of day
> Normal routine

d Interview **B** and fill in the form. Finally, tell **B** not to worry and that you are sure the person will turn up soon. You start:

> *Come in and take a seat. Now, you want to report a missing person, is that right?*

e Together, decide what happened to your friends.

6B WHAT'S IT CALLED? Student A

a   You are a customer at a DIY store. You want to buy the things below, but you don't know the word. **B** is a shop assistant. Have a conversation with **B**, explaining what you want. He / She will tell you the names of the things you want to buy and where to find them. Write the names. **B** will start.

> **Paraphrasing**
> Sorry, but I can't remember / don't know the word.
> I'm looking for a thing / things that you use for + verb + -ing.
> It's a kind of…   It's like…

b   Now you are the shop assistant. Listen to **B** explaining what he / she wants to buy. Ask questions and decide which of the things below they are. Tell **B** what they are called (spell the words if necessary), and where to find them. You start: *Can I help you?*

string /strɪŋ/   Sellotape /ˈseləteɪp/   stapler /ˈsteɪplə/

padlock /ˈpædlɒk/   pegs /pegz/   glue /gluː/

PE4 RENTING A ROOM Student A

a   You have a two-bedroom flat and you want to share it with someone. **B** would like to rent the other room. He / She is coming to see you. First, look at your house rules and decide if there is anything you'd like to add.

> **House rules**
> - No smoking
> - Share kitchen – keep food on 2nd shelf of fridge
> - Don't use washing machine or dryer after 10.00 p.m.
> - Make sure to lock door (two keys) when going out
> - _____

b   Greet **B**. Tell him / her about the house rules, and answer any questions. You start.

> *Hi, come in. Nice to meet you… If you don't mind, I'm going to start by telling you about the house rules…*

c   Decide if you would like to rent the room to **B**.

d   Swap roles. You are looking for a room to rent. **B** has a room in his / her flat. You are going to meet **B**. **B** will tell you about the house rules. You also have some questions to ask. Decide if there is anything you'd like to add.

> - How good is the wi-fi?
> - What's public transport like?
> - OK if you practise your electric guitar?
> - _____ ?

e   Go to meet **B** and talk about the flat. **B** will start.

f   Decide if you want to rent the room.

10B DESCRIBING A PHOTO Student A

a   Describe your photo to **B**. Say who the people are, where they are, and what is happening.

b   Listen to **B** describing his / her photo. What do the two photos have in common?

c   Discuss the questions together.
   1 Does this kind of thing often happen in exams or tests in your country? What methods do people use?
   2 Do people usually get caught? Why (not)?
   3 How do you think people should be punished for this behaviour?
   4 If you saw a friend cheating in an exam or test, what would you do?

7A GIVING IT AWAY Student A

a Read the article and answer the questions.
1 Who is Mr Lucky?
2 What is the we-are-lucky.com project?
3 What did Lucy do with some of her £1,000?
4 What kinds of people have received money from Mr Lucky?
5 Why does Mr Lucky think the project is creating positive feelings?

we-are-lucky.com

Mr Lucky is a mystery millionaire who gives away money to strangers. We know some things about him. He is from London, he worked abroad for an insurance company, and by the age of 37, he was so rich that he was able to retire. At first, Mr Lucky didn't know what to do with all his money. He thought about giving it to a charity. But in the end, he decided to start a project called we-are-lucky.com, in which other people choose how to spend his money for him. So far, he has given £1,000 in cash to more than 100 people all over the world to do 'something good'. Lucy, for example, runs a small bookshop in London. When Mr Lucky met her, he liked her openness and her dedication to her shop and gave her £1,000. Lucy then decided to pass on some of the money by giving a bonus to a colleague, which she couldn't previously afford to do. So far, the lucky people have included web designers, nurses, taxi drivers, bar owners, and photographers. Mr Lucky says he enjoys giving the money away, and people are enjoying giving the money to someone else, so there is a chain reaction of positive feeling.

b Tell **B** about Mr Lucky and his project. Use your answers in **a** to help you.

c Now listen to **B**'s story.

d Would you prefer to receive £1,000 which you have to spend on other people, or $100 which you can spend on yourself?

8B LOCAL HISTORY Student A

a Think about the area where you live and write down the information below. Write the names or places only. (Don't try to translate place names or names of festivals, etc.)
1 a famous person who has a connection here
2 an interesting or unusual historic building or site here
3 something that is or used to be made or grown here
4 a festival that is celebrated here every year
5 a typical dish which has been made and eaten here for many years

b Give your paper to **B**. **B** is a tourist. He / She will ask you about the names and places on your list. Give as much information as you can.

c Now you are a tourist. Look at **B**'s list of names and places, and ask **B** about them.

What's the Ponte della Costituzione?

It's a new bridge which was finished in 2008. It was designed by Calatrava…

10A MORE FACTS ABOUT THE USA? Student A

a Read sentence 1 to **B**. Try to use the correct stress. **B** will guess if it's true or false.

b Tell **B** if he / she is right, and explain why. Continue with sentences 2–5.

Texas is the largest state in the USA. True or false?

I think that's false.

That's right. Alaska is the largest. It's more than twice the size of the second largest state, which is Texas.

Are these statements true (T) or false (F)?

1 **Texas is the largest state in the USA.**
False. Alaska is the largest. It's more than twice the size of the second largest state, which is Texas.
2 **50% of Americans don't speak English at home.**
False. 20% speak a language other than English at home. About 8% don't speak any English at all.
3 **American workers have less paid holiday than workers in other countries.**
True. Most Americans have 10–20 days of paid holiday a year.
4 **Americans buy more Mexican salsa per year than ketchup.**
True. $680 million was spent on salsa last year, compared to $420 million for ketchup.
5 **No American has ever won the Nobel Peace Prize.**
False. Over 20 Americans have won the prize, including Martin Luther King, Jr. and Barack Obama.

c Now listen to **B**'s sentences and say if you think they're true or false.

2A CAROLINE'S HOLIDAY PLANS
Student B

a   Ask and answer questions with **A** about Caroline's holiday. Use the information below and the correct form of the verb, present simple or present continuous.

What time does she leave London?

At eleven forty in the morning. What time does she arrive in Ibiza?

At five past three in the afternoon.

Thursday	
11.40 a.m.	leave London Gatwick, flight EZ 8629
3.05 p.m.	arrive in Ibiza
Friday	
7.30 a.m.	have yoga class
10.00 a.m.	go waterskiing with _____ (meet at rental shop)
Afternoon	go sightseeing in Ibiza Town
Saturday	
8.30 a.m.	_____
9.00 p.m.	have dinner at Bambuddha (table booked in Emma's name)
Sunday	
8.00 a.m.	_____
6.00 p.m.	have massage at hotel spa
Monday	
_____	get bus to airport
8.35 a.m.	leave Ibiza, flight EZ 8630
_____	arrive London Gatwick

b   Check your answers by comparing your notes.

3A A REAL GROWN-UP? Student B

Hugo Rifkind   I'm pretty sure I'm an adult. I'm in my late-30s, and I have two kids, a mortgage, and a pension plan. Recently, I had a 20-minute conversation, which I thoroughly enjoyed, about my car. Today, there are no longer important events that mean you are an adult. A few generations ago, when a boy turned 16, he started wearing long trousers instead of shorts, and left home to raise a family. Now we stay longer in the family home, find it difficult to become financially independent, still listen to pop music, and still wear T-shirts. It took my wife and I a very long time before we had our own house. As for having kids, well, that doesn't make you feel like a grown-up. It just makes you panic. Maybe I'll only really become an adult when I stop wanting a big night out once a month, or four days a year at a music festival, that sort of thing.

a   Read about Hugo. Complete the sentences.

   Hugo
   - thinks he must be an adult because he has…
   - thinks that it was clearer in the past when you became an adult because at 16 a boy…
   - says that adults now still do teenage things like…
   - says that having kids doesn't…
   - thinks that he will become a real grown-up when…

b   Listen to **A** tell you about Carol.

c   Now tell **A** about Hugo. Use the prompts in **a**.

I read about Hugo. He's in his late-thirties. He thinks he must be an adult because he has…

d   Which of the two people do you think is more grown-up?

10B DESCRIBING A PHOTO Student B

a   Listen to **A** describing his / her photo.

b   Describe your photo to **A**. Say who the people are, where they are, and what is happening.

   What do the two photos have in common?

c   Discuss the questions together.
   1   Does this kind of thing often happen in exams or tests in your country? What methods do people use?
   2   Do people usually get caught? Why (not)?
   3   How do you think people should be punished for this behaviour?
   4   If you saw a friend cheating in an exam or test, what would you do?

5A TV DRAMAS Student B

a Read about the TV series and check your answers to **5b**.

> **E** *Engrenages – Spiral*
> A French legal drama.
> The show is set in Paris, and follows the lives and work of a team of Parisian police officers led by Laure Berthaud, as well as the lawyers and judges who work at the *Palais de Justice*.

> **F** *Bron / Broen – The Bridge*
> A Swedish / Danish crime drama.
> The first season begins with the discovery of a dead body exactly in the middle of the bridge that joins Sweden to Denmark, and further seasons continue to be set in both countries. One of the highlights of the series is the fascinating autistic detective Saga Norén.

> **G** *El Marginal – El Marginal*
> An Argentinian police drama.
> The series is set in Buenos Aires. Miguel Palacios, who used to be a policeman, infiltrates a dangerous prison to try to find the kidnapper of a well-known judge's daughter.

> **H** *Dupla Identidade – Merciless*
> A Brazilian crime drama.
> Edu is a young man who appears to be smart and sensitive, but is in fact a dangerous psychopath, who is behind a number of crimes that police are investigating in Rio de Janeiro.

b Read the texts again. Find the following information for each series, if it's available.

- what kind of series it is
- where it's set
- what it's about
- the name of the main character(s)

c Now work with **A** and take turns to tell each other about the series.

> *Spiral is a French legal drama. It's set in…*

3B SPOT THE DIFFERENCES
Student B

Describe the picture to your partner. Your partner has a very similar picture. Find nine differences between the pictures.

> *In my picture, there's a…in the foreground.*

> *There isn't one in my picture. There's a…*

6B WHAT'S IT CALLED? Student B

a You are a shop assistant at a DIY store. Listen to **A** explaining what he / she wants to buy. Ask questions, and decide which of the things below they are. Tell **A** what they are called (spell the words if necessary), and where to find them. You start: *Can I help you?*

broom /bruːm/   nails /neɪlz/   drawing pins /ˈdrɔːɪŋ pɪnz/

bucket /ˈbʌkɪt/   mop /mɒp/   screwdriver /ˈskruːdraɪvə/

b Now you are the customer. You want to buy the things below, but you don't know the word. **A** is a shop assistant. Have a conversation with **A**, explaining what you want. He / She will tell you the names of the things you want to buy and where to find them. Write the names. **A** will start.

> 🔍 **Paraphrasing**
> *Sorry, but I can't remember / don't know the word.*
> *I'm looking for a thing / things that you use for + verb + -ing.*
> *It's a kind of…   It's like…*

PE3 REPORTING A MISSING PERSON
Student B

a   You are a police officer. **A** is going to report a missing person. First, think about what questions you need to ask.

MISSING PERSON INFORMATION

Reported by Name
Address
Phone

Missing person
Name
Address
Description
(age and appearance)
Last seen
Wearing
Expected to see at _____ for _____
Plans for rest of day
Normal routine

b   Interview **A** and fill in the form. Finally, tell **A** not to worry and that you are sure the person will turn up soon. You start:

> Come in and take a seat. Now, you want to report a missing person, is that right?

c   Swap roles. Now you are going to report a missing person. Read your role and decide on the details.

> You are sharing a flat in London with a friend from your country. The address is 15 Vine Road, London, EC1 9AJ.
>
> - *Decide which of your friends it is and where you last saw them.*
>   You saw each other at lunchtime.
> - *Decide what time and where you had planned to meet.*
>   You had arranged to go to the cinema together.
>   The film started at 7.00 p.m. but your friend didn't turn up.
>   It is now 11.00 p.m., and he / she isn't answering his / her phone. You are worried and go to the police.
> - *Decide what your friend's normal routine is.*

d   **A** is a police officer. He / She will ask you questions about your friend, and write a report. **A** will start.

e   Together, decide what happened to your friends.

7A GIVING IT AWAY Student B

a   Read the article and answer the questions.
   1 Who is Jill Ginsberg?
   2 What does Jill write about on her blog?
   3 What did Mollie Dickson do after she read the blog?
   4 What did one child do in her project?
   5 How has Jill changed as a result of the project?

hundredsofhundreds.com

Jill Ginsberg, a doctor in Portland, Oregon, didn't use to like spending money on herself. So when she inherited some money from her mother, she decided to use it to make other people happy. Her plan was that every day for a month she would give $100 to a stranger. After the month ended, she didn't want to stop. She decided to continue, and to give away 100 more $100 bills to lucky strangers. On her blog, hundredsofhundreds.com, she wrote about the people she met. Many people who read Jill's blog wrote comments and shared her story on Facebook. She started receiving messages from people, many of whom wanted to do something to help others themselves. One teacher, Mollie Dickson, started a class project where children chose different things to do to help strangers, for example, one girl visited children with cancer in a local hospital. Jill was delighted to hear about the project, and wrote to the children to encourage them. Jill is surprised by how much she's changed. She's stopped being careful with money, and the project has helped her get over the death of her mother.

b   Listen to **A**'s story.

c   Now tell **A** about Jill Ginsberg and her project. Use your answers in **a** to help you.

d   Would you prefer to receive £1,000 which you have to spend on other people, or $100 which you can spend on yourself?

PE4 RENTING A ROOM Student B

a You are looking for a room to rent. **A** has a room in his / her flat. You are going to meet **A**. **A** will tell you about the house rules. You also have some questions to ask. Decide if there is anything you'd like to add.

- OK to bring cat?
- Where can you park motorbike?
- OK to have a shower about 6.30 every morning?
- _____ ?

b Go to meet **A** and talk about the flat. **A** will start.

c Decide if you want to rent the room.

d Swap roles. You have a two-bedroom flat and you want to share it with someone. **A** would like to rent the other room. He / She is coming to see you. First, look at your house rules and decide if there is anything you'd like to add.

House rules
- No smoking
- No pets
- Share kitchen – use recycling bins, one for glass, one for paper, one for all other rubbish. Don't leave washing-up overnight.
- No showers after 10.00 p.m.
- _____

e Greet **A**. Tell him / her about the house rules, and answer any questions. You start.

Hi, come in. Nice to meet you… If you don't mind, I'm going to start by telling you about the house rules…

f Decide if you would like to rent the room to **A**.

8B LOCAL HISTORY Student B

a Think about the area where you live and write down the information below. Write the names or places only. (Don't try to translate place names or names of events, etc.)
1 an interesting or unusual building, bridge, or monument that has recently been built here
2 a famous person who was born here
3 a special event that will take place here soon
4 typical souvenirs that are made or sold here
5 a popular tourist attraction here

b You are a tourist. Look at **A**'s list of names and places, and ask **A** about them.

Who's Joaquín Sorolla? — *He's a famous painter who lived here in the 19th century and did lots of paintings of the beaches…*

c Give your paper to **A**. **A** is a tourist. He / She will ask you about the names and places on your list. Give as much information as you can.

10A MORE FACTS ABOUT THE USA? Student B

a Listen to **A** reading some sentences about the USA. Say if you think they're true or false.

b Now read sentence 6 to **A**. Try to use the correct stress. **A** will guess if it's true or false.

c Tell **A** if he / she is right, and explain why. Continue with sentences 7–10.

The USA has more national parks than Europe. True or false?

I think that's false.

That's right. The USA has 59 national parks, and Europe has a total of 366…

Are these statements true (T) or false (F)?

6 **The USA has more national parks than Europe.**
False. The USA has 59 national parks, and Europe has a total of 366. However, the US parks cover 210,000 km^2, a larger area than all the European parks.

7 **The top holiday destination abroad for Americans is Britain.**
False. Mexico is the number 1 destination for Americans travelling abroad on holiday.

8 **The USA has 5% of the world's population, but 25% of the world's prisoners.**
True. The prison population has increased by 700% since 1971, to almost 2.2 million.

9 **The Declaration of Independence was signed in 1876.**
False. It was signed in 1776.

10 **Häagen-Dazs is an American company.**
True. It was started by the Mattus brothers in New York in 1976. They chose the name because they thought it sounded Danish and they admired Denmark and its culture.

Writing

1 DESCRIBING A ROOM

a Read Ana's description of her room. Would you like a room like this? Why (not)?

b Read the description again. Match the information to the paragraphs.

- [ ] the size and colour of the room
- [ ] what furniture there is
- [ ] which room it is and where
- [ ] why she likes it

c Complete the gaps in the description with a preposition from the list. Some prepositions are used more than once.

| above | ~~at~~ | from | in | inside | on | with |

d You're going to write a description of your favourite room. **Plan** the description. Use 1–4 in **b** to help you.

e **Write** the description of the room in four paragraphs. Use **Vocabulary Bank Adjective suffixes p.152** to help you.

f **Check** your description for mistakes (grammar, vocabulary, punctuation, and spelling).

← p.13

My pink room

1 I've just finished university, so I'm living ¹ _at_ my parents' house at the moment, ² _____ my old bedroom. It hasn't changed since I was a teenager.

2 It's quite a big room, with one window. The walls are pale pink and the door and the window frame are much darker pink. We painted the room when we first moved there when I was 13, and I'm 23 now but I still love the colour. Along one wall there's a huge wardrobe with a full-length mirror ³ _____ the door, so I have plenty of space for all my clothes and shoes and jewellery. There's a glittery disco ball hanging ⁴ _____ the ceiling ⁵ _____ the middle of the room.

3 My bed is painted bright pink, and has lots of cushions ⁶ _____ it. I have the same desk I've had since I was really little. It's pushed right up against the wall and ⁷ _____ the desk there are some wooden shelves that my dad put up. That's where I keep my diaries, books, and some plants. There's also a big pink and yellow rug ⁸ _____ the floor. There's an armchair ⁹ _____ the corner which my mum didn't want any more. It's got yellow and blue stripes. It's really comfortable but quite ugly, and the colours don't match the rest of the room. I've covered it ¹⁰ _____ a blanket which is also pink to hide it.

4 Some people might think my room is quite girlie because it has so many pink things. It's a bit like me, I suppose, and that's probably why I still like it!

Go online for more Writing practice   115

2 HOLIDAY MESSAGES

a   Read the holiday messages people have sent to their friends. Who is on holiday now? Who is going to have a holiday soon? Who has just finished a holiday?

b   Read the messages again. How does each person feel? What words and phrases or symbols do they use to express their feelings?

c   Read the **Writing messages** box. Then rewrite the last five messages using full sentences.

> 🔍 **Writing messages**
> When people write messages, they often leave out words in sentences, pronouns, for example, and auxiliary verbs like *I'm*, *I've*, *it's*, and *there is / are*. This is acceptable in messages and tweets but not in formal writing.
> *Having the most amazing experience* = I'm having the most amazing experience.
> *Another hard day* = It's been another hard day.
> *3 noisy children sitting behind me* = There are three noisy children sitting behind me.

d   Imagine you're having a four-day holiday. **Plan** where you are going and what you are doing on the days and times below.
   - the evening before your holiday
   - the first morning of your holiday
   - the second and third days
   - the last evening of your holiday
   - the day after your holiday is over

e   **Write** short messages to friends for each of the days and times in **d**. Write them first in normal sentences and then try to make them shorter, like the messages in **a**.

f   **Check** your messages to make sure they are clear. Can you make them any shorter?

← p.19

Caroline
Having the most amazing experience in Ibiza! Met fantastic people, but have put on 3 kilos in 4 days!   17.42

Mark
Another hard day: reading, having a nap by the pool, eating, and sunbathing. 🙂   17.58

Michael
Oh no! 3 noisy children sitting behind me on my plane to LA. Going to be the longest flight of my life.   18.02

Haylee
48 hours until I'll be in Rio sipping a piña colada – or is it a caipirinha? Can't wait!   18.05

Sheila
Just got to Cuzco! So beautiful here! After 13 hours on bus, am ready for a shower!   18.33

Andrew
Packing bags. Holidays really stressful! Not sure that want to go! 😖   18.45

Danielle
Got back an hour ago – plants dead and no milk in fridge. Please send me back to the beach.   19.11

Sam
Making the most of last glorious morning in sun. Going home this p.m. Back to work tomorrow. 😣   10.28

3 AN ARTICLE

Three tips for taking great portrait photos

1 _____

In most photos, the subject is looking at the camera. This is often a good idea, but there are other things you can try. You might ask the person to look at something outside the photo. This can make a photo more interesting – viewers want to know what the person is looking at. Or the person could be looking at something (or someone) that is in the picture.

2 _____

Many people are very uncomfortable when they are having their photo taken and don't know how to relax. One good idea to help them is to photograph them while they are doing something they enjoy, for example, working, or chatting to their friends or family. This will help them relax, and you will get better pictures. This is especially helpful if you are taking pictures of children.

3 _____

If you change the angle or the perspective of your photos, you can make them more interesting and unusual. Get up high, for example, stand on a table or chair, and look down on your subject. Another possibility is to sit on the floor and look up. Both of these angles will make the photo more original.

a Look at the photos in the article from a photography website. Which of them do you like? How are they different from ordinary portraits of people?

b Read the article and write the headings in the correct place. (There are two headings you do not need.)

Don't make them pose
Try different angles
Move away from the centre
Take a close-up
Don't look at me!

c Read the article again. Which tip do you think is the most useful? Have you ever used any of these tips yourself?

d You're going to write an article with three tips on <u>one</u> of the following topics:

   How to take good holiday photos
   How to plan a successful holiday
   How to use colour in decorating

With a partner, **plan** the content of each tip. Think of a heading and say why the tip is helpful.

> **Useful language: tips and instructions**
> **Imperatives**
> ***Get*** *up high and look down on your subject.*
> ***Don't make*** *people pose.*
>
> **Possibilities**
> *The person **could** be looking at something in the picture.*
> ***You might*** *ask the person to look at something outside the photo.*
> ***One good idea is to*** *photograph people while they are doing something…*
> ***Another possibility is to*** *sit on the floor.*

e **Write** your article. Use your plan and the **Useful language** to help you.

f **Check** your article for mistakes (grammar, vocabulary, punctuation, and spelling).

← p.31

Go online for more Writing practice

4 A LINKEDIN PROFILE

a LinkedIn is a website where you can connect with colleagues and school or university friends, who might be able to help you to find a new job. Read the beginning of Kate Lewis's profile. What kind of company do you think Shopping Spy Ltd is? What qualification do you think Kate is studying for?

Kate Lewis
Intern at Shopping Spy Ltd
London Retail

Current Shopping Spy Ltd
Previous Zara
Education Currently studying at University College London

b Now read the rest of Kate's profile and check your answers to **a**.

Summary
I am currantly studying at University College London for a degree in Comunications and Marketing and will gradaute in June. I am looking for a position in retail or marketing in the fashion industry. I am enthusiastic and hard-working, and keen to start in my new profesion.

I already have some expierence working in fashion. At present, I am working part-time as an intern at Shopping Spy Ltd., which is a website that helps shoppers find great shops and sales in London. I work in the online team, which provides essential information to customers and collegues. I have direct contact with customers, which I really enjoy. I have also had a part-time sales job at the Zara store in Covent Garden. I greeted customers and asisted them with purchases. I also brouhgt out new stock, and worked at the till.

Experience

Intern
Shopping Spy Ltd, London
September – present (9 months)

Sales assistant and cashier
Zara, London
June – September 2019 (4 months)

c Read the profile again. The computer has found eight spelling mistakes. Can you correct them?

d Imagine you are thinking of looking for a job. **Plan** your own profile.

> **Introduction**
> Give your name, employer's name, current and previous jobs, and your education level.

> **Summary**
> **Paragraph 1**
> Describe your present situation. Say what kind of job you are looking for and what kind of person you are.
> **Paragraph 2**
> Give details about your work experience.

e **Write** your profile for a site like LinkedIn. (Or go to linkedin.com and create a profile.) Use the **Useful language** and **Vocabulary Bank** Study and work p.157 to help you.

> 🔍 Useful language: writing a CV, covering letter, or LinkedIn profile
> I am currently working at / studying at…
>
> I am looking for a position in the… industry.
>
> I have…years' experience working in…
>
> **Punctuation**
> Use Capital letters for company names, countries, cities, and languages.

f **Check** your profile for mistakes (grammar, vocabulary, punctuation, and spelling).

← p.43

5 AN INFORMAL EMAIL

From: Bob Ayers 📎 2nd April 13.05
To: Sally Ayers
Subject: What happened to spring?

Hi Sally,

Thanks for your email. Glad you're well. We're so pleased to hear that you're enjoying London. Hope that you ¹_____ too hard.

When your mother and I woke up this morning, this is what we saw! The calendar says it's 2nd April, but the weather doesn't agree. It ²_____ for about four hours non-stop now. We ³_____ to clear the snow all morning, so that we can drive to the supermarket and buy some food. Luckily, I ⁴_____ to the weather forecast and they say it's all going to melt tomorrow.

Apart from the weather, there's not much news. Your mum ⁵_____ hard, as usual. This week I ⁶_____ the sheep to a different field. We also had a problem with the tractor and we ⁷_____ for the man to come and repair it. Fingers crossed he'll phone today…

What ⁸_____ you _____ apart from working? Miss you lots. Write soon, or at least send us a message!

Much love,

Dad

---

a Read an email from Bob to his daughter Sally, who is studying in London. What is the main subject of his email? How does he feel about it?

b Read the email again and complete it with verbs from the list in the present perfect continuous. Use contractions if possible.

| do   listen   move   snow |
| not study   try   wait   work |

c Find and underline three examples of sentences in which the subject pronoun (*I*, *you*, etc.) is missing.

d Imagine you're replying to an email from a friend or family member. **Plan** what you're going to write.
1 Thank him / her for writing, and react to the news in his / her email.
2 Say what your main news is.
3 Talk about other things that you've been doing lately.
4 Ask what the person you're writing to has been doing, and to reply to any questions in the email.

e **Write** the email. Use the **Useful language** to help you, and follow 1–4 in **d**.

> 🔍 **Useful language: informal emails**
> **Thanking someone for an email**
> *Thanks for your email / message.*
> *It was great to hear from you.*
> *Glad you're well.*
>
> **Mentioning previous emails**
> *I'm so pleased / happy / sad / sorry to hear that…*
>
> **Asking someone to reply**
> *Write (back) soon!*
> *Looking forward to hearing all your news.*
> *I can't wait to hear from you.*

f **Check** your email for mistakes (grammar, vocabulary, punctuation, and spelling).

← p.53

6 A RESTAURANT REVIEW

a Read two website reviews of the same restaurant. What do they agree about? What do they disagree about?

Bistro Giacomo

Cuisine: Italian | **Location:** Covent Garden, Central London

Reviews

Rafael, Barcelona

Value ●●●●● Atmosphere ●●●●○
Service ●●●●● Food ●●●●○

Great place for a pre-theatre dinner

My girlfriend and I had a lovely dinner here before going to the theatre.

The service was excellent. Although we hadn't booked a table and the restaurant was quite busy, we didn't have to wait long for a table. The atmosphere was lively, with great music and people chatting.

Our dinner was perfect for a summer evening. For our starter, we had a delicious brochette of cheese, mushrooms, herbs, and vegetables. For our main, we had tuna fusilli, then dessert and coffee. The bill was really very reasonable – quite a bit less than in other similar places – and we were able to get to the theatre in time for the performance. We'd definitely go back another time.

Zoe, Oxford

Value ●●○○○ Atmosphere ●○○○○
Service ●●●○○ Food ●●●●○

Good food, shame about the music

Pros: The service was friendly and helpful, and the food was very fresh and tasty. The house wine was also very good.

Cons: The music was too loud, so it was difficult for my friend and me to have a conversation. We asked our waitress to turn it down a little, but she said she couldn't. Also, there are a lot of tables for the size of the restaurant, so we felt a bit cramped. On top of that, it was a bit pricey – the bill was much higher than we'd expected.

Overall opinion: Did we enjoy it? Yes. Would we go again? Not sure. There are plenty of other restaurants in the area with a better atmosphere, good food, and quiet music.

b Read the reviews again. Which person…?
1 organizes their review into good points and then bad points
2 gives more details about what they had to eat
3 explains why they were there and who they were there with
4 summarizes their opinion

Which person do you think gives the most useful information?

c Look at the highlighted words in the reviews and work out their meanings. Then put the words in the correct place in the **Useful language** box.

🔍 Useful language: describing restaurants

	positive 🙂	negative 🙁
the service	friendly helpful efficient excellent	unfriendly rude slow dreadful
the atmosphere	¹ lively	dead
the room	cosy quiet spacious romantic	cold noisy ² _____
the food	³ _____ ⁴ _____ ⁵ _____	overcooked tasteless nothing special
the prices	good value for money ⁶ _____	expensive ⁷ _____

d You're going to write a website review of a café, bar, or restaurant you've been to recently. **Plan** your review.

Either follow the style of the first review and give the following information:
1 Say which place you went to, and who with.
2 Say why you decided to go there.
3 Describe the service and atmosphere.
4 Describe the food.
5 Say what you thought about the prices.
6 Say whether you would go back or not, and if not, why?

Or follow the style of the second review and use the following headings:

Pros   Cons   Overall opinion

e **Write** your review. Use the **Useful language** and **Vocabulary Bank** At a restaurant p.160 to help you.

f **Check** your review for mistakes (grammar, vocabulary, punctuation, and spelling). ⬅ p.59

7 DESCRIBING A BUILDING

1 The most beautiful building ¹**which** I've visited in my city is the Hagia Sophia. It is situated in a historic part of Istanbul called Sultanahmet.

2 The Hagia Sophia was constructed on the orders of Justinian I, ²**who** was emperor of Rome from 527 to 565 AD. It was built on the spot ³**which** two other churches had burned down. Construction began in 532 and the building was completed in 537. In 1453, it became a mosque, and it has been a museum since 1935.

3 The Hagia Sophia was the world's largest cathedral for nearly a thousand years and it is famous for its large dome. It is surrounded by four tall minarets, each of ⁴**that** is different. There is also a lovely park in front of the building, ⁵**where** you can relax and enjoy the view.

4 When you go into the Hagia Sophia, you can look up at the dome, ⁶**that** has beautiful Arabic writing in the centre. On the second floor, there are beautiful mosaics on the walls. Some of them are more than a thousand years old. In the north-west of the building, there is a column ⁷**that** has a hole in the middle called the Wishing Column, ⁸**who** people think has special powers.

5 The building is open from 9.00 a.m. to 5.00 p.m. (7.00 p.m. in summer). It is closed on Mondays. There is an entrance fee of 60 Turkish lira (about 10 euros), but children under 8 are free.

a Read the description of the Hagia Sophia. In which photo can you see a) a minaret, b) a mosaic?

b Read the description again and match the questions to paragraphs 1–5.
   a ☐ When is it open? How much does it cost to go in?
   b ☐ What does it look like outside?
   c ☐ What does it look like inside?
   d ☐ What's the most beautiful or interesting building in your town or city? Where is it?
   e ☐ Who was it built by? When was it built?

c Look at the highlighted relative pronouns. Are they right (✓) or wrong (✗)? Correct the wrong ones.

d Which relative pronoun could be left out?

> **Defining and non-defining relative clauses**
> Relative clauses add information to a sentence about a place, person, or thing. They are introduced with a relative pronoun (*who, which, where, whose* and sometimes *that*).
>
> - In **defining relative clauses**, the information is essential, and *that* can replace *who* or *which*.
>   *St Paul's is the cathedral which / that has a huge dome.*
>
> - We can omit the relative pronoun when the verbs in the main clause and the relative clause have a **different** subject. *where* and *whose* can never be omitted.
>   *There's the man (who) I saw yesterday in the park.*
>
> - In **non-defining relative clauses**, the information isn't essential and the sentence makes sense without it. We use a comma before and after the clause (or a full stop if the clause comes at the end of a sentence). We cannot omit the relative pronoun, and *that* cannot be used instead of *who* or *which*.
>   *Christopher Wren, who designed St Paul's cathedral, is buried in the crypt.*

e You're going to write a description of a building in your town or city for a tourism website. **Plan** what you're going to write. Answer the questions in **b** in the correct order. You may need to research some of the information.

f **Write** your description. Use the **Useful language** to help you.

> **Useful language: describing a building**
> It is situated in…
> It was designed / built by…
> Construction began / was completed in…
> It is famous for…
> When you go in / Inside, you can see…
> There is / are…

g **Check** your description for mistakes (grammar, vocabulary, punctuation, and spelling).

→ p.83

Go online for more Writing practice

121

8 A STORY

a Read Matt's story about his wedding day. What problem was there?

b Complete the story with an adverb or adverbial phrase from the list. Some can go in more than one place.

in fact   in the end   fortunately   luckily   unfortunately

> 🔍 **Adverbs**
> Adverbs can describe an action or modify adjectives or other adverbs. They can be one word or a phrase, and can help to make a story more vivid. Sentence adverbs refer to the whole sentence and not just part of it. They usually go at the start of a sentence and often show the writer's opinion.

c Correct the ten underlined mistakes (grammar, vocabulary, punctuation, and spelling).

d Look at the exam question below.

> - Your English teacher has asked you to write a story.
> - Your story must have one of the following titles:
>   **I won it!**
>   **It was so embarrassing!**
>   **A day I'd like to forget!**
> - Write your story.

You're going to write a story. Choose your title and think of some ideas for your topic.

e **Plan** your story. Think about:
1 where and when the event / moment happened
2 what was happening at the start of the story
3 what actually happened on that day
4 how you felt about it then, and how you feel now

f **Write** your story. Use the **Useful language** to help you.

> 🔍 **Useful language: telling a story with sentence adverbs**
> *Unfortunately / Sadly*, there was a big traffic jam before our wedding.
> *Fortunately / Luckily*, we had a map and found a faster way.
> *Eventually / Finally / In the end*, we arrived at the church just before the ceremony.
> *Surprisingly / Amazingly / Interestingly*, we were the first people to arrive at the church.
> *In fact / Actually*, we were the only ones there for 30 minutes.

g **Check** your story for mistakes (grammar, vocabulary, punctuation, and spelling).

← p.93

The most important day of my life

I think the most important day of my life was my wedding day. My wife and I got married five years ago in a little church in the countryside. The weather was perfect – sunny and warm. It wasnt a very big wedding – we only have about 20 gests – but it was very beautiful. However, there was one problem. We were hired a woman to play the violin at the wedding ceremony but ¹_____ she lost and never arrived. That was a stressed situation for all of us. ²_____, there was a piano in the church and one of the bridesmaids, my wife's niece, was an excellent piano player. She was prepared to play for us, but she didn't really know any wedding music. ³_____, my brother had his iPad so we downloaded the score for some wedding music, and ⁴_____, our niece played the music very good. ⁵_____, I think she was better than a proffessional musician because she was part of our family, and of corse it is a great story. Now we have two small children who love to here the story of our wedding music.

9 AN EXAM TASK

a Read the essay topic and the student essay. Does the writer agree or disagree with the statement?

> Your class has just had a discussion about exams and education. Your teacher has asked you to write an essay on the topic below. Write about 200 words.
>
> Exams are not a good way of testing what students know. Do you agree or disagree?

1 In most countries around the world, students are tested on what they know through exams, both at school and at university.

2 In general, I think testing through exams is a good thing. Firstly, it is a fair system ¹_____ all students have to do the same thing in the same period of time with no help. Secondly, having exams makes students work harder. It is well known that many students only really work hard ²_____ they know they have an exam in the near future. Thirdly, the only real alternative is continuous assessment. This system benefits young people whose parents are closely involved in their education and help them with projects, ³_____ it isn't as fair as an exam. In continuous assessment, it is also much more difficult to stop students from cheating by using other people's work from the internet ⁴_____ their own.

3 The only real disadvantage of exams is that some students get very nervous and don't do their best, ⁵_____ learning relaxation techniques is a good way of helping with this problem.

4 In conclusion, ⁶_____ the exam system is not perfect, it is, in my opinion, the best way there is of testing students' knowledge.

b Read the essay again. In which paragraph does the writer…?

Paragraph	give his / her opinion and three reasons for it
Paragraph	give a summary of his / her opinion
Paragraph	give an introduction to the topic
Paragraph	give a contrasting opinion

c Read the essay again and complete it with a connecting word or phrase from the list.

although   because   but   instead of   so   when

d You're going to write an essay for an exam. The topic is:

> It is not a good idea to cram the evening before an exam.

Think about whether you agree or disagree with the statement. **Plan** your essay in four paragraphs. Use **b** to help you.

e **Write** your essay. Use the **Useful language** to help you.

> **Useful language: essays**
>
> **Generalizing**
> In general,…
> It is well known that…
> Generally speaking,…
> In most countries around the world,…
>
> **Giving your opinion**
> I think…
> In my opinion,…
>
> **Organizing points**
> Firstly / Secondly / Thirdly,…
>
> **Contrasting opinions**
> The only real disadvantage of… is that…
> One disadvantage of… is that…
> On the other hand,…
>
> **Conclusions**
> In conclusion,…

f **Check** your essay for mistakes (grammar, vocabulary, punctuation, and spelling).

← p.101

Listening

🔊 **1.4**

1

Interviewer Excuse me, I'm doing a survey. Can I ask you some questions about your name?
Sean OK.
Interviewer So, what's your name?
Sean Sean Gibson.
Interviewer Is that S-E-A-N or S-H-A-U-N?
Sean S-E-A-N.
Interviewer Why did your parents call you that?
Sean I think I'm named after the actor Sean Connery, who played James Bond in the 60s. He was still very famous at the time when I was born.
Interviewer Do you have a nickname?
Sean Yes, at school they used to call me 'Gibbo' because of my surname, Gibson. I didn't really mind it because most people were called by some nickname or other.
Interviewer And are you happy with your first name?
Sean Mmm, I like it. I was usually the only Sean at school, which I think was quite a good thing. But people find it quite difficult to spell, especially as there are two possible spellings, and most foreign people find it really difficult to pronounce.
Interviewer Would you like to change it?
Sean No, no, I definitely wouldn't change it.

2

Interviewer So, what's your name?
Deborah Deborah.
Interviewer Is that with an h at the end?
Deborah Yes, D-E-B-O-R-A-H.
Interviewer Why did your parents call you that?
Deborah Ah, I'm actually named after the hospital where I was born, Deborah Hospital in New Jersey – near New York. My dad thought of that.
Interviewer Do you have a nickname?
Deborah No, but everyone calls me Debbie or Deb for short.
Interviewer Are you happy with your name?
Deborah Not really.
Interviewer Would you like to change it?
Deborah I don't know. When I was little, I started calling myself April and then Caroline, but now I don't like those names either.

3

Interviewer What's your name?
Khari Khari.
Interviewer How do you spell it?
Khari K-H-A-R-I.
Interviewer Sorry, K-A-H…?
Khari No, K-H-A-R-I.
Interviewer Why did your parents call you that?
Khari It was my mum's idea. When she was young she went travelling in the Himalayas and she stayed at a monastery in Nepal called 'Khari' – I think she said it was also the name of the lama.
Interviewer Lama?
Khari Yeah, the head priest there. You know, like the Dalai Lama. Apparently Khari means 'the precious one'.
Interviewer Oh, OK! Thanks, that's really interesting. Do you have a nickname?
Khari No I don't.
Interviewer Are you happy with your name?
Khari Yeah.
Interviewer Would you like to change it?
Khari No, no way. My name's unique, I'm proud of it.

4

Interviewer What's your name?
Anya It's Anya, A-N-Y-A.
Interviewer Why did your parents call you that?
Anya Well, my dad's half-Polish, and my parents wanted a Polish name. My mum originally wanted to call me Agnieszka, but my dad thought it would be too hard to spell, so they decided on Anya.
Interviewer Do you have a nickname?
Anya I do, but I don't want to tell you what it is – it's too embarrassing.
Interviewer Are you happy with your name?
Anya Yes, I am – it's quite an unusual name in the UK. I only know one other Anya. I think it's more common in Poland, but there it's spelt A-N-I-A.
Interviewer Would you like to change your name?
Anya No, I really like it. I often get compliments about it.

🔊 **1.8**

Interviewer Today we're talking to the Creative Director of a business that names companies and products. Welcome, John.
John Hello, Sarah.
Interviewer So, how do companies go about choosing their names?
John Oh, in all sorts of ways. Many, like Burberry clothes and accessories, and Ferrari cars, are named after the people who started them. Others are combination words, such as Vodafone, which is from letters in the words Voice, Data, and Telephone – though actually, they changed the P-H in telephone to F. And Microsoft comes from the words Microcomputer and Software.
Interviewer Interesting…
John And other names come from phrases in the local language. A good example of that is Samsung, the big Korean electronics company. In Korean, Samsung means 'three stars'. The name was chosen back in the year 1938, and at that time three stars was the most impressive rating that people could imagine for hotels and things like that.
Interviewer So if they'd started the company today they would probably have called it 'five stars' – whatever that is in Korean.
John Absolutely. Some names even come from Latin – the name of the cosmetics company Nivea comes from the Latin word 'niveus', which means 'snow white'. And talking of Latin, there's another famous brand name with a classical connection, which is Nike.
Interviewer I think I know this one. Nike is the Greek goddess of victory. Is that right?
John Yes, exactly. However, 'Nike' wasn't the company's original name. When it started in 1964, its original name was Blue Ribbon Sports. They changed their name to Nike a few years later in 1971.
Interviewer I didn't know that.
John And a name ideally needs to have a strong sound. Take the coffee chain Starbucks, which was founded by two teachers and a writer, who decided to set up a business selling high-quality coffee beans and roasting equipment. Their advertising agency advised them that the letters S-T were powerful, and so they brainstormed words beginning with these letters and thought of a character called Starbuck from a 19th century novel. The name didn't have anything to do with coffee, but they said that 'the sound seemed to make sense'.
Interviewer And do you have a favourite brand name?
John Well, one of my favourites is Bluetooth. This one comes from the name of a Viking king, Harald Blatand, so called because he had a dead tooth which had turned blue – Blatand means 'blue tooth' in Danish. This king believed in good communication between people, which is an excellent model for a company developing new communication technologies. But also, the logo for Bluetooth on your phone screen, the B-shape, is made up of the two Viking letters for the king's initials – the symbols for H (Harald) and B (Blatand). I love that.
Interviewer Brilliant. Thank you so much, John, for speaking with us this afternoon.
John You're very welcome.

🔊 **1.13**

Look around you. Colour is everywhere in our lives. Did you know that, according to some experts, there are as many as 10 million possible colours in our world, though many are too complex for the human eye. So how much do you really know about colour? Here are some fascinating facts.

Research shows that the world's most popular colour is blue, followed by purple, red, and green, while white, orange, and yellow are our least favourite colours.

Works of art using the colour red tend to be more expensive. This is because it's a powerful colour, which is considered lucky in many countries, such as China. The most expensive works by the artist Mark Rothko, for example, whose paintings are mainly just blocks of colour, are his two red paintings.

The word orange didn't describe a specific colour in English until the 16th century, when it was named after the fruit. Instead, people used the old English word 'geoluhread' which meant 'yellow-red'. This is why we have the word 'redhead' for people with this colour of hair.

Pink has a calming effect and reduces anger and anxiety. Many prisons and hospitals paint their walls pink, to make prisoners and patients less anxious.

In Imperial Rome, the colour purple was produced with an extremely expensive dye made from thousands of seashells. The colour symbolized the power and wealth of the Roman Empire, and by the fourth century AD, only the emperor was allowed to wear it.

Mosquitoes are attracted to dark colours, especially blue. So, if you're planning to be outside in the evening in an area with a lot of mosquitoes, be careful what colour clothes you wear.

There is no such thing as a green mammal, even though it's a perfectly common colour for birds, reptiles, fish, and insects. One reason might be that most mammals can't see this colour, so it doesn't help with camouflage.

Van Gogh said that yellow was the colour of happiness, and it's the main colour of many of his paintings between 1880 and 1890. The Dutch painter suffered from epilepsy, and doctors may have given him the drug 'digitalis', which can cause people to see this colour very strongly.

The safest colour for a car is white. Studies show that it is the most visible colour in all driving conditions except snow.

Most diamonds in their natural state are brown. These are used in industry as cutting tools rather than in jewellery. The largest cut diamond in the world is this colour. It was found in 1985 in South Africa and weighs 109 grams.

The name for the colour black hasn't always meant 'dark'. It comes from the root word *bhleg-*, which meant 'to burn, gleam, or shine'. This may explain why in languages like French and Spanish, *blanc* or *blanco* are actually the words for white.

These are just a few of the fascinating facts I discovered when I was researching colour. The next time you make a choice about colour, for example, for a new car, do some research first to find out exactly what it means.

2.7

In reverse order, here's the list of the things that the British most often leave behind when they go on holiday. At number ten we have – passports. At number nine, flip-flops. Number eight, mobile phones. At number seven, toothbrushes, and at number six, toothpaste. At number five, sunglasses, and at number four, a good book. So, to the things people forget the most often. At number three, sunscreen. At number two, phone chargers. And finally, the number one thing people forget to bring is… comfortable shoes!

2.9

The holiday season is here, and many of you will be about to travel, and that means that you need to start thinking about packing. Packing is often something we do at the last minute, and we frequently get it wrong – we take too much and then have to pay for extra luggage, or we forget some really important items. Often when we arrive and unpack, our clothes need ironing before we can wear them. So, to make things easier, here are my top eight tips for perfect packing.

My first tip is 'Don't pack too much'. Put all the clothes you think you want to take on your bed. Then put a third of them, yes, a third, back in the cupboard. And only pack things you really love, otherwise you probably won't wear them.

Now to my second tip. 'Keep some space in your suitcase for shopping.' If you're planning to do some serious clothes shopping when you're away, or if you love buying souvenirs, or you want to buy presents for the family, make sure there's some empty space in your case. Think about what you might want to buy, and how much space you'll need.

My third tip is 'Pack in the right order'. Think about your itinerary, and put your first day's clothes at the top and your last day's clothes at the bottom. Then, if you don't have space to unpack everything, you can just leave your suitcase under the bed, and every morning you'll easily find what you want to wear.

OK, tip number 4. 'Make sure your clothes arrive looking good.' Learn to pack your clothes like a professional. Roll your jeans, T-shirts, and pyjamas. The only things you really need to fold are shirts and jackets. Where possible, travel with clothes that don't need ironing.

My fifth tip is 'Keep your chargers and adaptors together'. We all need chargers for our gadgets these days. Pack them all together in a separate small bag, with adaptors if you're going to need them. It's also a good idea to put this bag in your hand luggage, and not in your checked-in luggage, to avoid losing it.

Tip number 6. 'Use shoe bags.' Never allow your shoes to have direct contact with your clothes – use shoe bags to keep them separate, and put socks and underwear inside your shoes.

Tip number 7. 'Think about airport security.' If you're travelling with hand luggage only, put your wash bag at the top or in an outside pocket of your case, so you can easily take it out at security. The same is true of laptops, tablets, and anything you might need to put on a separate tray.

And finally, my eighth tip. 'Buy a travel wallet.' It's a good idea to print out all your important documents, like your itinerary or travel insurance, and keep them with your passport in a special wallet. It's true that nowadays you can keep a lot of documents on your phone, including boarding passes. But you might lose your phone, or it may run out of battery just when you need it. So now you're ready to go. Have a great holiday!

2.21

1 **Carol** I do a lot of shopping online. I love how convenient it is you know, I can be in my pyjamas and do the food shopping for the week or clothes shopping, but one thing I hate about it though is how difficult it is to sort out any problems because, you know, if you buy something in a shop, you go back to the shop and you sort it out, but if you've bought something online, returning it can be a pain, especially getting something replaced or changed if it's broken – it's just a huge nightmare.

2 **Alex** I love online shopping. I guess because it's so convenient, because I can do it at any time of day or night and I can do it from home. I don't particularly like going shopping so that's a real bonus for me. But I hate having to send things back, particularly shoes. They never seem to fit when I buy them online.

3 **David** I do quite a lot of shopping online. Mainly food – I usually do my supermarket shopping online. What I like best is that I don't have to take the shopping home. I live at the top of a hill and I used to have to walk up the hill with a whole load of shopping bags. It was a real pain. The only thing I really don't like is that online, it's easy not to notice what size the packets are, so you can end up with a huge packet of things when you only want a tiny amount. For example, I ordered a box of tea bags and I wanted a small box of 40 bags, but I didn't read the description properly and I ended up with a huge box with 460 tea bags.

4 **Anna** I do a lot of online browsing, looking for things I might buy. Not really for clothes, more shopping for, kind of, cooking things, or things on Amazon, presents for friends, that sort of thing. I love the fact that you have access to all kinds of shops, and access to brands that you can't necessarily find in shops that are near where you live. But I don't like not being able to feel things or know exactly what the colours are – they're often different from what you see online.

5 **Chris** I do a lot of shopping online because I'm not very keen on going to places where there are crowds of people and it's really busy. It's great being able to avoid the big department stores and shopping streets especially at weekends, where you can hardly walk on the pavement because there are so many people there.

The only thing I hate is people delivering things when I'm not in. Some companies are really good and give you a one hour delivery window, but with others they say they'll deliver between eight in the morning and seven in the evening, so you stay in all day but then just when you need to go out for an hour, that's when they come. That's so annoying.

3.2
Part 1

Interviewer Welcome back. Up next, age and the generation gap. We know how hard it can be to tell someone's age, but in fact it turns out there may be a way that's quite simple. It's called the 'Mosquito Tone Test', and Mark is here to tell us more.

Mark Thanks, Sue. The Mosquito Tone is a sound – a very high pitched, very annoying sound, which is why it's named after the insect. What's interesting is that apparently as we age, we slowly lose our ability to hear this sound. According to scientists, almost everyone under the age of 25 can hear the Mosquito Tone, but almost no one over 25 can hear it!

Interviewer Really! Is that right?

Mark Yes. And to test this out, I actually played the tone for my family last night. My wife and I heard absolutely nothing at all, but our teenage daughters could hear it, and in fact they complained that it was an irritating sound that was quite painful to hear.

Interviewer Oh no! Well, at the risk of irritating some of our younger listeners' ears, why don't we play the tone briefly now?

Mark OK, here goes. I'm playing the tone in 3, 2, 1…

Interviewer Have you played the tone yet?

Mark I just did. Or, at least, I think I did.

Interviewer Well, I suppose that just confirms that neither of us are under 25!

3.3
Part 2

Interviewer Now Mark, apart from testing a person's age, what is the Mosquito Tone being used for?

Mark This has actually become an interesting controversy. Because the sound is so annoying, and because only the young can hear it, the Mosquito Tone is being used to keep teenagers away from certain places.

Interviewer What kinds of places?

Mark Well, for example, from shopping centres. As you know, in some towns you get large groups of young people hanging around shopping centres and causing trouble. And some shop owners say that these gangs can annoy other customers, or frighten them away, which is obviously not good for business. So now these centres can play the Mosquito Tone over their audio system, and the groups of teenagers will feel uncomfortable and leave the area. But of course the sound won't annoy the other customers at all, as they don't hear it.

Interviewer Have you spoken to any of these shop owners?

Mark Yes, I have, and they said that the Mosquito Tone has worked very well for them. And they also said that although it's true that the Mosquito Tone is certainly very annoying, it doesn't hurt the teenagers.

Interviewer It sounds like rather a good idea to me. But you said this was a controversy. Who's against it?

Mark Well, there are some groups of people who are trying to ban the Mosquito Tone. They've pointed out a number of problems with it. Firstly, they worry that the sound really is harmful, but more to the point they say that the Mosquito Tone affects all young people, some of whom are well-behaved and just want to go shopping. And finally, they say that the Mosquito Tone doesn't actually stop the problem of teenage gangs, it just drives them from one place to another.

Interviewer Those do seem like good points.

Mark Yes, indeed. And there's also an interesting twist. Some teenagers have discovered an advantage to the Mosquito Tone.

Interviewer Oh yes?

Mark Well, the Mosquito Tone has also been released as a ringtone for your mobile. So in secondary schools that don't permit mobile phones, teens can use their phones in class. They can receive calls and messages during lessons and teachers don't have any idea what is happening.

Interviewer Because the teacher can't hear it! That must really annoy them.

Mark That's right. And if they can't hear it, they can't…

🔊 3.14

You don't need expensive photographic equipment to take amazing photos. The camera on your phone can be just as good. Here are my top ten tips for taking great photos on your phone.

Tip 1 Be ready. It may be an obvious thing to say, but remember to charge your phone and to keep your lens clean. I carry a charger with me most of the time. Also, keep your phone in your hand, not in your bag. I always keep my phone in camera mode so that when I unlock it, it's ready to take pictures.

Tip 2 Don't think twice. Take photos whenever you want and of whatever you want! There's nothing to lose. Some moments will never be repeated. If you don't like your picture, you can always delete it, but you can't turn back time.

Tip 3 Learn about your phone camera. Read your phone manual, and make sure you're using your camera in the best way. Sometimes little tips can really help you to improve your photos. Learn how you can control the exposure, or focus on the objects better. Know the strengths and weaknesses of your phone camera. My iPhone isn't good at night photography, so I try to only use it in the day time.

Tip 4 Don't use zoom. Don't forget that this is just a phone. It doesn't work like a camera with a DSLR lens. If you want to take a close-up of something, use your legs and move nearer!

Tip 5 Light is important. Good photography is all about using light well. Even the most boring composition will be saved by good use of light, whether it's day or evening.

Tip 6 Use the grid. Imagine your picture is divided into nine equal squares. This is called 'the grid'. The important parts of your photo should be positioned where the lines cross. Learn to use the grid, and then, just as importantly, learn to do without it.

Tip 7 Choose unique angles. Try looking at objects from a new perspective. Take a picture from the dog's view!

Tip 8 Don't stick to one style. A lot of people nowadays try to take photos in the same style or colours. Don't do this! Show your creativity. Take any photos you like, landscapes, portraits, or unusual compositions. Your own unique style will develop.

Tip 9 Select and edit. Be selective! Choose only your best pictures and then edit those. There are many apps that will help you to do this. But remember that sometimes a picture can be better without any filters.

Tip 10 Make your pictures come alive. Print your pictures, send them as postcards, give them to your friends, and hang them on your walls. Holding your photos in your hands is such a lovely feeling, much nicer than looking at them on a screen.

🔊 3.19

1 Chris I took this photo last year when I was in Uganda. I was there working for three weeks with a charity, and before going back to London, the two friends I was working with and I decided to go and see the mountain gorillas which live in the rainforest on the border of Uganda. On the day of the trek, I was feeling very nervous because I wasn't sure whether I would manage it. I'm not very fit, and we basically had to walk up the mountain in the rainforest until we found the gorillas, which could take as long as five or six hours. Luckily, after two hours, just when I was wondering if I could carry on, we found them. The first gorilla we saw was this Silverback, which is the large dominant male in the group. I couldn't believe my eyes – he was so close, only about a couple of metres away. I'll never forget that moment. We stayed with the gorillas for an hour, and then walked back down again. I love this photo because it reminds me of that moment, how proud and relieved I was to have got there, and probably the most amazing wildlife experience I've ever had. I keep it on my computer as my desktop background and when I'm sitting working in rainy England, it reminds me of another world.

2 Tom So, I took this photo in Australia, when I was visiting my girlfriend, Roz. She was studying out there for a year. It was taken in Byron Bay, which is the most easterly point of the Australian mainland. We were out walking along the beach, and in Byron, when the sun sets, it's a really special occasion, lots of people go out onto the beach and watch the sun set over the bay, and so I took this photo just as the sun was setting. I really like the photo because I have some great memories of Byron Bay and Australia, because I'd been there before on my own, and I was really glad to go there with Roz. It was a really happy time of my life and we were having a lovely holiday. And I like that you can see the silhouettes of people on the sand and in the water and I love the way the light comes off the sea and sand. It's one of several photos, actually, from that trip, that we printed and it's in a frame on a wall in our house.

3 Kate This is a photo I really like. Me and my partner, David, were staying with friends who live on the edge of Dartmoor, a really wild and beautiful place in Devon, in the south west of the UK. We had a big lunch, and then we all decided to walk up to the top of the hill behind their house. The weather wasn't very good on most of the walk, in fact at one point it rained quite hard, but when we got to the top, the sun came out and there was a glorious blue sky, and we could see the most fantastic view of the countryside. We asked another walker up there to take the photo for us. That's me and David in the middle, in red and green, with our little black dog. I like this photo because it's so colourful and we all look really happy – it was just a lovely, memorable day. I have the photo on my phone and my iPad – at the moment, it's my Facebook profile photo.

🔊 4.8

Part 2

Interviewer So how did you come up with the idea?

Tessa Well, I've always been worried about food waste. My parents have a farm in the north of England, in North Yorkshire, and I learnt as a child how much hard work goes into producing the food that we all eat. And so I grew up with the belief that food should be eaten, it ought not to be thrown away. But I got the idea for the app when I was living in Switzerland and I was packing up my flat because I was going to move back to the UK. When the removal people came to take all my things, I still had in my fridge some potatoes, a cabbage, and some pots of yogurt. The men told me to throw away the food, but it seemed such a terrible thing to do, to throw away good food. The removal men didn't want it and my neighbours were out, and I thought to myself, 'This is absolutely crazy…this food is delicious. Why isn't there an app where I can share it with someone nearby who wants it?' And so the idea for OLIO was born… When I told my friend Saasha about it…

Interviewer You co-founded OLIO with your friend Saasha, is that right?

Tessa Yes. Saasha has always been passionate about recycling, and when I told her my idea, her eyes immediately lit up – she got very excited. In just an hour of talking, we'd come up with a name and made a plan.

🔊 4.9

Part 3

Interviewer So what happened next?

Tessa The first thing we did was some research, in order to understand how big the problem of food waste was, and what we discovered truly shocked us. For example, did you know that in the UK, the average family throws away £700 worth of food each year? That adds up to 12.5 billion…£12.5 billion that's going straight in the bin! But our research also showed that one in three people feel really terrible when they throw away good food. But just because people hate throwing away food, that doesn't mean they'll take the next step, which is to share food. We needed a cheap and quick way to test whether our food sharing idea would work.

Interviewer How did you do that?

Tessa We invited 12 people from our research survey who said they hated throwing away good food, and we put them all in a closed WhatsApp group. We asked them to post photos of any surplus food they had into the group for two weeks, and see if anyone wanted it. Eventually, someone posted an item – half a bag of onions! And then more and more items of food were shared. Then, when the trial was over, we met face to face with everybody who took part, and asked for feedback. The conclusion was unanimous – 'it's an amazing idea'.

Interviewer So when did you actually launch the app?

Tessa We launched it on 9th July 2015. The very first version of the app could only be used in North London. But now it's being used in 41 countries.

Interviewer So people love it and are using it?

Tessa Absolutely. We get loads of messages on our website, and there was one the other day from this guy – I'm going to read it to you – he said, 'I had some vegetables I knew I wouldn't have time to eat and within an hour they'd been collected and I suddenly felt like a hero!' That's so great. People are helping each other, and helping the planet, and feeling good all at the same time.

🔊 4.16

Part 1

Interviewer Recently in the news, students and graduates have been complaining about how interns are treated, basically about the fact that many people doing internships are either very badly paid or not paid at all. We asked Jake Butler from the website savethestudent.org to give us the facts. Hello Jake, nice to have you on the programme.

Jake Hi there.

Interviewer So what's the current situation with interns getting paid?

Jake Well, I'd like to make it clear that at Save the Student, we're strongly against unpaid internships. And thankfully, the situation is better than it used to be.

Interviewer But are unpaid internships actually legal?

Jake They can be. It all depends on your status as an intern: that is, whether you qualify as 'a worker' or not. And the law isn't completely clear about what being 'a worker' means.

Interviewer So how do you know if you should be getting paid?

Jake Well, if you're promised a contract for future work once the internship period is over, then you are an employee, so you're entitled to the National Minimum Wage – that's £7.70 an hour – or the National Living Wage if you're over 25, which is £8.21 an hour.

Interviewer Are there any other situations in which you should definitely be paid?

Jake Yes. If you spend your day doing jobs that would usually be done by a paid employee, then you should also be paid the Minimum or Living wage.

Interviewer So when is it legal for an employer not to pay an intern?

Jake You don't have to be paid if you're doing an internship as part of your university course, or if you're doing school work experience. And of

course, if you're volunteering for a charity.
Interviewer Any other situations?
Jake Yes, you also don't have to be paid if the role you have is similar to work experience or shadowing – where you are in an office or another workplace just to observe and learn about what's going on rather than actually working. But, and this is very important, if you're not getting paid for doing an internship, you shouldn't be given fixed working hours.
Interviewer So the important thing is to know your rights?
Jake Absolutely!
Interviewer Thank you very much, Jake.

4.17
Part 2
Interviewer We're now asking people who either are interns, or have just been interns to phone in and tell us about their experiences. Our first caller is Rosie. Hi Rosie, and thanks for calling. So, what's your experience?
Rosie Well, I wanted to work in fashion, making hats, to be precise, and in the fashion industry, it's almost impossible to get a job unless you do an internship first, so I did several.
Interviewer And did you get paid?
Rosie The most I got was about £15 a day for lunch and transport. Companies get so many applications for internships that they don't need to pay you.
Interviewer So it wasn't a good experience?
Rosie Actually, it was. It was very hard work, but I learnt loads about designing and making clothes. I sometimes worked later than 11 p.m., and that wasn't easy, but then I'd look in the newspapers and I'd see a model wearing a hat that I'd helped to make, and then I felt great.
Interviewer But it can't have been easy to survive, financially?
Rosie No, it wasn't. My parents were able to help me a bit, but I had to earn money by working in a bar as well.
Interviewer Would you recommend doing an internship?
Rosie Oh yes, overall, I think they're brilliant. I'd definitely advise someone to do one – despite the hard work and the debt, you learn so much that it's worth it.
Interviewer Thank you, Rosie. Our next caller is Lauren. Hi Lauren.
Lauren Hello.
Interviewer So what was your experience like?
Lauren I've done four internships in Publicity. My last one was two months at a small Public Relations agency. They paid for my travel expenses and lunch, and I learnt a lot. It really helped me when I applied for jobs because I knew what I was talking about.
Interviewer So, a good experience.
Lauren Absolutely. But in the other three, I worked ten-hour days, six days a week, and I got no money at all, so I also had to work in a pub to support myself. And each time they told me, 'Do well and there'll be a job at the end of it.' But then there were no jobs. It made me so angry.
Interviewer And were you working during these internships, or was it more observing others?
Lauren I was working really hard. In fact, during one of those internships, the manager went on holiday for a month and I had to manage everything. And in another one, I worked from home, using my own phone, and I wasn't paid a penny, not even to cover the phone bill. I only met the boss once – it was all done by email. She promised me a job after three months, but it never happened.
Interviewer So you felt you were being exploited?
Lauren Yes, totally.
Interviewer I'm really sorry to hear that, Lauren…

5.7
1 Interviewer How do you watch TV programmes, on a television or on another device?
I watch programmes on TV if I'm at home, or on my laptop, or on my iPad. I might watch something on my phone, if I was, I don't know, I suppose when something has happened on the news, I might watch it live, or something like that.
2 Interviewer Do you 'two-screen' while watching TV? What kinds of things do you do?
Yes, I can often be guilty of perhaps checking emails on my phone, or perhaps even doing a bit of online shopping while I'm watching TV. In fact, yesterday I was watching *Masterchef*, you know, the cookery competition, and I bought some small cake tins that you needed to make, to make a chocolate thing that one of the contestants was making.
3 Interviewer Do you normally watch live TV or catch-up?
Both, though nowadays I watch more catch-up. But I watch the news live and football, or tennis – Wimbledon – things like that.
4 Interviewer Have you ever binge watched a TV series? How many episodes did you watch in one go?
I haven't done it for a long time, but I did once watch eight episodes in one sitting of *Mad Men* the American series. But as I say, it was a long time ago.
5 Interviewer Do you use a streaming service like Netflix? What do you like about it?
I have Netflix and I also buy things off Amazon Prime Video – is that a streaming service? I don't really use them for films, more for TV series, like old ones I missed when they first came out. For example, a few months ago, I watched all the episodes of *Brideshead Revisited*, the original series from the 80s, because I didn't see it then, but I'd heard that it was very good.
6 Interviewer How often do you watch YouTube, or online channels like Apple? What kinds of things do you watch?
I sometimes watch YouTube – it's usually if I have a problem with my laptop or my phone and I want to find out how to fix it, and I sometimes, sometimes, use it for watching people cook recipes. In fact, I've just watched someone preparing a fish dish, because I'm going to cook it this evening.
7 Interviewer Do you ever interact with TV shows by voting for contestants?
Not very often, but I do like *Strictly Come Dancing* and I have voted several times for contestants, when they've done a really good dance. And once, I was addicted to a TV show where the contestants were auditioning for a part in a West End musical and I really liked one young singer, so I voted for him every week. And eventually, he won, and I remember shouting and jumping off the sofa when the results were announced!

5.10
I used to live in a village in the province of Sakarya. It was an amazing place to live – just so beautiful. There's a large lake nearby and the hills are covered with pine trees – people go to picnic there. The coast is also not far away. When I lived there, it was as if time had stood still. People worked in the fields. Some things were annoying…there was no running water or electricity – we had our own well and generator – and there was only one shop. We had to wait for a minibus from the nearest town to bring fresh bread and the newspapers every morning! I worked in a school in a nearby town – in fact, the one that sent the bread and papers. I used to think, when I was living there, that there wasn't much choice of things to do, things to buy, but I made my own entertainment – I played tennis, went for walks, played the piano. In the end, I had to move for work, to Istanbul, which is the biggest and noisiest city in Turkey, and now I really miss the fresh food and fresh fish, the peace and quiet.

5.17
Liz When I moved in, the house was cold and absolutely filthy, and the cooker didn't work. I discovered everything in the countryside is more expensive: you have to drive miles to find a shop where everything costs twice as much as in my local supermarket in London. Local restaurants are really expensive and if you tell the waiter that you're a vegetarian, they look at you as if you were from Mars. I never fitted in. I think that in the country, if you're a woman, you'll never be accepted unless you're a full-time mum. Another thing I hated was the shooting! I love animals, I had two horses and two dogs, and I just couldn't pass a group of men with guns, shooting rabbits and deer, without getting out of my car and saying, 'Do you really have nothing better to do on a Saturday morning?' That didn't make me very popular. I became so lonely, I often used to sit in my car and listen to the kind voice of the satnav lady. After five years, I decided to go back to London. I'd learnt that an amazing view and a pair of nesting herons were not enough to make me happy. On my last night in the country, I sat outside underneath millions of stars and I thought to myself, 'I've come to the end of a five-year prison sentence.' I promised myself I would never, ever go back.
Bob The first thing we had to do was find new jobs. Jean got part-time work with a local company that sells meat products, and I did work as a lawyer. Two years later, we had a barn built, and my wife always wanted to have a donkey or a horse, but in the end we thought sheep were less destructive to the land, so we kept with the sheep, better for the land. So we started with four sheep, which we kept in the garden at first, and then we bought a field, and then we bought ten more sheep and sold six for meat, and that was the start of our sheep business. Now we've got 68 sheep and seven fields. At the moment, we've got 25 sheep that are expecting lambs, ready for the next season. In addition to that, we've got free-range hens which we rescued from battery farms. It hasn't all been easy. Um, it rains a lot where we live now, and, um, it gets incredibly muddy, and of course the work with the animals – it can get physically very hard. At first, we had a little bit of resistance – there were some local farmers who didn't really like newcomers – but we've always employed local people and we buy food in the local shops, and we try and engage with the local community as much as we possibly can. We sell our meat and eggs to neighbours and friends, and we produce wool from the sheep as well now. We haven't really ever considered moving back, because we really enjoy it. We loved life in the city, but we would never think about going back now.

6.6
1 I remember we once went to a restaurant in Portugal, beautiful location, upstairs overlooking the River Douro. We ordered some grilled sardines to share, and after a few minutes, the waiter came with a big plate of fried sardines and put them down on our table. And we thought, well, we'd ordered grilled sardines but hey, they're really busy and these look really nice. So we each took a fried sardine and ate it, at which point the waiter came back, and said, 'These aren't yours' and took them away, and in a few minutes came back with a plate of grilled sardines. So this was all fine, and we had a nice meal, but when we got the bill we saw that we'd been charged for both the fried sardines and the grilled sardines. So we complained to the waiter and then to the manager and said, you know, 'This was your mistake.' But the manager said, basically, 'you ate them so you have to pay for them' and we had quite a long argument.

Eventually, when we said that we wanted to make a formal, written complaint, very reluctantly he agreed to take them off the bill. We didn't leave a tip.

2 We went to lunch one Sunday in a place, a Parisian brasserie called Delaville. It's a beautiful place, it's from about 1900 with wonderful old furniture, mirrors and all that, really nice. We ordered very simple things like lasagne, which is easy to just heat up, but we waited and waited and it didn't come. The place was crowded, but not completely full, and there were quite a few waiters, but when we realized that we had been waiting for two hours, we went to speak to them and we asked them, 'What about our food, have you forgotten us?' And instead of apologizing, they were really aggressive with us, so we became more and more angry with them. And finally, we got our dishes and ate them and left. We should have left earlier, but we kept thinking that the food would come and also it was too late to find somewhere else. But it was a terrible experience, because it was a very famous place, very, with a good reputation where all the famous people go. But that's the type of service they offer. First I thought, maybe they were treating us like that because we're not famous, but in fact, I heard lots of other people complaining.

3 I had a table recently at the restaurant I'm working at in London and I went to all sorts of trouble with them. It was a group of six and there was a vegan and a coeliac – you know, someone who can't eat wheat, and anyway, I went through the menu with them and explained what they could have – there was even a woman who said she didn't like onions so I had to check all the dishes to make sure they didn't have any. There was also a little boy and I got the kitchen to make a plain omelette for him. Anyway, one of them, an elderly woman, asked for the bill, and she paid in cash, and when I came back with the change, she said, 'Don't worry about that, you've been great. Keep it.' It was 16p. I mean, I know service was included, but in that case, much better not to tip at all. I left the 16p on the table.

🔊 6.12

Presenter In many countries, tipping is an optional extra. But in the USA, it's a serious business! There are no actual laws on tipping, but the unwritten rule is that you should always leave a tip in a restaurant unless you want to deal with some very unhappy waiters. But how much is reasonable, and who exactly do you have to tip? Sally from the US is here to help us. Hello, Sally.
Sally Hi.
Presenter So first of all, why is it so important to leave a tip?
Sally I absolutely get that in countries where servers are paid well, you shouldn't have to tip at all, unless you want to because the service was great. But in the US, many servers earn just two to three dollars per hour for their services, because it's assumed that the tips will make it up to the minimum wage, which varies between the different states, but is generally around eight dollars per hour, in tips. Now I know you may think this is wrong, and many Americans, myself included, would agree, but that is the situation right now, until the law changes.
Presenter And how much should you tip?
Sally A normal gratuity is around 15 to 20 per cent of the check. But it can be as much as 25 per cent for amazing service, or in very expensive restaurants. It sounds a lot, but servers work really hard and I think generally they deserve it!
Presenter OK, so it doesn't often happen often, but what about if the service is bad? Do you still have to tip?
Sally I'd say you do, but if it really was bad maybe just 10% – that will give the message. And if you feel you don't want to leave even that, then you should probably call the manager and complain, and explain why you're not leaving a tip.
Presenter Do you need to tip even if the restaurant has already added a service charge to your bill?
Sally There's no automatic service charge added in the US, but some restaurants will add a gratuity to your check if you're in a big group of eight people or more, if it's a public holiday or sometimes if you're in a busy tourist area. You don't have to leave any more money if the check already includes the service charge.
Presenter Do you have to tip for fast food or takeaway coffee?
Sally No, no. If you buy food or drinks over the counter, people don't usually leave any gratuity, but there's always a tip jar close by if you'd really like to!
Presenter And what should you do in bars?
Sally Well, take lots of dollar bills with you because the normal gratuity in bars is $1 a drink. Order and pay for your drink at the bar, and leave the dollar bill on the bar. Don't worry about putting it in the bartender's hand.

🔊 6.20

1 I love IKEA. Especially the bookshelves. We have several. And I'm usually pretty good at putting their stuff together. But I've had a few problems over the years. I remember I once had some trouble with a wardrobe. After hours and hours, and a lot of swearing, I finally managed to put it together. But I'd assembled it in my study, next to the bedroom, which was where the wardrobe was going, because I had more space there. And when my husband and I tried to move it into the bedroom, we couldn't get it to fit through the door. So I had to take it to pieces, move all the bits into the bedroom, and start all over again. I suppose it was my fault though, not IKEA's. And the wardrobe looked very nice and has lasted for ages.

2 About three years ago, my girlfriend and I went to IKEA to buy a kitchen. The units were cheap and cheerful, but they also looked quite well-designed, and we were very excited by how good it was all going to look. The guy in the store said they were easy to put up, that it wouldn't take long, etc. etc., and I'm quite handy, quite practical, so I thought, no problem, though I admit my girlfriend was a bit sceptical. Anyway, when we got home, I thought I'd assemble one cupboard, just to see how easy it was going to be. It was a nightmare. The instructions were incomprehensible – it took me the whole afternoon just to do this one cupboard and when it was finished, I realized I'd put the door handle on the wrong way round. In the end, we had to pay someone to come and do it all for us. But at least they looked good.

3 I have lots of things from IKEA – it's great for students because generally speaking it's pretty cheap. Anyway, I bought a table there with my boyfriend not long ago. We started putting the table together and at one point we had three legs screwed in. Then we reached for the screws to attach the fourth leg – and realized there were no more screws. We had to take off the other three legs, take one screw off every one of them and reassemble the table. So now at least it has four legs, but it's rather wobbly, and I'm not very happy with it. It does annoy me when they don't give you the right number of nails or screws or whatever, and it's not the first time it's happened to me. Now I always check before I bring stuff home.

🔊 7.2

Story 1 Tonight, we're going to start with a good news story – well, good news for some people! Yesterday, bank customers in a village in Hampshire were thousands of pounds richer after an ATM started giving out double the money people had asked for.
When people heard the news, they rushed to take money out of the faulty machine, and long queues formed. For two hours, around 200 residents continued to withdraw money. It was mostly middle-aged people, but a few children arrived on their bikes with their parents' bank cards. One villager, who asked not to be named, said that some people had used five or six bank cards and had got £300 free with each card. At first people thought it was funny, but then some people became a bit aggressive when other people started pushing into the queue.
Finally, after two hours, the police arrived and switched off the ATM. They even posted a message on Twitter to stop more people arriving. They warned that receiving too much money from a cash machine might be a crime, and that the bank would ask people to pay back the money. However, later, the bank said that it wasn't the customers' fault and that no one would have to return the money.
Story 2 And finally on Texas News this Wednesday evening, the man who got trapped inside an ATM. Customers who were using an ATM in Corpus Christi earlier today got a big surprise. While they were withdrawing money from the machine, several people received handwritten notes, asking for help.
A man, who asked not to be named, had locked himself in while he was changing the lock to the ATM room at the bank. Unfortunately, he'd left his cellphone and the swipe card he needed to get out of the room outside in his van. When he realized that he couldn't get out and couldn't phone for help, he started passing notes through the ATM receipt slot to customers who were taking out cash. One of them read, 'Please help. I'm stuck in here and I don't have my phone. Please call my boss!'
At first, the customers thought the notes were a trick. But eventually, one of them called the police. When the police arrived, they heard a very quiet voice coming from inside the ATM. An officer went into the bank, broke down the door to the room behind the cash machine, and found the man. Senior Officer Richard Olden said, 'We thought it was a joke. It was just crazy that somebody was stuck in the ATM. Luckily, the man is OK.'

🔊 7.12

1 Hi. Yeah, not bad… Yeah, it's half time… One-all. Yeah, there's a really good crowd. The stadium's packed… No, no trouble. The Liverpool fans are making a bit of a noise, but nothing major… OK, I'll call you when it's over. With a bit of luck, we'll be in the semi-final in an hour's time.
2 **A** So, tell me all about it!
  B It was absolutely brilliant. We were in the second row, just near the stage, and when he was singing, I swear, a few times he looked right at me!
  A Did he sing *Baby Baby*?
  B Of course! All the best songs. It was just an amazing performance.
  A Were Sandy and Annette there?
  B Yeah, we met for a drink in the interval.
  A Gosh, you're so lucky you got tickets!
3 **A** OK, I'm looking for tickets now… There's a matinee at 3 o'clock and then it's on again in the evening at 8.00.
  B Let's go at 8.00 if we can get seats.
  A Well, there aren't any in the stalls, but there are two upstairs in the circle, in the second row.
  B OK. Go for it. It's a small theatre anyway, so we should have a good view wherever we sit.
  A OK. Right, we've got them. We can pick them up at the box office.

7.18

1 Andy A few years ago, I went to Wimbledon, the tennis championships, which take place in June in south-west London, and it's quite difficult to get tickets, but I was very lucky and got two tickets for the men's quarter-final matches on Centre Court, which are usually fantastically exciting with lots of big names. The tickets were very expensive, but I was really pleased because they were right in the front row. And on the day, my partner and I, we got up and drove to Wimbledon, it took about two hours. And as we were driving, it started to rain – the weather forecast was for showers, and at that time there was no roof on Centre Court, and the players couldn't play if it was raining. But we got there, parked the car and went in and found our seats and sat under our umbrella. Play was supposed to start at 2.00, and at 1.30 the rain stopped, then at 2.00, the players came on and the atmosphere was brilliant, and then at 2.15… the rain started again! The match was stopped and the court was covered over, and that was all the tennis we saw all day. We just sat there for four hours, hoping to see some more, but in the end we just went home, very cold and very disappointed. It was a very expensive 15 minutes.

2 Cathy Once, when my daughter was about 14, our local theatre, the Playhouse in Oxford, put on a play called *The Woman in Black*. It's a classic ghost story, full of suspense and quite scary – it's been made into a film starring Daniel Radcliffe, you know, who played Harry Potter. Anyway, I decided to take my daughter, and I got quite good seats in the stalls so she could see well. When we got there, we found our seats and sat down. The theatre wasn't full, but then just before the play was going to start, the rows of seats in front of us suddenly filled up with a group of about 30 teenagers. They were obviously a school group, and they were a bit noisy, but I thought they'd settle down when the play started. So the curtain went up and the audience went very quiet, and there was spooky music, and the tension started to grow, but then, every time anything happened on stage, the teenage girls in front of us screamed, even though nothing was really happening yet, so then we couldn't hear what the actors were saying for a few minutes until they quietened down again. In fact, they carried on doing this all the way through the first half, and it totally ruined the atmosphere for absolutely everyone. Their teachers obviously said something to them during the interval, or maybe someone had complained, but they weren't much better during the second half. It basically ruined the whole evening.

3 Clive I'd been a fan of Leonard Cohen since I was a teenager, but I'd never ever heard him sing live. But then, in I think about 2009, I read that he was going to do a world tour and that he was coming to Valencia in Spain where I lived. I was really excited and I thought, 'Even though he's in his mid-seventies, I'm finally going to get to hear him!' The concert was in September, in the velodrome in Valencia, so in the open-air. I went with a group of friends, and when he came on stage and started singing, I was amazed at how great his voice still was. We were having a wonderful evening, but then when he was on his fourth song, one of his old classics called *Bird on the Wire*, he suddenly collapsed on the stage! The other musicians all rushed up to help him and carried him off. We waited there, hoping that he was OK and that the concert would continue, but after almost an hour there was no announcement, nothing, and we thought maybe he'd died. Finally, someone came on and said that he'd been taken to hospital and so the concert wouldn't continue. We went home terribly disappointed. I'd waited all my life to hear him sing live, and we just got three and a half songs. Luckily, he recovered, and went on with his tour, but he never came back to Valencia, and then he died in 2016, so I never got to hear him live again.

8.5

Interviewer Dino, what made you choose hairdressing?
Dino Er, I always liked it from when I was child. I remember being taken to the barber's by my dad when I was a child in Greece, and I really loved the atmosphere there.
Interviewer He wasn't a barber himself though?
Dino No, but my aunt was a hairdresser.
Interviewer What sort of training did you do?
Dino When I came to London, I went to the Vidal Sassoon Academy. It was a two-year course – absolutely fantastic, very intense. I loved it!
Interviewer What sort of things do you love or hate doing in hairdressing?
Dino I love everything. There really isn't anything I don't like. And I do everything, cut, colour, highlights, straightening. Nowadays, some hairdressers specialize in maybe just colour, or just styling, but I think it's important to do everything.
Interviewer What do you think are important qualities for a hairdresser?
Dino Well, as I just said, I think being able to do everything – colour, styling, cutting – is very important. I don't believe in specializing in just one area.
Interviewer Any other important qualities?
Dino I think you need to be sociable, to be able to talk to people, calm them down if they're stressed, listen to them if they want to talk.
Interviewer Do you enjoy that?
Dino Yes, I do. The sociable side of hairdressing was one of the things that attracted me to it. Even women who want to tell me all their problems – I don't mind it at all, it doesn't distract me.
Interviewer Are women clients very different from men?
Dino Yes, definitely. They are normally the ones who want to talk, and they are much more worried – stressed – about their hair. Men are more quiet and relaxed, and they're not normally very fussy about their hair.
Interviewer What do you do if a client doesn't like the results?
Dino I try to correct it immediately. That's easy if it's the colour, less easy if it's a cut.
Interviewer Have you ever had a really bad experience, I mean one where you couldn't correct it?
Dino Only once, when I was still at college. I cut a woman's hair shorter than she was expecting it – not much, only about one centimetre shorter, but she burst into tears – and I couldn't correct that.
Interviewer Is it true that hairdressers always want to cut off more hair than their clients want?
Dino I think maybe it is. Many hairdressers want to make the hair healthier, and cut off all the parts that are, you know, damaged. Or sometimes they have a style in mind and they just want to do it. But obviously, normally I try to do what the customer wants. You have to be flexible. That's another important quality in a hairdresser.
Interviewer So, if you completely disagreed with what a client wanted, would you still do it?
Dino Well, if a client wanted a treatment that I thought was going to damage her hair, for example, if she wanted to have her hair bleached when it was already in bad condition, then I would say no. But if it was a question of style – for example, a woman who wanted to have her head shaved completely – I would try to convince her that it wasn't a good idea, but if she insisted, I would do it. It's her choice after all.
Interviewer Do you have any tips for having good hair?
Dino Yes – use good products, ones which are right for your type of hair. I notice that a lot of people take a lot of trouble choosing the right face cream – you know for dry skin, or problem skin. For day, for night, and so on. But with shampoo, they just buy the first one they see in the supermarket.
Interviewer Thank you very much, Dino. I won't forget this.

8.9

The body polish
Joanna So? What did you think?
Stephen It was just horrible! Horrible. First, they covered me in fruit puree, then they wrapped me in plastic film, then in blankets, and then I was left on a water bed. I mean, come on! Fruit's for eating, not for putting on your body. It was hot and sticky, and incredibly uncomfortable. And I felt so stupid. I'd never have that again. I give it zero out of ten.
Joanna Sticky? It was fruit, for goodness sake! I thought it was wonderful. It smelled amazing, and the head massage was divine. I mean, how could anybody not like it? That was one of my favourite spa treatments ever. Ten out of ten.

The foot treatment
Stephen Wow!
Joanna Don't tell me – you liked it!
Stephen It was wonderful!
Joanna I must say, your feet look…well, better. Clean anyway.
Stephen Well, I've never liked my feet much, to be honest, but now they look great. Definitely worth the time and money. Nine out of ten. What do you think?
Joanna Yes, it was great. A real luxury. And I love the colour they painted my nails. I agree – nine out of ten. You see…

8.15

Guide Good afternoon, everybody, everyone, and welcome to St Paul's, which, as you probably know, is one of the most famous and most historic cathedrals in Britain. The previous church on this site burned down in 1666, in the Great Fire of London, and the famous architect Sir Christopher Wren was asked to design a new cathedral. It took nearly 40 years to build and was completed in 1710.
Just behind you is the great West Door, you can see the great West Door. The magnificent doors are nine metres tall. They're normally closed, except when someone very special arrives, for example, her Majesty the Queen. And now in front of you, you see the Nave, which gives you the most wonderful view of the full length of St Paul's Cathedral. Maybe some of you watched Prince Charles and Princess Diana walk down the Nave when they married here in 1981.
OK, now please follow me. We're going to walk down the Nave, and you'll see the north and south aisle on either side…

8.16

Guide Right. Can we just stop here? Could we stop here? We're now in the centre of the cathedral. Look up above you, and you can see inside the wonderful Dome. It is one of the largest domes in the world, and I personally think the most beautiful. Now, you remember the outside of the Dome, which you saw when you arrived, can anyone tell me what was on top of the Dome?
US tourist A cross?
Guide Yeah that's right, a cross. In 1710, the year the cathedral was finally completed, Christopher Wren was 81 years old, and he was lifted up in a basket and was able to watch his own son place the cross on the top of the Dome. Another thing

about, fascinating thing about the Dome is that from the top of the Dome to the floor, down where you're standing, is exactly 365 feet, one foot for every day of the year.

Foreign tourist How much is that in metres?

Guide It's 1-1-1, 111 metres. In fact, St Paul's was the tallest building in London right up until the 1960s, because until that time, no one was allowed to build anything taller near St Paul's. We're going to move on shortly, but just spend a few minutes now looking at the magnificent paintings…

We are now in the area called the South Transept. Over there you can see the monument to Britain's great naval hero, Horatio Nelson, who died at the Battle of Trafalgar in 1805. Yes, yeah, he's the one on the top of the Nelson's column in Trafalgar Square.

We're now in the South Quire Aisle, and we're just going to stop for a moment to look at this marble statue of John Donne. Donne was a Dean of the Cathedral and one of Britain's finest poets – he died in 1631. But this statue is also important because it's one of the few monuments that survived the Great Fire of London. And you can still see the burn marks at the bottom of the statue there…

Now, are you all feeling energetic? I hope so, because we're going to go up these stairs here, to the Whispering Gallery, which goes around the inside of the great Dome, and I do need to tell you that there are 257 steps, so if there are any of you who don't think you can manage it, just wait for us here in the South Quire Aisle…

So, that wasn't too bad, was it? We're now in the Whispering Gallery. The gallery gets its name because if you whisper, talk very quietly, on one side, your voice can be heard very clearly on the other side. When there are a lot of tourists, it doesn't always work, but as there aren't so many of us today, why don't you try it…?

So, did any of you try out the whispering? We're now going to go back along the Nave, and then down into the Crypt to see some of the tombs of famous people who are buried in St Paul's. Right, now, the tomb over there is Lord Nelson's – you remember you saw his monument earlier – and then here we have the tomb of the Duke of Wellington, who defeated Napoleon at the Battle of Waterloo. And finally, this tomb here belongs to the great man himself, Sir Christopher Wren, the architect of St Paul's. It's just a simple stone monument, but can you see the Latin words on it? Anyone speak Latin here? No, well I'll translate it for you. It says, 'Reader, if you seek his monument, look around you.' Because of course, the whole of St Paul's is really Wren's monument.

9.1

1 Sarah My husband Rick always forgets where he's put things, and last night he came home very late from work and then had to leave very early again this morning, at 5.00, while I was still in bed. I heard him crashing about downstairs getting ready, and then he shouted up the stairs, 'Sarah, have you seen my car keys?' So I shouted back, 'No', and I tried to go back to sleep, but then he came running up the stairs into the bedroom and said, 'I can't find them. I left them on the table when I went to bed last night. You've moved them.' And I said, 'I didn't move them, I was in bed when you came home. Have you looked in your coat pocket?' So he went downstairs again and shouted, 'They're not there'. So I got up, in a very bad mood, and went downstairs, and looked in his coat pocket, and, surprise surprise, there were his car keys. I was really quite angry because by now I was completely awake. But at least he apologized.

2 Kim It was my mum's 70th birthday last week and I suggested to my sister Caro that it would be nice to have a birthday lunch for her. I said I'd organize it, because my sister isn't very good at that kind of thing – she works full time and has a very important job (so she says), but anyway she said, 'I want to do something to help. I'll bring a birthday cake.' I said, 'Fine', even though I quite wanted to make the cake myself. Anyway, on the day, everyone arrived and Mum was really surprised and pleased, and we had lunch, and then I said to my sister, 'Where's the cake?' She went pale, and said, 'OMG, I completely forgot about it.' Mum said, 'Oh don't make a fuss, Kim. It's no problem.' – she thought it was very funny – but I was seriously annoyed.

9.5
Part 1

Continuity announcer Can you remember exactly what you did on any day 10, 20, or even 30 years ago? Now it's Mind Matters, and we're going to hear about a woman who can do just that.

Presenter Ask Jill Price to remember any day in her life, and she can usually come up with an answer. When I met her, she asked for my date of birth, which is 24th January 1986.

Jill OK, 24th January 1986 was a Friday. It was four days before the *Challenger* explosion. I was working in an ice cream shop. I hated my job. That night I went out with some friends, Tim and Candace.

Presenter Jill could also tell me what she ate and what time she got home that evening. I tried another date. What did she do on 29th August 1980?

Jill It was also a Friday, I went to Palm Springs with my friends Nina and Michelle and their family.

Presenter Then I asked her, 'When was the third time you drove a car?'

Jill That was 10th January 1981. A Saturday.

Presenter Jill Price has HSAM, or 'Highly Superior Autobiographical Memory', which means she can remember exactly what happened on most days in her life. She remembers the day of the week for every date since 1980 – what she was doing, who she was with, where she was. She can recall a memory of 20 years ago as easily as a memory of two days ago.

Jill was born on 30th December 1965 in New York. Her first memory is when she was 18 months old and she lived with her parents in an apartment in Manhattan. She remembers the traffic, and staring out of the window down 9th Avenue. When she was five, her family moved to New Jersey, and then when she was eight, they moved to a rented house in Los Angeles. That was 1st July 1974 – and on that day, she says, her 'brain snapped', and she began to be able to remember everything that happened to her in great detail. Her memories come without her trying to recall them.

Jill People have called it a gift, but for me it's a nightmare. My entire life goes through my head every day – it drives me crazy.

9.6
Part 2

Presenter So what do we know about how Jill's superior memory works? Dr James McGaugh, who is an expert in memory research, met her for the first time in June 2000. He first tested her memory using a big history book. Jill answered the questions quickly and confidently.

Dr McGaugh What happened on 16th August 1977?

Jill Elvis Presley died in his Graceland bathroom. It was a Tuesday.

Dr McGaugh When did Bing Crosby die?

Jill Friday, 14th October 1977, on a golf course in Spain. I heard it on the radio while my Mom was driving me to soccer practice.

Presenter It's often difficult for scientists to confirm whether autobiographical memories are accurate, but McGaugh was able to check with Jill's detailed diary. He also checked Jill's memories with her mother.

Dr McGaugh's research was focused on showing that strong emotional experiences are the most memorable ones, and Jill had the most vivid memories that McGaugh had ever encountered. However her memory only stores the things that she finds important. When it comes to remembering things that don't relate to her personally or to her interests, Jill is no better than the average person.

Jill At school, I couldn't remember facts and figures, and I can't memorize a sequence of random numbers.

Presenter McGaugh and other experts have now discovered around 60 people with HSAM. These people often say that there was a specific point in their lives that triggered their ability to remember in such detail. For Jill, it was her family's stressful move to Los Angeles. Most people would think that having HSAM is an advantage, but Jill says there are two big problems.

Jill The first is that there's so much information running through my head all the time, and the second is that I find it difficult to forget unpleasant things. For example, I can remember bad moments from my childhood as if they'd just happened, and they make me feel unhappy all over again.

Presenter No one else in Jill's family has a memory like hers. She's published an autobiography, *The Woman Who Can't Forget*, but her brother hasn't read it. He says that there might be things in it that he doesn't want to know.

9.10
Part 2

Narrator When George arrived at Singapore he found a telegram waiting for him.

Reader 'Quite understand. Don't worry. Love Mabel.'

George 'My God, I believe she's following me,'

Reader he said. He checked the passenger list of the next ship on its way to Singapore, and sure enough her name was on it. There was not a moment to lose. He jumped on the first train to Bangkok. But he was uneasy; she would have no difficulty in finding out that he had gone to Bangkok. Fortunately there was a French boat sailing the next day for Saigon. He took it. At Saigon he would be safe. It would never occur to her that he had gone there. It was five days' journey from Bangkok to Saigon and the boat was dirty, crowded and uncomfortable. He was glad to arrive and went straight to the hotel. A telegram was immediately handed to him. It contained only two words:

Mabel 'Love Mabel'.

Reader He started to tremble.

George 'When is the next boat for Hong Kong?'

Reader he asked. He sailed to Hong Kong but was afraid to stay there. Then he went to Manila, and from there he went on to Shanghai. Shanghai made him feel nervous; every time he went out of the hotel he expected to run straight into Mabel's arms. No, Shanghai would never do. The only thing was to go to Yokohama. At the Grand Hotel in Yokohama a telegram awaited him.

Mabel 'So sorry I missed you at Manila. Love Mabel.'

Reader Where was she now? He went back to Shanghai. This time he went straight to the club and asked if he had received any telegrams. One was handed to him.

Mabel 'Arriving soon. Love Mabel.'

9.16

Alex My girlfriend Chloe and I had been together for just over a year. Soon after we met, I'd told her that I didn't want to get married or have children, and she seemed fine with that. But then, Chloe began to talk about moving in together. I tried not to discuss it, and we went on like that for a couple of months. Then one afternoon, it was the 29th February, Chloe invited me to her house. When I arrived, she was making a bracelet. I sat down and she passed me a box which contained some small beads with letters on them. When I looked into the box, I realized that the letters spelled 'Will you marry me?' I was horrified. I didn't want to embarrass her, so I started putting the letters on the bracelet thread in the wrong order – I made words like 'owl' and 'yellow', but then she started crying. So we went out for a walk and she explained that 29th February only happens once every four years, and it's the day when, traditionally, women can propose to men. I didn't say anything and went home. I felt awful. It's probably the worst thing that's ever happened to me, and I didn't see her for three days afterwards. But we got over it, and we're still together. We're not married, but who knows? Maybe in a few years' time, I'll propose, and Chloe will say no.

Emma When I first started going out with Tom, I was completely in love. He was ten years older than me, very good-looking, and he had been an Olympic athlete. He was also a really lovely guy. In theory, he was my perfect man, but after two years, our relationship became very difficult, so I decided to end it. Not long afterwards, Tom phoned me to say that he wanted to meet at the cathedral. I thought, OK, fine. When I got there, Tom was waiting for me outside. He was holding a bottle of champagne and a bunch of flowers. And then before I had a chance to say anything, he got down on one knee and proposed. He gave me a necklace – not a ring, a necklace. Then a crowd of Japanese tourists rushed towards us and began taking photos – Tom was down on one knee and I was looking white and shocked. It was awful. I asked him to get up, and explained to him, in front of all the tourists, that we were not together any more, and we were definitely not going to get married. We left the cathedral, and as I was walking with him to the station, Tom said he had hoped that if he proposed to me, it would solve all our problems. But it was never going to work. We're not together now.

🔊 10.6

1 **Yannis** Um, so I've lived in New York for, uh, 12 years now, and one thing that I think I will always appreciate is the diversity of the place and the people. And every time I go away it's so nice to come back here and, and be on the subway and see all the different faces and hear different accents. Um, and, you know, my English is pretty good, but I have never felt judged here, you know, for having a foreign accent, and nobody is surprised, you know, if you have a strange surname, um, or if you sound different. I have never felt that. And I could say that sometimes in Europe, I did, so… This is one thing that I will always appreciate about living here.

2 **Cristina** Um, one thing that, um, I don't particularly like here is the culture around American Football. And maybe this has something to do with me being European and liking, uh, European football, or soccer, um, more than American football. And I did try, um, but I think, uh, the game is way too complicated – though I tried to understand the rules. And I find the atmosphere around American football, I…just…I find it a bit too aggressive? For example, recently the Philadelphia Eagles won the Superbowl and, um, the celebrations, so to speak, if we can call them celebrations, were more like riots.

3 **Louisa** I know from having travelled a lot and having lived overseas, having an Italian husband, it's very complicated to get sort of bureaucratic tasks done in places like Italy. So I think the one thing that I like most about living in the United States is that things are pretty easy to do and even living in a big city it's, um, it's easy to get things done. So it's pretty easy to, you know, change your phone company, and it's easy to renew your driver's licence.

4 **Laura** Um, something that I like about America is that I find people are very keen to help, even without being asked. 'cause I lived in Germany for four years and I remember every time I flew there, at the airport, I would always really struggle to get my bag off the luggage carousel and no one would ever help me. And every time I flew back home to the US, immediately someone would come over and offer to help. And I've noticed the same thing with opening doors, with helping people carry things up the stairs in the subway.

5 **Peter** Something I really like about America is the sense of opportunity here. Um, I feel like as a new immigrant I've been able to come into the country and get jobs that I couldn't get back home in the UK because I don't think I would have had the same opportunities there, I think that you can move here and make something of yourself very quickly, and I really like the sort of entrepreneurial spirit there is here, um, the feeling that if you have a good idea and you work hard, you can be successful, I think it really is the land of opportunity and I really like that.

6 **Sarah** I've lived in the US for three years, and something that I really dislike about American culture has to be the fascination with guns, er, growing up in the UK, growing up in Europe, I've never seen people really want to own guns themselves. For me, it's up to the police to take care of people and to make sure everyone's safe. I can't understand why a civilian would want to own their own gun and keep it in their house. For me that means that the country is less safe not more safe, so that's something I don't think I'll ever be able to understand.

🔊 10.13

Interviewer What's the hardest exam or test you've ever taken?
Mark My A Level physics exam – I didn't understand at least half the questions.
Interviewer Have you ever done an exam where everything went wrong?
Mark I'm afraid so. For a history O level there were five questions – all short essays. I'd prepared five questions from previous exam papers, but nothing else. So I was gambling that at least three of the questions would come up. But none of them did, so obviously I failed it.
Interviewer How did you usually prepare for a big exam?
Mark I remember it generally involved a lot of coffee and late nights!
Interviewer Did you find exams stressful?
Mark No, I never got that stressed about exams but that may have had a negative effect on the results, come to think of it. I was never the world's best at exams. I usually passed, but the results were never brilliant.
Interviewer What's the hardest exam or test you've ever taken?
Sophie I think the hardest was probably my driving test – the practical part. I got so nervous each time I just couldn't drive. In fact, I failed three times before I finally passed.
Interviewer Have you ever done an exam where everything went wrong?
Sophie Yes, in the beginning of my first driving test, I refused to stop where the examiner asked me to stop. I just didn't think it looked safe and I thought it was a trick – I mean, I thought that he was asking me to do something dangerous, to test me. Anyway it wasn't a trick and he wasn't happy at all.
Interviewer How did you usually prepare for a big exam?
Sophie I used to spend a lot of time writing notes; I probably spent more time making them look nice, using different coloured pens and so on, than I did actually learning the information. But I found it really helpful to stick the notes up on posters all over the house so that I could see them every day.
Interviewer Did exams use to stress you out?
Sophie Yes. I hated exams and used to get very nervous and stressed beforehand. But once the exam had started I usually relaxed.
Interviewer What's the hardest exam you've ever taken?
Diane I think it has to be the eleven plus because that was the first time I had ever felt any pressure to succeed.
Interviewer How did you do?
Diane I passed it.
Interviewer Have you ever done an exam where everything went wrong?
Diane Yes, my A level French oral exam went horribly wrong. Some friends had said, 'Whatever you do, don't say that you've been to France, otherwise they'll expect your French to be quite good', and so what happened was, I got in there and the examiner said, 'Have you ever been to France?' (in French) and I said 'Non' and then I starting talking about driving to Gibraltar with my parents, and then the examiner said, 'Well, how did you manage to drive from the UK to Gibraltar without driving through France?', at which point I just completely froze and couldn't say anything else at all! But I guess I'd spoken enough previously, so I passed.
Interviewer How did you usually prepare for a big exam?
Diane Well, for literature exams I used to memorize loads and loads of famous passages from the books we were studying, so I could put them in my answers, and that seemed to work, because I passed.
Interviewer How did you usually feel about doing exams?
Diane Not great, but I was usually reasonably confident, I'd say.
Interviewer What's the hardest exam or test you've ever taken?
Paul Probably the exam at the end of the first year of my geography course at university. Not because the questions were very difficult but because I'd done so little work for it.
Interviewer Have you ever done an exam where everything went wrong?
Paul Oh yes. I thought I'd done quite well in my GCSE Chemistry exam but I failed it. So something must have gone very wrong.
Interviewer How did you usually prepare for a big exam?
Paul I used to read notes over and over again, right up till the last possible minute. Yeah, I relied heavily on short-term memory, I think.
Interviewer Did exams use to stress you out?
Paul Not really, though they probably would now. When I was at school and university it was just part of life – so not particularly stressful.

1A GRAMMAR BANK

pronouns

Revise the basics
1 **I** live in London. **NOT** *I live*
2 My parents don't visit **me** very often.
3 **My** name's Anna.
4 They have a flat in north London, but **mine** is in south London.

pronouns and possessive adjectives

1 subject pronouns	2 object pronouns	3 possessive adjectives	4 possessive pronouns
I	me	my	mine
you	you	your	yours
he / she / it	him / her / it	his / her / its	his / hers
we	us	our	ours
you	you	your	yours
they	them	their	theirs

direct / indirect object pronouns and word order

1 He bought **me** a rose. 🔊 1.5
 I'm going to lend **her** my camera.
 They showed **us** their new flat.
 I'll send **you** the document.
 We brought **him** some books.
2 He bought it **for me**.
 I'm going to lend it **to her**.
 They showed it **to us**.
 I'll send it **to you**.
 We brought them **for him**.

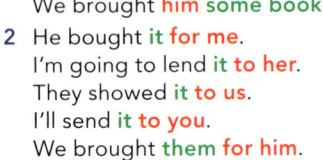

1 Some verbs can have two objects, usually a thing (the **direct object**) and a person (the **indirect object**). If the direct object is a noun (*a rose, my camera*, etc.), we usually use verb + **indirect object** + **direct object**.

- The order can also be verb + **direct object** + *for* or *to* + **indirect object**, e.g. *He bought a rose for me, I'm going to lend my camera to her.* See list of verbs with *for* and *to* below.

2 If the direct object is a pronoun (*it, them*), we usually use verb + **direct object** + **indirect object**, with either *for* or *to* before the indirect object. Some common verbs which can have two objects are:

- With *for*
 bring sth for/to sb, buy sth for sb, cook sth for sb, find sth for sb, get sth for sb, make sth for sb
- With *to*
 give sth to sb, lend sth to sb, offer sth to sb, read sth to sb, sell sth to sb, send sth to sb, show sth to sb, take sth to sb, write sth to sb
- If the indirect object is a pronoun, we use the object pronoun, not the subject pronoun:
 I'm going to lend it to her. **NOT** *I'm going to lend it to she.*

a Circle the correct form.

 My cousin's name's James, but we call *his /* **him** Jim.
1 My brother doesn't have a tablet. *He / She* prefers to use *his / her* laptop.
2 **A** Are these *your / yours* books here?
 B Yes, they're *my / mine*.
3 Most people are happy with *theirs / their* names, but Sarah doesn't like *her / hers*.
4 **A** What are *hers / her* children called?
 B I don't know, she's never told *me / my*.
5 I gave *them / their* my phone number, but they didn't give me *theirs / their*.
6 **A** Are these *ours / our* coats?
 B No, *ours / our* are on the bed.
7 This is *your / yours* pen, so that one must be *my / mine*.
8 She'll call *us / we* when *her / hers* flight arrives.
9 Can you send *he / him* the information? I can give you *his / him* email address.
10 *It's / They're* a really good restaurant, but I can never remember *his / its* name.

b Rewrite the highlighted phrases. Replace the **bold** words with a pronoun and use *for* or *to*.

 I gave you **that pen** for your birthday. *I gave it to you.*
1 They sent me **a new password** yesterday.
2 I gave my mum **some flowers**, but she's still angry with me.
3 She found me **some hotels** online.
4 My grandmother wrote me **these letters** when I was at boarding school.
5 Will you lend him **the money**?
6 My son made me **a birthday card** at school.
7 Our car broke down, so my parents offered us **their old one**.
8 We didn't buy our daughter **a phone** because we think she's too young.
9 I read the children **the first Harry Potter book** last week.
10 A friend sold me **these headphones** for £20.

↩ p.8

132

1B GRAMMAR BANK

adjectives

Revise the basics
1 It's a **poisonous snake**. **NOT** *snake poisonous*
2 They're very **powerful people**. **NOT** *powerfuls people*
3 I'm **older than** my brother. **NOT** *more old that*
4 Rome isn't **as expensive as** Paris. **NOT** *as expensive than*
5 It's **the most difficult** exercise in the book. **NOT** *the difficultest*

comparative and superlative adjectives

adjective	comparative	superlative
tall	taller	the tallest
hot	hotter	the hottest
bored	more bored	the most bored
stressed	more stressed	the most stressed
modern	more modern	the most modern
busy	busier	the busiest
dangerous	more dangerous	the most dangerous
interesting	less interesting	the least interesting
good	better	the best
bad	worse	the worst
far	further (or farther)	the furthest (or the farthest)

adjective + *one* / *ones*

1 I've lost my suitcase. It's a **big blue one**. 🔊 1.14
   Expensive laptops are usually more reliable than **cheap ones**.
2 I'm looking for white bread, but I can only find **brown**.
   We don't have any skimmed milk, only **semi-skimmed**.

1 We use *one* / *ones* after an adjective instead of repeating a singular or plural noun.
2 We don't use *one* with uncountable nouns.

more rules for comparatives and superlatives

1 I'm **less busy** this week than I was last week. 🔊 1.15
   Alan is **the least interesting** person in the office.
2 She's **the cleverest** girl in the class.
   The old road was much **narrower** than the new one.
   It would be **simpler** to go back to the beginning.

1 We can use *less* and *the least* with adjectives of any number of syllables.
2 Some two-syllable adjectives can make comparatives and superlatives with *-er* and *-est*. Common examples are *clever, narrow, polite, quiet, simple, stupid*. A good dictionary will tell you the usual comparative and superlative form for a two-syllable adjective.

a *bit* and *much* + comparative adjective

1 It's **a bit cloudier** today than yesterday. 🔊 1.16
   This phone's **a bit more expensive** than that one.
2 Your job is **much more stressful** than mine.
   The airport is **much busier** than it was a few years ago.

1 We use *a bit* + comparative adjective to say that a difference is small.
2 We use *much* + comparative adjective to say that a difference is large.

---

a Are the highlighted forms right (✓) or wrong (✗)? Correct the wrong ones.

He's **happier than** he was yesterday. ✓
She's **a person very ambitious**. ✗
She's a very ambitious person.

1 That's **the most bad film** I've ever seen.
2 I'm not **as sporty than** my brother.
3 Cats are **much more selfish than** dogs.
4 We can't decide between Mexico and Sicily. Mexico is **further** to travel, but the hotels are **less expensive**.
5 I always lose my phone, so I bought **a cheap**.
6 My wife's **a more good driver** than I am.
7 These shoes are **the more comfortable ones** I have.
8 My brothers and sisters are all **very successfuls**.
9 This exercise **is easyer than the other one**.
10 It's **the biggest room** in the house.

b Complete the second sentence so that it means the same as the first.

Adam is friendlier than Chris.
Chris isn't <u>as friendly</u> as Adam.

1 Tom isn't as lucky as his brother.
   Tom's brother _____ he is.
2 Their house is much bigger than ours.
   Our house is _____ theirs.
3 My new password is easier to memorize than my old one.
   My old password was _____ to memorize than my new one.
4 This flat is nicer than the other two we've seen.
   This flat is _____ of the three we've seen.
5 My sister's children are more helpful than mine.
   My children aren't _____ my sister's.
6 The weather wasn't as good as we'd expected.
   The weather was _____ we'd expected.
7 The film was a bit less dramatic than the book.
   The book was _____ the film.
8 Yellow will look better than red for your kitchen walls.
   Red won't look _____ yellow for your kitchen walls. ⬅ p.12

> Go online to review the grammar for each lesson

133

2A GRAMMAR BANK

present tenses

Revise the basics

present simple and frequency
1 She **goes** abroad a lot. NOT *She go*
2 **Does he know** Paris well? NOT *Do he know*
3 We **don't like** camping. NOT *We not like*
4 They **never go** swimming. NOT *Never they go*
5 He's **always** late. NOT *Always he's late*
6 I **go** for a walk **every morning**. NOT *I go every morning for a walk.*

present continuous
7 He's **working** today. NOT *He working*
8 They **aren't** / **They're not watching** TV, they're **playing** a video game. NOT *They not watching*
9 **Are you going** away this weekend? NOT *Do you go / You are going*

action and non-action verbs

1 A What **are** the children **doing** now? 🔊 2.10
   B Mark'**s playing** tennis and Anna'**s reading**.
   A Hi, Marta. **Are** you **waiting** for someone?
   B Yes, I'**m waiting** for Tim.
2 I **like** vegetables now, but I didn't use to.
   Oh, now I **remember** where I left my glasses.

1 Many verbs describe actions. These verbs are used in the present continuous to talk about actions happening now or in the future.
2 Some verbs describe states and feelings, not actions. Examples are *agree, be, believe, belong, depend, forget, hate, hear, know, like, look like, love, matter, mean, need, prefer, realize, recognize, remember, seem, suppose, understand, want*. These verbs are normally used in the present simple, not the continuous, even if we are referring to now.

verbs which can have action and non-action meanings

Do you **have** any sunscreen? = possession (non-action) 🔊 2.11
He's **having** a shower at the moment. = an action
Do you **think** we should have lunch in the hotel? = opinion (non-action)
They're **thinking** of going on a cruise. = an action
I **see** what you mean. = understanding (non-action)
I'm **seeing** the hotel manager tomorrow morning. = an action

- Some verbs have two meanings, an action meaning and a non-action meaning, e.g. *have, think, see*. If they describe a state or feeling, not an action, they are not usually used in the present continuous. If they describe an action, they are used in the present continuous.

present continuous for future arrangements

I'm **leaving** tomorrow and I'm **coming back** on Tuesday. 🔊 2.12
We're **seeing** our grandparents this weekend.
When **are** they **coming** to visit us?
Ella **isn't going out** tonight. She's **staying in**.

- We often use the present continuous where there is an arrangement to do something in the future.

present simple for 'timetable' future

The train **leaves** at 6.30 in the morning. 🔊 2.13
Our flight **doesn't stop** in Hong Kong. It **stops** in Singapore.
What time **does** your flight **arrive** in New York?

- We use the present simple to talk about things which will happen according to a timetable, especially travel times. We are usually referring to things which always happen on certain days at certain times, like flight times or classes, and are not people's personal plans or decisions.

a (Circle) the correct form.

We're going / We go to New Zealand on Saturday. The flight ¹*leaves / is leaving* at 6.50 in the morning. ²*We need / We're needing* to check in two hours ahead, so ³*we go / we're going* to the airport the night before, and ⁴*we stay / we're staying* in an airport hotel (£200 a night, but it's better than getting up at 2.00 a.m.!). The first part of the flight, to Singapore, ⁵*takes / is taking* 14 hours, and ⁶*we break / we're breaking* the journey there for a couple of days. Then it's on to Auckland. The flight ⁷*gets in / is getting in* at nearly midnight, but our friends ⁸*meet / are meeting* us at the airport, and ⁹*they look after / they're looking after* us for a week or so. Then ¹⁰*we travel / we're travelling* round North and South Island – ¹¹*we rent / we're renting* a camper van. ¹²*We have / We're having* to be back in Auckland on 22nd February, but I don't think I'll want to come home!

b Complete the sentences with the present simple or present continuous form of the verbs in brackets.

Do you *know* Andrew's sister? (know)
1 _____ you _____ camping or staying in hotels? (prefer)
2 We _____ of going on a safari next year. (think)
3 _____ we _____ to pack insect repellent? (need)
4 She _____ to Frankfurt for a business meeting next week. (fly)
5 A Can I help you?
   B Yes, I _____ a charger for my phone. (look for)
6 A This hotel _____ a restaurant. (not have)
   B It _____, we can eat in town. (not matter)
7 A Hi. Can you hear me? What _____ you _____? (do)
   B I _____ by the pool and Tanya _____ a spa treatment. Where are you? (read, have)
8 A What time _____ our flight _____? (leave)
   B It _____ at 9.50 and it _____ at 12.10. (leave, arrive)

→ p.18

134

2B GRAMMAR BANK

possessives

Revise the basics

possessive 's and of

1 That's **Mark's** jacket.
  He's my **sister's** boyfriend.
2 What's **the name of the street** where you live?
  They sat at **the back of the bus**.

more rules for possessive 's

1 I asked **Chris'** advice. / I asked **Chris's** advice. 🔊 2.14
2 This is a photo of my **parents'** house.
  That's the **children's** bedroom.
3 We spent the weekend at **Paul's**.
  I went to my **grandmother's** yesterday.
  Can you get me some aspirin when you go to the **chemist's**?
4 We saw **Tom and Mary's** parents.
  Is that **Kate and David's** house?

1 If a name ends with -s, we form the possessive with ' or 's. Both are pronounced /ɪz/.
2 Possessives are different for regular and irregular plurals.
- After a plural noun ending in -s, we form the possessive with a final ' (but no extra s).
- After an irregular plural not ending in -s, we form the possessive with 's.
3 We can use *name / person* + 's to mean that person's house or flat.
- We also use 's after words for certain jobs to refer to their shop or business, e.g. *chemist's, hairdresser's* etc.
4 When we are talking about something belonging to two people or things, we put the 's only after the second name.

more rules for *of* to show possession

That man over there is **a friend of mine**. 🔊 2.15
This is **an interesting book of Sarah's**.
Tell me about **this plan of theirs**.
Where's **that husband of yours**?

- We often use noun + *of* + possessive pronoun or name / noun + 's after *a / an* or *this / that*.

own

I'd love to have **my own** business. 🔊 2.16
That's my magazine. Why don't you buy **your own**?
Our town is going to get **its own** shopping centre.
Small bakers often sell **their own** bread and cakes.

- We can use *own* after a possessive adjective for emphasis.
- We can also use *of my / his / her*, etc. + *own*, e.g. I'd love to have **a business of my own**.

---

a Circle the correct form.

What's *the name of the shop* / *the shop's name* where Suzy works?
1 That's *the car of my friend / my friend's car* over there.
2 My *brother's / brothers'* names are Peter and Michael.
3 I live in the flat at *the top of the building / the building's top*.
4 The only *travel agents / travel agent's* in our village closed down last year.
5 I can't remember *Jim and Marie's / Jim's and Marie's* address – do you have it?
6 **A** Who's Samantha?
   B She's *my husband's sister / my sister's husband*.
7 We often have lunch at *my parents' / my parent's*.
8 Tim's a colleague *of my / of mine*.
9 Not many people live in *the centre of London / London's centre*.
10 I quite like supermarket pizza, but I prefer to make *my own / mine own*.

b Are the highlighted forms right (✓) or wrong (✗)? Correct the wrong ones.

We went to Annes for dinner last night. ✗ to Anne's
1 There are lots of expensive womens' clothes shops round here.
2 James's brother is much younger than him.
3 They'd really like to have his own flat.
4 **A** Who are those women?
   B The blonde one is my sister Alice, and the dark one is a colleague of her.
5 There's been a hairdressers on that corner for years.
6 Two of my friend's mothers run online businesses.
7 Simon is a distant cousin of ours.
8 If you want to work from home, you need to have a study of your own.
9 Keith's and Brian mother works in the shop with them.
10 There was a beautiful painting of Monet's at the exhibition.

← p.20

Go online to review the grammar for each lesson

3A GRAMMAR BANK

past simple, past continuous, or *used to*?

Revise the basics

past simple
1 When I **was** young, I **loved** playing outside.
2 We **didn't live** in a big city. **NOT** we didn't lived
3 Where **did** you **go** to school? **NOT** did you went

past continuous
4 I **was watching** TV when you arrived.
5 She **wasn't studying** when I called her.
6 What **were** you **doing** at 9.00 this morning?

used to
7 Luke **used to have** long hair.
8 They **didn't use to live** in London. **NOT** didn't used to
9 What music **did** you **use to like** when you were young?
NOT did you used to

past simple and past continuous

1 I only **saw** him for a few minutes before he **left**.   ◆ 3.4
Most people **didn't own** a computer until the 1980s.
Where **did** you **grow up**?
2 What **were** you **doing** at 7.00 yesterday evening?
He **was texting** a friend when the accident **happened**.
While we **were having** our picnic, it **started** to rain.
Sorry, what **did** you **say**? I **wasn't listening**.

1 We use the past simple for finished past actions or states (when we say, ask, or know when they happened). We can use the past simple for things which happened at any time in the past – very recently or a long time ago. The important thing is that we see them as finished.
- For irregular past simple verbs, see **Irregular verbs** p.165.
2 We use the past continuous:
- to talk about an action or situation in progress at a specific time in the past.
- to describe a past action in progress which was interrupted by another action (expressed in the past simple).

***used to* and past simple**

1 I **used to be** very shy when I was a child.   ◆ 3.5
Tim **used to go** to the theatre a lot when he lived in London.
We **used to live** in Rome.
2 I **was** very shy when I was a child.
Tim **often went** to the theatre when he lived in London.
We **lived** in Rome for ten years.

1 We use *used to* (not the past continuous) to describe a habit or state that was true for a significant period in the past, and that has now finished.
2 We can also often use the past simple instead of *used to* especially with an adverb of frequency, e.g. *usually, often,* etc.
- We use the past simple (not *used to*) when we specify how long we did an action **NOT** We used to live in Rome for ten years.

---

a Are the highlighted forms right (✓) or wrong (✗)? Correct the wrong ones.

Where **did you use to go** on holiday when you were young? ✓
1 This time last week I **was sitting** on a beach.
2 When **did they use to get** married?
3 I **worked** in a pizza restaurant when I first met my wife.
4 **We used to love** going to concerts when we were students.
5 **I used to travel** round Asia for a year before I decided to go to university.
6 My brother and I **didn't used to get on** very well when we were young.
7 Andrew **was never studying** much at school.
8 **A** Where **did you go to school**?
B In Manchester.
9 Sorry, I didn't hear what you said, I **watched** the news.
10 **I used to be** much thinner when I was a teenager.

b Complete the sentences with the correct form of the verbs (past simple, past continuous, or *used to*). Sometimes more than one form is possible.

I *grew up* in a little village. (grow up)
1 They _____ dinner when I _____. (already have, arrive)
2 When we were young, our parents _____ us to the beach every weekend. (take)
3 We _____ when the taxi _____. (still pack, come)
4 _____ your brother _____ you to play the guitar when you were young? (teach)
5 When I was a child, I _____ vegetables. (not like)
6 He _____ a beard when he _____ at university. (have, be)
7 We _____ all day playing together when we _____ children. (spend, be)
8 He _____ on his phone when the police _____ him. (talk, stop)
9 I _____ to a boarding school for two years, from the age of 13 to 15. (go)
10 They _____ a car when I first _____ them. (not have, know)

← p.28

136

3B GRAMMAR BANK

prepositions

prepositions of place

She sat **in** the square and watched the tourists. 🔊 3.16
There's a box **under** your bed.
You'll find some cash **inside** my purse.
The cups are **on** that shelf there.
There's a man standing **in front of** the gate.

- Prepositions that describe place, like *in* and *on*, can be used with different verbs and places and the meaning doesn't change.

prepositions of movement

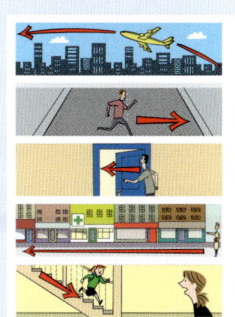

The plane flew **over** the city. 🔊 3.17
He ran **across** the road.
He walked **through** the door.
Go **along** the street, **past** the chemist's.
Don't run **down** the steps. You'll fall.

- Prepositions that describe movement, like *over* and *through*, can be used with different verbs of movement and the meaning doesn't change.

dependent prepositions after verbs and adjectives

1 We **waited for** the film to start. 🔊 3.18
  Everybody **laughed at** me.
2 I'm **worried about** my camera – the flash isn't working.
  Lily's **interested in** astrology.
3 Tony's **good at spending** other people's money.
  She **believes in taking** lots of pictures and then **choosing** the best.

1 Some verbs are always followed by the same preposition.
2 Some adjectives are always followed by the same preposition.
3 If there is a verb after the preposition, we use the *-ing* form, not the infinitive.

> The verbs *ask*, *discuss*, *enter*, *marry*, and *tell* have no preposition, e.g.
> I **asked Jack** a question. **NOT** ~~asked to~~
> We **discussed the situation**. **NOT** ~~discussed about~~
> The police officers **entered the building**. **NOT** ~~entered in~~
> She **married her personal trainer**. **NOT** ~~married with~~
> The photographer **told everyone** to smile. **NOT** ~~told to everyone~~

- For a list of **prepositions after verbs and adjectives**, see p.164.

---

a Complete the story with the correct preposition.

across   onto   under   into (x2)   ~~down~~   off   towards
next to   round   on   between   in

The mouse ran _down_ the stairs, ¹_____ the corridor, and ²_____ the kitchen. It jumped ³_____ the table, and ran ⁴_____ the salt and pepper and ⁵_____ the coffee pot. There was some cheese ⁶_____ a plate. The mouse took a piece, jumped ⁷_____ the table, and disappeared ⁸_____ the door. Then it ran ⁹_____ the garden and stopped ¹⁰_____ the gate. But unfortunately, two cats were hiding ¹¹_____ the grass, and they started to creep ¹²_____ the mouse…

b Complete the sentences with the correct preposition. Write – if no preposition is needed.

She paid _for_ my flight home.
1 I'm tired _____ all this work – I'm ready _____ a holiday!
2 I'm not looking forward _____ apologizing _____ what happened.
3 He's very proud _____ his new phone.
4 We need to discuss _____ the problems with our IT department.
5 Mum! Josh won't share his sweets _____ me!
6 You can't always rely _____ the buses here – they're often late.
7 I don't know what you're talking _____.
8 The pilot told us not to worry _____ the turbulence.
9 Who's responsible _____ updating the website?
10 Let's not argue _____ it now – let's wait _____ the boss to get here.
11 Sarah married _____ Anthony in July this year.
12 I'm interested _____ photography, but I'm not very good _____ taking photographs!

← p.32

Go online to review the grammar for each lesson

4A GRAMMAR BANK

future forms: will / shall and be going to

will / shall

1 **Predictions** 🔊 4.11
Who do you think **will win** tomorrow's game?
The climate probably **won't change** much in the next five or ten years.

2 **Future facts**
I**'ll be** at work on Monday.   The election **will be** on 6th May.

3 **Instant decisions**
A Do you want coffee or tea?   B I**'ll have** a coffee, please.

4 **Promises**
A Have you been using my laptop? You didn't turn it off.
B Oh sorry. I**'ll remember** next time.
A The battery's almost run down!
B Sorry. I promise I **won't do** it again.

5 **Offers and suggestions**
I**'ll cook** dinner tonight.
Shall I **throw away** this bread?
What **shall** I **do** with my old phone?
Where **shall** we **go** for lunch today?

- We use *will / won't* + infinitive:
  1 to ask for or make predictions about what we think or believe will happen.
  2 for future facts which are beyond our control.
  3 for instant decisions that you make at the time of speaking.
  4 to make promises.
  5 to offer to do something. If the offer is a question, we use *Shall I / we…?*
- We also use *shall* with *I* and *we* to make suggestions.

be going to

1 **Plans and intentions** 🔊 4.12
I**'m going to buy** a new phone this weekend.
Tom**'s going to make** pizza for dinner.

2 **Predictions**
You **aren't going to like** this film – it's very violent.
It's a bit cloudy – the weather forecast says it**'s going to rain** this afternoon.

- We use *be going to* + infinitive:
  1 when there is a plan to do something – a decision has been made.
  2 to make predictions when we have visible or other evidence of what is going to happen.
- We can often use either *will* or *be going to* for predictions.

> 🔍 **The future in the past**
> When we talk about the future from the point of view of a time in the past, we use *was / were going to*. This often describes failed plans.
> *I was going to call you, but I forgot.*
> *We were going to go shopping, but we didn't have time.*

---

a Are the highlighted forms right (✓) or wrong (✗)? Correct the wrong ones.

  A Is that the doorbell?
  B Yes, it is. I'm going to get it. ✗ *I'll get*
1 A What are your plans for the weekend?
  B I'm going to do lots of gardening, and we're going to see my parents on Sunday.
2 A This cardboard box is empty. Will I put it in the recycling bin?
  B No, I'm going to use it.
3 A I've decided to buy a new camera. I'll get one with a good zoom.
  B Will I help you choose one? I know a lot about cameras.
4 A Is Katie going to be at the party?
  B I don't know. Pass me my phone and I'm going to text her.
5 A Did you finish all the biscuits?
  B Yes, sorry. I'll buy some more this afternoon.

b Complete the sentences with the correct form of *will*, *shall*, or *be going to* and the verb in brackets.

  We've decided that we **'re going to stay** in the UK for our holiday this year. (stay)
1 A It's really hot in here!
  B I _____ the air conditioning. (turn on)
2 Can I borrow £10? I _____ you back tomorrow. (pay)
3 A What are you planning to do with these old books?
  B I _____ them to the charity shop. (give)
4 A _____ I _____ some more bread when I go out? (buy)
  B Yes, please. I've decided I _____ sandwiches for lunch. (make)
5 Are you going home by bus? I _____ you a lift if you like. (give)
6 A Let's go to the cinema tonight.
  B OK. What film _____ we _____? (see)
7 A What _____ you _____ with all those old bottles and jars? (do)
  B I _____ them to the bottle bank for recycling. (take)
8 After 2040, diesel cars _____ in most European countries. (not sell)

➜ p.38

138

4B GRAMMAR BANK

first and second conditionals

first conditional

1. If I **have** time, I'**ll write** my CV tonight. 🔊 4.19
   If you **don't work** hard, you **won't get** promoted.
2. If he **does** well at school, he **can go** to a good university.
   I **might (may) go back** to college if I **can't find** a job.
   If you **apply** for a job, you **must prepare** an up-to-date CV.
   If you **want** to do well in the exam, you **should work** hard this weekend.
3. If you **get** an interview, **think** carefully about what to wear.

- We use the first conditional to talk about a possible future situation and its consequence.
  1. The first conditional normally uses *if* + present simple, *will / won't* + infinitive.
  2. We can also use other modal verbs instead of *will*, e.g. *can, might, may, must,* or *should*.
  3. We can also use an imperative instead of *will*.

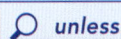

🔍 **unless**
We can use *unless* instead of *if...not* in conditional sentences.
I won't go unless you go, too. (= I won't go if you don't go, too.)

second conditional

1. If I **had** more money, I **wouldn't need** to work overtime. 🔊 4.20
   If they **offered** you a part-time job, **would** you **take** it?
2. I **might meet** more people if I **lived** in a hall of residence.
   You **could apply** for a scholarship if you **got** a place to study in the USA.
3. If John **was (were)** here, he'**d know** what to do.
   I'**d take** it back to the shop if I **were** you.

- We use the second conditional to talk about a hypothetical or imaginary present / future situation, or one that we *don't* think is a possibility.
  1. The second conditional normally uses *if* + past simple, *would / wouldn't* + infinitive.
  2. We can use *might* or *could* instead of *would*.
  3. When we use *be* in the *if* clause, we can use *was* or *were* after *I / he / she / it*.

- However, in the phrase *if I were you*, which is often used to give advice, only *were* is used. **NOT** *If I was you.*

🔍 **First or second conditional**
The conditional we use depends on how likely the condition is. Compare:
If I have time, I'll help you. (I think it's a real possibility that I'll have time.)
If I had time, I'd help you. (I think it's unlikely or impossible that I'll have time.)

---

a Circle the correct form.

If I go to university, *I'd study / ~~I'll study~~* engineering.
1. If she had her own car, she *doesn't / wouldn't* need to borrow yours.
2. If I *got / get* a good degree, I'll find a better job.
3. I'd take the job if I *am / were* you.
4. We can't help you unless you *tell / told* us what the problem is.
5. If you *think / thought* you're going to be late, please send me a text.
6. *You might / You'll* give a better impression if you wore a suit.
7. I *won't / wouldn't* go there unless I really had to.
8. Dana would enjoy life more if she *didn't / doesn't* study all the time.
9. If I can't find a cheap bike, I *won't / wouldn't* buy one.
10. If I *earned / earn* more, I could afford to rent a flat.

b Complete the sentences with the verb in brackets.

I *wouldn't do* research if I didn't enjoy working on my own. (not do)
1. If I _____ to stay at university, I'll probably do a PhD or a master's degree. (decide)
2. If you didn't spend so much on clothes, you _____ borrow money all the time. (not have to)
3. I think my sister and her boyfriend _____ sooner if they could afford to pay for the wedding. (get married)
4. If I have time over the summer, I _____ for an internship. (apply)
5. I think Andy might get a scholarship if he _____ on working hard. (keep)
6. If we _____ a bigger house, we could rent a couple of rooms to students. (buy)
7. I might enjoy my job more if I _____ such awful colleagues. (not have)
8. If I don't like the job after six months, I _____. (not stay)
9. My tutor says I must attend all the seminars if I _____ to fail my exams. (not want)
10. I'd get more job offers if I _____ better qualified. (be)

◀ p.41

▶ **Go online** to review the grammar for each lesson

139

5A GRAMMAR BANK

present perfect simple

Revise the basics

+	–	past participle
I **have** You **have** He / She / It **has** We **have** They **have**	I**'ve** You**'ve** He / She / It**'s** We**'ve** They**'ve**	I **haven't** You **haven't** He / She / It **hasn't** We **haven't** They **haven't**	seen the news.

Have you **seen** the news?   Yes, I **have**. / No, I **haven't**.
Has he **seen** the news?   Yes, he **has**. / No, he **hasn't**.

🔊 5.9

1 I**'ve used** Netflix, but I **haven't used** Amazon Prime.
  Have you **ever watched** a foreign TV series?
  She**'s never liked** quiz shows.
2 I don't believe it! We**'ve won** £500 on the lottery!
  He**'s just sent** me a text – I'll tell you what it says.
3 **Have** / **Haven't** you **started** work yet?
  I **haven't talked** to her yet – I'm going to call her later.
4 A **Have** you **started** painting the kitchen?
  B Yes, and I**'ve already finished** it.
5 Sally**'s known** him for 20 years.
  We**'ve** only **had** a smart TV since last month.
  I**'ve been** out all morning.

1 We use the present perfect simple for past experiences if we don't say when they happened. If we say when they happened (*five minutes ago, yesterday, last week*, etc.) we use the past simple, e.g. *I've watched Netflix a few times. I watched six episodes of The Crown last weekend.*

2 We use the present perfect simple to give news. If something has happened very recently, we often use *just*.

3 We use the present perfect simple with *yet* to ask if something has happened, or to say that it hasn't happened, but that it will.
   • Negative questions *Haven't you…yet?* often express surprise or criticism.

4 We use the present perfect simple with *already* to say that something has happened, sometimes earlier than expected.

5 We can use the present perfect simple, especially with non-action verbs, to talk about situations that started in the past and have continued to the present. We don't use the present simple or the present continuous, e.g. *I've lived here for three months.* **NOT** *I live here for three months. / I'm living here for three months.*
   • To express a period of time we often use *for* or *since*.
   • We use *for* + a period of time, e.g. *for two minutes / ten years / ages / a long time*.
   • We use *since* + a time in the past, e.g. *since this morning / 5.00 / September / 2010 / I was a child*.
   • We can use phrases with *all* to express a period of time, e.g. *all my life, all day, all year*, etc. We don't use *for* with *all*, e.g. *I've been here all day.* **NOT** *I've been here for all day.*
   • For irregular past participles, see **Irregular verbs** p.165.

---

a Circle the correct form.

  Oh no! We're late! The film **has already started** / hasn't started yet.
1 This programme's been on **for** / **since** an hour.
2 I've **already had** / **haven't had** breakfast, so I'm not really hungry.
3 I've been to Canada, but **I never went** / **I've never been** to the USA.
4 We've known them **since we were at university** / **since five years**.
5 I've only been at work for an hour, but I've **just** / **already** done a lot.
6 They got married in May, so **they're married** / **they've been married** for six months.
7 You'll love New York – **have you been** / **did you go** there before?
8 He's lived here **since all his life** / **all his life**.
9 We've never been to Sweden, but **we went** / **we've been** to Norway last year.
10 Sorry, I can't meet you after work. I've **just** / **yet** had an email from my boss.

b Complete the sentences with the present perfect or past simple form of the verbs in brackets.

  Have you *ever been* to the Edinburgh Festival? (ever / be)
1 A _____ you _____ that wildlife documentary last night? (see)
  B No, I _____ it. (miss)
2 A When _____ you _____ here? (get)
  B I arrived at the weekend, so I _____ here for a few days. (only / be)
3 A _____ you _____ the match results? (check)
  B It _____ yet. It _____ late. (not finish, start)
4 A Bad news – Ben _____ a bike accident. (have)
  B Oh no! When _____ that _____? (happen)
5 A Where's Linda? She isn't at her desk.
  B I think she _____ for lunch. (just / go out)
6 A _____ you _____ him at tennis? (ever / beat)
  B No, but I _____ a set last time. (win)
7 A _____ Marcus _____ his new job? (already / start)
  B Yes, his first day _____ last Monday. (be)
8 A How long _____ you _____ a motorbike? (have)
  B Not long! I _____ it six months ago. (buy)

➔ p.47

5B

GRAMMAR BANK

present perfect continuous

Revise the basics

+	−	
I **have** You **have** He / She / It **has** We **have** They **have**	I**'ve** You**'ve** He / She / It**'s** We**'ve** They**'ve**	I **haven't** You **haven't** He / She / It **hasn't** We **haven't** They **haven't**	**been sleeping** well recently.

Have you **been sleeping** well recently?   Yes, I **have**. / No, I **haven't**.
Has he **been sleeping** well recently?   Yes, he **has**. / No, he **hasn't**.

1 A What **have** you **been doing** lately?   🔊 5.18
  B I**'ve been studying** for my exams.
  She**'s been going** for a walk every morning this week.
  John**'s been working** very late recently.
2 A You look tired.
  B I**'ve been working** in the garden.
  A You're covered in paint.
  B Yes, I**'ve been decorating** the kitchen all day.
3 How long **have** you **been looking for** a new job?
  We**'ve been living** here since last year.
  It**'s been raining** all day.

1 We use the present perfect continuous with action verbs for repeated actions that started in the past and have continued till now. We often use time expressions like *recently / lately*.

• With non-action verbs we use the present perfect simple, e.g. *I've known them for 10 years.* **NOT** *I've been knowing them for 10 years.*

2 We use the present perfect continuous for continuous actions which have visible present results.

3 We use the present perfect continuous to ask or talk about situations which started in the past and are still happening now. We often use *for / since* or time expressions like *all day / all morning / all week*. We don't use the present continuous or the present simple, e.g.

I've been waiting since 10 o'clock.
NOT *I'm waiting since 10 o'clock.*
I wait since 10 o'clock.

• If you say *when* something happened, use the past simple, not the present perfect continuous, e.g. *I've been watching a lot of TV lately. I saw a great programme last night.* **NOT** *I've been seeing a great programme last night.*

> 🔍 **work and live**
> These verbs can usually be used in either the present perfect simple or the present perfect continuous with no difference in meaning, e.g.
> *I've been living here for three months.*
> **OR** *I've lived here for three months.*

a Complete answers a–i with the present perfect continuous. Then match them to the questions.

  Why are your clothes so wet?   d
1 Why are you so late?
2 Do you want a coffee?
3 Are you going to move to London?
4 Are the children hungry?
5 Is her English good?
6 How's your new camera?
7 Why is Sally crying?
8 Do you think it's safe to drive?

 a She _____ a sad film on TV. (watch)
 b No, thanks. I _____ too much caffeine lately. (drink)
 c I don't think so. It _____ very heavily. (snow)
 d I *'ve been washing* the car. (wash)
 e No. They _____ biscuits all afternoon. (eat)
 f I hope so. We _____ a flat we can afford. (look for)
 g Yes, she _____ it for a long time. (learn)
 h It's great – I _____ pictures all day. (take)
 i I _____ in a traffic jam for two hours. (sit)

b (Circle) the correct form.

  (I've been working) / *I'm working* too hard lately.
1 *I've been living* / *I'm living* in a small village for five years.
2 Ania is really tired – *she's travelling* / *she's been travelling* a lot for work since February.
3 *I haven't been doing* / *I'm not doing* much exercise lately.
4 I arrived yesterday and *I've been staying* / *I'm staying* for two weeks.
5 He's not answering his phone – maybe *he's driving* / *he's been driving*.
6 At last! *I'm waiting* / *I've been waiting* for you for ages.
7 I can't stand this weather – *it's raining* / *it's been raining* all week.
8 Be quiet! *I've been trying* / *I'm trying* to concentrate.
9 *I've been seeing* / *I'm seeing* a lot of my family recently.
10 We need to get someone to look at the central heating. *It isn't working* / *It hasn't been working* properly for ages.

⬅ p.53

▶ Go online to review the grammar for each lesson

141

6A

GRAMMAR BANK

obligation, necessity, prohibition, advice

obligation and necessity

1 I **have to** work every evening. 🔊 6.7
  Do we **have to** leave a tip?
  They **had to** wait for two hours at the airport.
2 You **must** be more careful.
  Must I show ID at the door?
  You **must** pay him back as soon as possible.
3 I **need to** buy some food for tonight.
  Do we **need to** book a table?

1 We use *have to* to talk about all kinds of obligation. *have to* can be used in all tenses.
2 We also use *must* to talk about obligation. *must* is only used in the present tense. The meaning is similar to *have to*, but *must* is especially used when the speaker sees something as a personal obligation. Compare:
  I **have to** start work at 9.00. (an external obligation, the rule where I work)
  I **must** remember to book a table. (a personal obligation, one that I impose on myself)
3 We can use *need to* to talk about things that are necessary. *need to* can be used in all tenses.

no obligation / no necessity

1 You **don't have to** pay me now. 🔊 6.8
2 We **won't need to** take the car – it's walking distance from here.
3 You **needn't** hurry. We have plenty of time.

1 We use (*not*) *have to* when there is no obligation to do something.
2 We use (*not*) *need to* when it is not necessary to do something.
3 We can also use *needn't* + infinitive **without** *to* to say that it is not necessary to do something.

prohibition

You **mustn't** be rude to customers. 🔊 6.9
You **mustn't** serve alcohol to people under 18.

- We use *mustn't* when something is prohibited, dangerous, or wrong.
- *mustn't* and *don't have to* are completely different. Compare:
  You **mustn't** drive. You've been drinking. = Don't drive. (It's dangerous / wrong to do it).
  You **don't have to** drive. We can get the bus. = It's not necessary to drive. (There's no obligation or necessity.)

advice

1 You **should** try that new Vietnamese restaurant. 🔊 6.10
  He **shouldn't** drink so much coffee.
2 You **ought to** get a new phone.
  She **oughtn't to** spend so much on clothes.
3 When you're in Venice, you **must** / **have to** have a drink at Harry's Bar!

1 We use *should* / *shouldn't* to give someone advice, or to say what we think is the right thing for ourselves or for someone else to do.
2 We can also use *ought to* / *oughtn't to* to give advice. The meaning is the same as *should* / *shouldn't*.
3 We can use *must* and *have to* to give strong advice when we think it's very important that someone does something.

---

a Circle the correct form. Tick (✓) if both are possible.

  I **had to** / **must** buy a new fridge last week.
1 We **don't have to** / **mustn't** be at the airport until 5.00. Our flight isn't until 7.00.
2 You **needn't** / **don't have to** worry about getting a ticket in advance – you can pay on the train.
3 He **shouldn't** / **doesn't have to** have any more cake. He's already had three pieces.
4 You'll **have to** / You'll **need to** book a table if you want to go to Gino's on Saturday evening.
5 I **should** / **ought to** try to eat more vegetables.
6 We **don't need to** / **mustn't** leave yet. The show doesn't start until 7.30.
7 You **mustn't** / **don't have to** spill anything on the sofa – it's leather.
8 We **must** / **have to** go to the supermarket later. We've run out of coffee.
9 You **don't need to** / **needn't** phone me unless your train is delayed.
10 You **oughtn't to** / **don't have to** arrive late on your first day at work.

b Complete the sentences with one word. Contractions count as one word.

  I definitely think you *should* sell your house. It would be a really good idea.
1 You _____ turn your phone on until the plane has landed.
2 Here's the form. You _____ to sign it at the bottom.
3 I think perhaps you _____ to buy a new table, and maybe you should get some chairs as well.
4 We _____ have to leave until 2.30. It'll only take an hour to get there.
5 She _____ come if she doesn't want to. Nobody will mind.
6 Our journey back was a nightmare. We _____ to wait hours for the bus.
7 You _____ read his new book! You'll love it.
8 You _____ to drink so many fizzy drinks. They're really not good for you.
9 Do I _____ to write a thank-you letter or can I just send an email?

← p.58

6B GRAMMAR BANK

can, could, and be able to

ability, possibility, and permission

1 You **can** use a toothbrush to clean jewellery. 🔊 6.13
  I **can't** understand these instructions.
  We **can't** park here. It's a no-parking zone.
  She **could** swim when she was three years old.
  They **couldn't** come to the concert last night.
2 **Can** you give me a hand?
  Could I borrow your car?
3 I'**ve been able to** drive since I was 17.
  The technician **will be able to** fix it.
  I'd love to **be able to** ski.
  I like **being able to** try clothes on, so I never buy things online.
4 Unfortunately, we **are not able to** supply the missing parts.
  I'm very sorry that I **wasn't able to** attend the interview on Friday.
5 I **couldn't** find the book I wanted in the shops, but I **was able to** buy it online.
  The mark on the carpet was really bad, but in the end I **was able to** get it out.

1 We use *can* to talk about ability, possibility, and permission. *can* is a modal verb, and it only has a present form (which can be used to talk about the future) and a past / conditional form (*could*).
2 We often use *Can you / I…?* or *Could you / I…?* to make requests or ask for permission. *Could…?* is more polite.
3 For all other tenses and forms, we use *be able to* + infinitive.
4 We sometimes use *be able to* in the present and past if we want to be more formal.
5 If we want to talk about ability on **one specific occasion** in the past, we can use *couldn't* but **not** *could*. Instead, we use *was / were able to*.
• We can also use *managed to* instead of *was / were able to*, e.g. *I managed to buy it online.*

deduction

It **can't** be broken! I only bought it last week. 🔊 6.14
They **can't** be back yet. They said they were coming home on Sunday.

• We use *can't* to say we are sure that something is impossible / not true.
• In this sense, the opposite of *can't* is *must*. Compare:
  She can't be at work yet. It's only 7.30 a.m. (= I'm sure it's not true.)
  She must be at work now. It's 9.30 a.m. (= I'm sure it's true.)

---

a Are the highlighted forms right (✓) or wrong (✗)? Correct the wrong ones.

   I'm afraid it's broken and I won't can mend it. ✗
   I won't be able to
1 He can to sew really well – he makes all his own clothes.
2 The office is closed now, but you will can phone them on Monday.
3 He loves music – he could play the violin when he was four!
4 You couldn't be serious! The ball was definitely out.
5 I love this shopping centre. It's great to be able to buy everything in one place.
6 Ask the shop assistant – she might can help you.
7 I tried to phone the bank, but I wasn't able to speak to the manager.
8 Will I be able use my UK credit card when I'm in the USA?
9 I bought a new bike yesterday – I could get 10% off by paying cash.
10 This camera's really cheap – it can't be very good.

b Complete the sentences with the correct form of *can*, *could*, or *be able to*.

   I got a puncture, but I *was able to* change the wheel myself.
1 This screw is much too short – it _____ be the right one.
2 I prefer real clothes shops to shopping online. I hate not _____ try things on.
3 If we _____ afford it, we'd eat out every week.
4 _____ you see if they have these jeans in my size?
5 If it doesn't fit you, you should _____ change it.
6 They _____ find the book anywhere in the UK, so they ordered it from a US website.
7 I've never _____ pronounce her name correctly.
8 Fifty pounds for two pairs of socks? They _____ cost that much!
9 I spent ages looking for the right paint, and in the end I _____ find the perfect colour.
10 She's got a beautiful voice. I'd love _____ sing like that.

→ p.61

💬 Go online to review the grammar for each lesson

143

7A GRAMMAR BANK

phrasal verbs

Type 1 – phrasal verbs with no object

I **get up** at 6.00.
I'm going to **be away** for three days next week.
What time are you **coming back** tonight?
They **set off** early in the morning.
The plane **took off** late, but we still arrived on time.

- Some phrasal verbs have no object. The verb and the particle can't be separated. **NOT** *I get at 6.00 up.*

Type 2 – phrasal verbs with an object – separable

1 Can you **fill** this bank form **in**?
  Can you **fill in** this bank form?
  Please **put** your clothes **away**.
  Please **put away** your clothes.
  Did you **switch** the computer **off**?
  Did you **switch off** the computer?
2 Can you **fill** it **in**?
  Please **put** them **away**.
  Did you **switch** it **off**?

1 Some phrasal verbs have an object and can be separated – we can put the object before or after the particle.
2 If the object is a pronoun (*it*, *them*, etc.), it *always* goes between the verb and the particle.
  I switched it off. **NOT** *I switched off it.*

Type 3 – phrasal verbs with an object – inseparable

1 My sister and I both **take after** our father.
  A Where's your phone?
  B I don't know. I'm **looking for** it.
  A How are you managing until you find a job?
  B We're **living on** my wife's salary.
2 My boyfriend doesn't **get on with** his parents.
  Jane's **looking forward to** her holiday.

1 Some phrasal verbs have an object but can't be separated – the verb and the particle must stay together, even if the object is a pronoun.
  We take after our father. We take after him.
  NOT *We take our father after. We take him after.*
2 Some phrasal verbs have two particles – they are never separated.

---

a Circle the correct form. Tick (✓) if both are possible.

Shall I *switch on the air conditioning / switch the air conditioning on*? ✓

1 I went to the cashpoint and *took out €100 / took €100 out*.
2 The pasta was cold, so I *sent back it / sent it back*.
3 Could you *turn down the music / turn the music down*? It's very loud.
4 They *live off their parents / live their parents off*.
5 I decided I didn't like my new coat, so I *took back it / took it back* to the shop.
6 I *picked up the man's wallet / picked the man's wallet up* for him.
7 My sister lent me some money, but I haven't *paid back her / paid her back* yet.
8 I *set up our new computer / set our new computer up* at the weekend.
9 I *grew up in Wales / grew in Wales up*.
10 I'm afraid we're *out of these trousers / out these trousers of*.

b Complete the sentences using a pronoun and the correct form of the phrasal verb in brackets.

Your phone's ringing. Quick, *turn it off*. (turn off)
1 My parents are arriving at 11.15. Could you _____ at the airport? (pick up)
2 A When do you leave on your trip to China?
  B Next Saturday. I'm really _____. (look forward to)
3 A Do they still have their website?
  B No, they _____ a month ago. (close down)
4 A Excuse me madam, have you finished your steak?
  B Yes, I can't eat any more. Please _____. (take away)
5 A Have you found your glasses yet?
  B No, and I've been _____ for half an hour! (look for)
6 A What did you do with your old computer?
  B I _____. (give away)
7 This cheese is past its sell-by date. I'm going to _____. (throw away)
8 She was with her husband for 20 years, and she _____ during his final illness. (look after)
9 A Have they brought the bill?
  B No, but I've _____. (ask for)
10 A Is the TV loud enough?
   B No. Could you _____ a bit? (turn up)

p.68

144

7B GRAMMAR BANK

verb patterns

Revise the basics

infinitive with to
1 It's very difficult **to read** his writing.
   NOT *It's very difficult read…*
2 I need **to go** to the supermarket.
   NOT *I need go…*
3 I went to the cinema **to see** the new James Bond film.
   NOT *I went to the cinema for to see…*
4 Be careful **not to stay** in the sun too long.
   NOT *Be careful to not stay…*

infinitive without to
5 He can **speak** five languages.
   NOT *He can to speak…*
6 We mustn't **be** late.
   NOT *We mustn't to be late.*

gerund (verb + -ing)
7 **Watching** TV helps me to relax in the evening.
   NOT *Watch TV helps me…*
8 I'm not very good at **remembering** names.
   NOT *I'm not very good at remember…*
9 I love **getting up** early in the summer.
   NOT *I love get…*
10 I hate **not seeing** the children at bathtime.
   NOT *I hate not see the children…*

- For a list of **verb patterns**, see p.164.

verbs + infinitive (with or without to)

1 Mandy **agreed to come** with me. 🔊 7.20
  They **decided to go** home early.
  We **wanted to visit** the Tate Gallery.
2 We **can't buy** the tickets till tomorrow.
  There's a lot of traffic – we **might be** a bit late.
  You **shouldn't drink** so much coffee.

1 We use the infinitive with *to* after many verbs. See p.164 for examples.
2 We use the infinitive without *to* after all modal verbs (except *ought*).

verbs + gerund (verb + -ing)

1 They **enjoy watching** films at home. 🔊 7.21
  I**'ve finished reading** the paper if you want it.
2 She**'s given up working** on Saturdays.
  I'm **looking forward to hearing** from you.
  Are you going to **carry on studying** English next year?

1 We use the gerund after some verbs, e.g. *enjoy, finish, hate*.
2 We use the gerund after phrasal verbs.

verbs + object + infinitive (with or without to)

1 They **want us to go** on holiday with them. 🔊 7.22
  Liam **told me not to tell** anyone his news.
  My parents don't **allow me to wear** make-up.
2 His parents **let him go** to the concert.
  Our boss **makes us work** late on Fridays.

1 We use an object + the infinitive with *to* after some verbs.
   NOT *They want that we go with them.* See p.164 for examples.
2 We use an object + the infinitive without *to* after *let* and *make*.

---

a Complete the sentences with the correct form of the verbs in brackets.

   We really enjoy *going* to concerts. (go)
1 We went to the box office _____ the tickets. (pick up)
2 _____ to a live sporting event is much more exciting than _____ it on TV. (go, watch)
3 I hate _____ to visit my family more often, but they live so far away. (not be able)
4 I tried _____ tickets for the concert, but I didn't manage _____ any. (buy, get)
5 Nowadays, it's cheaper _____ to the theatre than to a football match. (go)
6 She moved from London to a small village and she really misses _____ to plays and exhibitions. (go)
7 They told me _____ in the front row. (not sit)
8 We needn't _____. Amy's always late. (hurry)
9 I can't afford _____ in the city centre. (live)
10 Now it's difficult _____ _____ a mobile phone. (imagine, not have)

b Complete the second sentence so that it means the same as the first.

   I didn't remember to turn my phone off.
   I forgot *to turn my phone off*.
1 They asked me to go to the cinema, and I agreed.
   They persuaded _____.
2 He said he wouldn't help her.
   He refused _____ her.
3 Karen's teacher allowed her to leave school early.
   Karen's teacher let _____ school early.
4 My husband said, 'You should go to the dentist's.'
   My husband wants _____ to the dentist's.
5 The police ordered him to move his car.
   The police made _____ his car.
6 I practise the piano for 20 minutes a day.
   I spend 20 minutes a day _____ the piano.
7 They asked if we wanted to have dinner with them.
   They invited _____ with them.
8 We don't go to concerts any more.
   We've given up _____ concerts.

↩ p.72

Go online to review the grammar for each lesson

8A

GRAMMAR BANK

have something done

How often **do** you **have** your car **serviced**?
I **don't have** the flat **cleaned**. I clean it myself.
She **has** her house **repainted** every few years.
I**'m having** my hair **cut** tomorrow.
We**'ve had** a new bathroom **put in**.
The flat was in good condition, so we **didn't have** it **redecorated**.
When **did** you **have** those photos **taken**?
We're **going** to **have** the carpets **cleaned** next week.
You ought to **have** your roof **repaired**.

- We use *have* + object + past participle when we arrange (and usually pay) for someone to do something for us, either because we can't or don't want to do it ourselves. Compare:

I cleaned my car yesterday.
(= I did it myself.)

I had my car cleaned yesterday.
(= I paid someone to clean it for me.)

8.1

- We can use *have something done* in any tense and with modal verbs and other verb patterns, e.g. gerunds or infinitives.
- *have* is the main verb and is stressed. We use auxiliary verbs (*do*, *did*, etc.) to make questions and negatives.
- If we want to say who did the work, we use *by*, e.g. *We had our wedding photos taken **by the same photographer you used**.*
*I had the central heating checked **by British Gas**.*

> **Using *get* instead of *have***
> In this structure, we can also use *get* instead of *have*, e.g. *I'm going to have my hair cut = I'm going to get my hair cut.*

a Put the words in the correct order to make sentences.

I (my hair had yesterday cut).
I had my hair cut yesterday.

1 Have (eyes your tested had recently you)?
2 We (to repaired don't have roof the need).
3 I (never whitened teeth have my would).
4 My sister (hair to cut not told short my me have).
5 It's (expensive the to have too replaced carpets).
6 He's (have to his taken going photo).
7 My (faces at children had festival the their painted).
8 We (have ought air conditioning to fixed the).
9 I (shopping the had cleaned my at centre car).
10 I (have before renewed passport go I holiday on to my have).

b Write sentences about the people in the pictures. Use the correct form of *have something done*.

He / hair / cut   *He's having his hair cut.*
1 She / need / her car / service
2 He / his front door / replace
3 I / the lock / change
4 They / should / their windows / clean
5 She / ought to / her shopping / deliver
6 He / not want / his photo / take
7 She / her portrait / paint
8 He / want / his suit / dry-clean

↩ p.76

146

8B GRAMMAR BANK

the passive
forms of the passive

present simple	The site **is visited** by thousands of people every year.
present continuous	The castle **is being restored** at the moment.
present perfect	The King's body **has never been found**.
past simple	10,000 soldiers **were killed** in an hour at the Battle of Gettysburg.
past continuous	The bridge was closed because it **was being repaired**.
past perfect	The hospital **had been opened** by the Queen three years before.
will and be going to	When **will** the new museum **be built**? We **are going to be given** our exam results tomorrow.
infinitive with to	The city centre has **to be closed** to all traffic next weekend.
infinitive without to	The President must **be elected** by a clear majority.
gerund	Most people hate **being woken up** in the middle of the night.

🔊 8.11

- We often use the passive when it's not said, known, or important who does an action. *My phone has been stolen.* (= Somebody has stolen my phone, but we don't know who.)
- If we want to say who did an action in a passive structure, we use *by*. *The Sagrada Familia was designed by Antoni Gaudi.*
- The subject of a passive sentence can be the direct or the indirect object, e.g.
  Active: They are going to give **us** (indirect object) **our exam results** (direct object) tomorrow.
  Passive: We are going to be given our exam results tomorrow. OR Our exam results are going to be given to us tomorrow.
- We often use the passive to talk about processes, for example, scientific processes, and in formal writing, such as newspaper reports.
  The chemicals are combined at very high temperatures.
  Parts of Windsor Castle have been damaged in a fire.

> 🔍 **Active or passive?**
> We can often say things in two ways, in the active or the passive.
> 1 Using active or passive changes the focus.
>   Compare:
>   The royal family **owns** Windsor Castle.
>   (**Active:** The focus is more on the owner.)
>   Windsor Castle **is owned** by the royal family.
>   (**Passive:** The focus is more on the castle.)
> 2 The passive is often used for a more formal style.
>   Compare:
>   They **grow** rice in Valencia.
>   (**Active:** informal – they = people, farmers)
>   Rice **is grown** in Valencia.
>   (**Passive:** a more formal style)

a Complete the sentences with the correct passive form of the verb in brackets.

The Guggenheim Museum in Bilbao *was opened* in 1997. (open)
1 Many roads _____ to traffic for the carnival last month. (close)
2 In recent years, many books _____ about the American Civil War. (write)
3 A new shopping centre _____ in the town centre at the moment. (build)
4 I think you should _____ to take photos in the museum if you don't use flash. (allow)
5 The last battle on British soil _____ at Culloden in 1746. (fight)
6 Washington, DC _____ by nearly 20 million people every year. (visit)
7 I love _____ round a city by someone who knows it well. (show)
8 The gallery was closed because a TV series _____ inside. (film)
9 I _____ by the neighbour's noisy dog three times already this week. (wake up)
10 Picasso's famous painting *Guernica* can _____ in the Reina Sofia Museum in Madrid. (see)

b Complete the second sentence so that it means the same as the first.

Someone's stolen my bike!   My bike *'s been stolen*.
1 They had to close the palace for renovations.
  The palace _____.
2 You can find more information on the website.
  More information _____.
3 Martin Luther King gave the famous 'I have a dream' speech in 1963.
  The famous 'I have a dream' speech _____.
4 A seat belt must be worn at all times.
  You _____.
5 Do you think they're going to offer you the job?
  Do you think you're _____?
6 The previous church had been destroyed by a fire.
  A fire _____.
7 Your phone has to be turned off during take-off and landing.
  You _____.
8 They're going to open a new visitor centre next year.
  A new visitor centre _____.
9 They won't finish the new hospital until July.
  The new hospital _____.
10 They grow tea in Sri Lanka.
  Tea _____.   ➔ p.80

> 🔗 **Go online** to review the grammar for each lesson

147

9A GRAMMAR BANK

reported speech

Revise the basics

direct statements	reported statements
'I **have** a good memory.'	She said (that) **she had** a good memory.
'I**'m not** leaving.'	He told me (that) **he wasn't** leaving.
'We**'ll** never forget you.'	They told me (that) **they'd never forget** me.
'I **can't** remember.'	He said (that) **he couldn't** remember.
'We **might / may** be a bit late.'	They told us (that) **they might** be a bit late.
'I **must** go.'	She said (that) **she had to** go.

word changes in reported speech

'I'll see **you tomorrow**.'	He said (that) **he**'d see **me the next day**.	9.2
'I did it **yesterday**.'	She told me (that) **she**'d done it **the day before**.
'I went skiing **last week**.'	He said (that) **he**'d been skiing **the week before**.
'**We** don't like it **here**.'	She told us (that) **they** didn't like it **there**.
'**This** is **your** station.'	She said (that) **that** was **our** station.

- Remember that when we report direct speech some time after the original words were said, we change pronouns and possessive adjectives, time expressions, and words like *here* and *this*.

reported questions

1 'What **do you want** to do?' She asked me what **I wanted** to do. 9.3
  '**When's your** birthday?' She asked me when **my** birthday **was**.
2 '**Have you been** to Australia?' He asked us if / whether **we'd been** to Australia.
  '**Are you coming** with me?' She asked him if / whether **he was coming** with **her**.

1 In reported questions, we change the tenses as with reported statements.
- Reported questions have normal word order, auxiliaries *do/did* are not used, nor are question marks: *She asked me what I wanted to do.*
  NOT ~~She asked me what did I want to do?~~
- The verb *ask* in reported questions can be used with or without a subject or object pronoun. e.g. *She asked what I wanted to do.*
- With the verb *be*, the word order changes in the reported question.
2 We use *if* or *whether* to report questions which start with an auxiliary verb.

reported imperatives and requests

1 '**Wait** in the car.' 9.4
  She **told me to wait** in the car.
  '**Don't forget**.'
  He **told me not to forget**.
2 '**Could you close** the window?'
  She **asked me to close** the window.
  '**Can you wait** here, please?'
  He **asked us to wait** there.

1 We can use *tell* + object pronoun + infinitive to report imperatives and instructions.
- The verb *tell* can mean *give information* or *give an instruction*. Compare:
  He told me (that) his name was Rob. (= information)
  He told me to close the door. (= instruction)
2 We can use *ask* + object pronoun + infinitive to report requests (when you ask someone politely to do something). We must use an object pronoun, e.g. *me, us*.
- The verb *ask* can mean *ask a question* or *make a request*. Compare:
  He asked (me) what I was doing. (= question)
  He asked me to close the door. (= request)

---

a Complete the sentences using reported speech.

'I don't know your email.'
He said (that)…*he didn't know my email.*
1 'I can't find my purse.' She said (that)…
2 'I'm not coming to class on Friday.' He said (that)…
3 'We probably won't go on holiday this summer.' They said (that)…
4 'I've finished my exams!' Jane said (that)…
5 'The film will be on tomorrow.' They told us (that)…
6 'I haven't been here before.' Robert told me (that)…
7 'I must leave at 6.30.' She said (that)…
8 'We've never forgotten our visit.' They told me (that)…
9 'I saw a man hiding in the bushes.' He said (that)…
10 'I don't really want to see you.' She told me (that)…

b Complete the reported questions, requests, and imperatives.

'Where do you live?' He asked me…*where I lived.*
1 'How many children do you have?' She asked him…
2 'Could you take a photo of us?' They asked the woman…
3 'Will you be able to come?' They asked us…
4 'Please fill in the application form.' He told me…
5 'Did you arrive on time?' He asked her…
6 'Bring plenty of food.' She told us…
7 'Can you help me with the cooking?' She asked me…
8 'How long have you been waiting?' He asked them…
9 'Can you confirm your date of birth?' He asked her…
10 'Don't worry about anything.' They told us…

p.87

9B

GRAMMAR BANK

third conditional and other uses of the past perfect

third conditional

If I**'d known** his number, I **would have called** him. 🔊 9.13
They**'d have been** much happier if they **'d** never **married**.
If I **hadn't gone** to university, I **wouldn't have met** my wife.
What **would we have done** if we **'d missed** the flight?

- We use the third conditional to talk about how things could have been different in the past, i.e. for hypothetical / imaginary situations and their consequences. In the third conditional, we use *if* + past perfect, *would have* + past participle.

🔍 **'d**
In third conditionals, *'d* is the contraction of both *had* and *would*, e.g. *If I'd known his number, I'd have called him.*
↑ ↑
had would

other uses of the past perfect

1. When we arrived at the departure gate, the flight 🔊 9.14
   had already **closed**.
   When the film started, I realized that I**'d seen** it before.
   We still **hadn't had** breakfast when the taxi arrived.
   How long **had** they **been** engaged before they got married?
2. 'We haven't been married long.'
   She said (that) they **hadn't been** married long.
   'My boyfriend proposed to me in Paris.'
   She told me (that) her boyfriend **had proposed** to her in Paris.
   'I'd already seen the film.'
   He said (that) he**'d** already **seen** the film.

1. We use the past perfect in narratives when we are talking about the past and we want to talk about something that happened earlier in the past.
- Compare:
  *When we arrived at the departure gate, the flight **closed*** (= we were on time).
  *When we arrived at the departure gate, the flight **had closed*** (= we were too late).
2. We use the past perfect in reported speech when the original speech uses the present perfect or the past simple.
- If the original speech is past perfect, there is no change in reported speech.

---

a Complete the third conditional sentences with the correct form of the verbs in brackets.

If we *'d missed* the bus, we *wouldn't have got* home till midnight. (miss, not get)
1. She _____ in love with him if he _____ her laugh so much. (not fall, not make)
2. If they _____ to the wedding, they _____. (invite, go)
3. I _____ our anniversary if you _____ me. (forget, not remind)
4. If we _____ earlier, we _____ our train. (leave, not miss)
5. If you _____ in advance, you _____ your money. (not pay, not lose)
6. If they _____ enough money, they _____ a flat instead of renting one. (have, buy)
7. I _____ better if I _____ a coffee after dinner. (sleep, not drink)
8. Jane and I _____ touch if she _____ abroad. (not lose, not move)
9. If I _____ you had a problem, I _____ to help. (know, offer)
10. If he _____ at the policeman, he _____. (not shout, not be arrested)

b Complete the sentences with the past simple or past perfect form of the verbs in brackets.

When she *woke up*, the house was empty – he *'d gone*. (wake up, go)
1. I _____ that play very much, even though I _____ it three times before. (enjoy, see)
2. He _____ he _____ for the company for six months. (say, work)
3. She still _____ at 10.00, so I _____ the house without her. (not get up, leave)
4. We _____ an hour looking for Carol, but she _____. (spend, disappear)
5. He _____ across the road, but the taxi _____ by someone else. (run, already / take)
6. I _____ get on the flight because they _____ it. (not can, overbook)
7. I _____ in Sydney for a week when I first _____ Sally. (only / be, meet)
8. She _____ me if I _____ China before. (ask, visit)
9. They _____ me they _____ engaged. (tell, just / get)
10. The shop _____ yet, but there _____ already a lot of people waiting outside. (not open, be)

⬅ p.91

🔵 Go online to review the grammar for each lesson   149

10A

GRAMMAR BANK

be, do, and have: auxiliary and main verbs

be – main verb and auxiliary

1 **A** Where**'s** my bag? **B** It**'s** over there. 🔊 10.2
  I **was** very sensitive when I **was** a child.
  They haven't **been** here before.
2 I**'m** sitting on the bus.
  They **aren't** coming to the party.
  I **was** cycling to work when I saw him.
  Were they waiting for you when you arrived?
  She**'s been** learning Japanese for two years.
  They **haven't been** working here for very long.
  A new concert hall **is being** built – it will open next year.
  My car **has been** stolen!

1 We can use *be* as the main verb in a sentence.
2 *be* is also an auxiliary verb.
- We use *am / is / are* as auxiliaries in the present continuous.
- We use *was / were* as auxiliaries in the past continuous.
- We use *has been / have been* as auxiliaries in the present perfect continuous.
- We use all tenses of *be* as auxiliaries in passives.

do – main verb and auxiliary

1 What are you **doing**? 🔊 10.3
  I **did** my homework last night.
2 She **doesn't** speak English. Where **do** they live?
  They **didn't** go to the theatre. **Did** you enjoy the film?

1 We can use *do* as the main verb in a sentence.
2 We use *do / don't / does / doesn't* as auxiliaries in the present simple, and *did / didn't* as auxiliaries in the past simple.

have – main verb and auxiliary

1 I **have** two brothers and a sister. 🔊 10.4
  He**'s having** a shower at the moment.
  What did you **have** for dinner?
2 I **have to** be at the airport at 11.00.
  We **had** our computer repaired last week.
3 They**'ve** bought a new car.
  I **haven't** seen him recently.
  Has he ever been to Spain?
4 I was sure I**'d** seen him before.
  We were hungry because we **hadn't** had breakfast.
  Had she tried to phone you before she arrived?

1 We can use *have* as the main verb in a sentence. It can be an action or non-action verb. See **2A** p.134.
2 With *have to* and *have something done*, *have* is a main verb.
3 We use *have / haven't / has / hasn't* as auxiliaries in the present perfect.
4 We use *had / hadn't* as auxiliaries in the past perfect.

---

a Complete the sentences with the correct form of the auxiliary verb *be*, *do*, or *have*.

Does he like living in the UK, or *is* he feeling homesick?

1 **A** _____ you ever been to the USA?
  B No, my husband _____ like flying.
2 **A** _____ you miss the beginning of the film?
  B No, luckily it _____ started yet.
3 _____ he know we _____ coming, or do we need to give him a ring?
4 I'm sorry I _____ answer the phone when you called, but I _____ having a meeting.
5 We _____ often travel outside Europe, but we _____ been to Chile twice.
6 He _____ been working since 7.00 this morning, but now he _____ gone home.
7 **A** Where _____ Melanie going on holiday this year?
  B Rome, I think. She _____ never been there before.
8 They're in New York, but they _____ have much time for sightseeing – they _____ only staying for two days.

b Complete the sentences with the correct form of the main verb *be*, *do*, or *have*.

What *have* you *been doing* since I last saw you? (do)

1 I would have finished the exercise if I _____ more time. (have)
2 She _____ to Africa before, so she's really looking forward to our trip to Namibia. (not be)
3 I _____ steak for lunch and it was delicious. (have)
4 Nothing _____ at the moment to solve the problem. (do)
5 Where _____ you at 10 o'clock this morning? (be)
6 I _____ a shower when the hot water stopped working! (have)
7 I _____ really annoyed if you'd repeated what I told you. (be)
8 The reception was a great success, and a good time _____ by all. (have)
9 I _____ the washing-up as soon as I finish my homework. (do)

← p.96

150

10B GRAMMAR BANK

revision of verb forms

a Complete the conversation with the correct form of the verb in brackets.

Tina Hi Roger, how <u>are</u> (be) you?
Roger Hi Tina. I'm exhausted – I ¹_____ (work) really hard all week.
Tina Is that why you ²_____ (not come) out with us last night?
Roger Yes, I ³_____ (not can) come because I ⁴_____ (study). My last exam ⁵_____ (start) at 9.00 tomorrow morning.
Tina Really? I ⁶_____ (finish) all my exams!
Roger Lucky you! What ⁷_____ you _____ (plan) to do now they're over?
Tina I ⁸_____ (fly) to Australia in three days. I ⁹_____ (always / want) to go there, ever since my aunt and uncle ¹⁰_____ (move) there five years ago, but I ¹¹_____ (not have) time until now.
Roger Fantastic – I'm sure you ¹²_____ (love) it.
Tina I hope so! What about you? I ¹³_____ (see) Mary yesterday and she ¹⁴_____ (say) you ¹⁵_____ (invite) her to go to France.
Roger Yes, but unfortunately she ¹⁶_____ (already / make) other plans.
Tina And what about tomorrow evening? ¹⁷_____ you _____ (celebrate)?
Roger Yes, I ¹⁸_____ (think) of going to that new pizzeria with some friends. ¹⁹_____ you _____ (want) to come along?
Tina Yes, that would be great – I ²⁰_____ (see) you tomorrow. And good luck with the exam!

b Complete the second sentence so that it means the same as the first. Use the correct form of the verbs in brackets.

He cleaned the windows and earned £20. (pay)
He <u>was paid</u> £20 for cleaning the windows.

1 She first met him 20 years ago. (know)
She _____ him for 20 years.
2 It's not necessary for you to bring any money. (need)
You _____ to bring any money.
3 I can't repair the chair because I don't have any glue. (have)
If I _____ some glue, I could repair the chair.
4 I learnt to swim when I was five. (be able, swim)
I _____ since I was five.
5 What are your plans after you graduate? (go)
What _____ to do after you graduate?
6 He says it would be good to include a covering letter. (suggest, include)
He _____ a covering letter.
7 The President opened the concert hall in 2019. (open)
The concert hall _____ in 2019.
8 I had much longer hair when I was younger. (used, have)
I _____ much longer hair when I was younger.
9 You can pay me back tomorrow. (not have to)
You _____ pay me back until tomorrow.
10 She started learning Russian two months ago. (learn)
She _____ Russian for two months.
11 Somebody had stolen his car so he phoned the police. (steal)
He phoned the police because his car _____.
12 My boss said I could leave work early. (let, leave)
My boss _____ me _____ work early.
13 She accepted the wedding invitation. (say, can)
She _____ come to the wedding.
14 The photo was out of focus because I moved the camera. (move)
The photo would have been in focus if I _____ the camera.
15 They shouldn't be so careless. (ought, be)
They _____ more careful.

← p.103

Go online to review the grammar for each lesson

151

Adjective suffixes

VOCABULARY BANK

1 DESCRIBING PEOPLE

a Add an ending to the nouns and verbs below and make any other small changes necessary to form adjectives. Write them in the correct column.

a<u>ffec</u>tion /əˈfekʃn/   a<u>ssert</u> /əˈsɜːt/   a<u>ttract</u> /əˈtrækt/
com<u>pass</u>ion /kəmˈpæʃn/   con<u>sider</u> /kənˈsɪdə/
cre<u>ate</u> /kriˈeɪt/   <u>envy</u> /ˈenvi/   <u>glamour</u> /ˈglæmə/
help /help/   <u>impulse</u> /ˈɪmpʌls/   love /lʌv/
po<u>ssess</u> /pəˈzes/   <u>power</u> /paʊə/   re<u>bel</u> /rɪˈbel/
re<u>ly</u> /rɪˈlaɪ/   res<u>ponse</u> /rɪˈspɒns/   thought /θɔːt/

> 🔍 **Word endings for adjectives**
> Many adjectives are formed by adding suffixes (= endings) such as *-able / -ible* to a noun or verb. Sometimes another small spelling change is required, e.g. losing a final *e* (*fame – famous*).
> Check the spelling changes in your dictionary.
> Knowing typical suffixes will help you to recognize that a new word is an adjective.

-able / -ible	-ate	-ive	-ous	-ful
so<u>cia</u>ble sen<u>si</u>ble	<u>passion</u>ate affectionate	<u>sensi</u>tive	am<u>bi</u>tious	su<u>ccess</u>ful

b 🔊 1.9 Listen and check.

ACTIVATION Cover the chart and look at the nouns and verbs in **a**. Say the adjectives.

'I was a very rebellious teenager.'

2 DESCRIBING PLACES AND THINGS

a Add an ending to the nouns and verbs below and make any other small changes necessary to form adjectives. Write them in the correct column.

a<u>fford</u> /əˈfɔːd/   <u>colour</u> /ˈkʌlə/   <u>comfort</u> /ˈkʌmfət/
de<u>sire</u> /dɪˈzaɪə/   dirt /dɜːt/   ex<u>pense</u> /ɪkˈspens/
health /helθ/   im<u>press</u> /ɪmˈpres/   <u>luxury</u> /ˈlʌkʃəri/
mess /mes/   noise /nɔɪz/   peace /piːs/   <u>profit</u> /ˈprɒfɪt/
rest /rest/   risk /rɪsk/   space /speɪs/   stress /stres/
suit /suːt/

-able	-y	-ive	-ous	-ful
recog<u>ni</u>zable affordable	<u>ea</u>sy	a<u>ddic</u>tive	<u>dange</u>rous	<u>use</u>ful

b 🔊 1.10 Listen and check.

ACTIVATION Cover the chart and look at the nouns and verbs in **a**. Say the adjectives.

3 -FUL AND -LESS

> 🔍 **-ful and -less**
> *-ful* and *-less* are suffixes which add the meaning 'with' or 'without' to the base word, e.g. *careful* = with care, *careless* = without care, *hopeful* = with hope, *hopeless* = without hope.
> However, not all words which can form an adjective with *-ful* can also form one with *-less*, e.g. we can say *successful* but **NOT** *successless*, and not all words which can form an adjective with *-less* can also form one with *-ful*, e.g. we can say *endless* but **NOT** *endful*.

a Look at the *-ful* adjectives in the charts in **1** and **2**. Tick the ones that <u>can</u> form an adjective with *-less*.

b 🔊 1.11 Listen and check.

⬅ p.10

152

Packing

VOCABULARY BANK

1 THINGS TO TAKE ON HOLIDAY

a Match the words and photos.

Electronics
- [ ] adaptor /əˈdæptə/
- [ ] batteries /ˈbætriz/
- [ ] (phone) charger /ˈtʃɑːdʒə/
- [1] earphones /ˈɪəfəʊnz/
- [ ] hairdryer /ˈheədraɪə/
- [ ] headphones /ˈhedfəʊnz/
- [ ] travel iron /ˈtrævl aɪən/

Toiletries
- [ ] brush /brʌʃ/
- [ ] comb /kəʊm/
- [ ] deodorant /diˈəʊdərənt/
- [ ] insect repellent /ˈɪnsekt rɪpelənt/
- [ ] make-up /ˈmeɪk ʌp/
- [ ] razor /ˈreɪzə/
- [ ] (nail) scissors /ˈsɪzəz/
- [ ] shampoo /ʃæmˈpuː/
- [ ] sunscreen /ˈsʌnskriːn/
- [ ] toothbrush /ˈtuːθbrʌʃ/
- [ ] toothpaste /ˈtuːθpeɪst/
- [ ] washbag /ˈwɒʃbæg/ (also sponge bag /ˈspʌndʒ bæg/)

Clothes and shoes
- [ ] bathrobe /ˈbɑːθrəʊb/ (or dressing gown /ˈdresɪŋ gaʊn/)
- [ ] flip-flops /ˈflɪp flɒps/
- [ ] pyjamas /pəˈdʒɑːməz/
- [ ] rain jacket /ˈreɪn dʒækɪt/ (or raincoat /ˈreɪnkəʊt/)
- [ ] slippers /ˈslɪpəz/
- [ ] sun hat /ˈsʌn hæt/
- [ ] swimming trunks /ˈswɪmɪŋ trʌŋks/
- [ ] swimsuit /ˈswɪmsuːt/
- [ ] underwear /ˈʌndəweə/

Others
- [ ] beach bag /ˈbiːtʃ bæg/
- [ ] first-aid kit /ˌfɜːst ˈeɪd kɪt/
- [ ] guidebook /ˈgaɪdbʊk/
- [ ] pack of cards /ˌpæk əv ˈkɑːdz/
- [ ] towel /ˈtaʊəl/

b ◆ 2.1 Listen and check.

ACTIVATION Cover the words and look at the photos. Say the words.

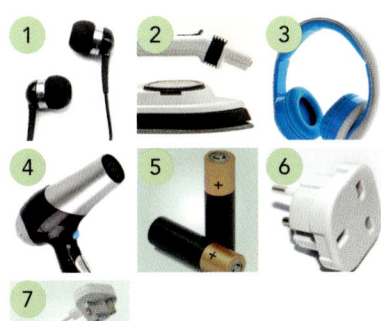

2 DOCUMENTS YOU MAY NEED

a Match the documents to the reasons why you need them on holiday.

1 [ ] passport or ID card
2 [ ] visa
3 [ ] travel insurance documents
4 [ ] driving licence
5 [ ] booking confirmation

a if you are travelling to a country which requires one, e.g. the USA
b if you want to rent a car
c in case you have an accident or another problem
d to allow you to leave and enter a country
e to prove to a hotel or airline that you have paid for a room, flight, etc.

b ◆ 2.2 Listen and check.

ACTIVATION Which of these documents do you usually take with you when you travel?

3 PACKING VERBS

a Match the words and photos.
- [ ] fold (clothes) /fəʊld/
- [ ] pack (a suitcase) /pæk/
- [ ] roll up (clothes) /ˌrəʊl ˈʌp/
- [ ] unpack /ʌnˈpæk/
- [ ] wrap (fragile things) /ræp/

b ◆ 2.3 Listen and check.

← p.16

Go online to review the vocabulary for each lesson

153

Shops and services

VOCABULARY BANK

1 PLACES

a Match the words and photos.

- baker's /ˈbeɪkəz/
- barber's /ˈbɑːbəz/
- butcher's /ˈbʊtʃəz/
- car showroom /ˈʃəʊruːm/
- chain store /ˈtʃeɪn stɔː/
- chemist's /ˈkemɪsts/
- deli /ˈdeli/
- DIY store /ˌdiː aɪ ˈwaɪ stɔː/
- dry-cleaner's /ˌdraɪ ˈkliːnəz/
- estate agent's /ɪˈsteɪt eɪdʒənts/
- fishmonger's /ˈfɪʃmʌŋɡəz/
- florist's /ˈflɒrɪsts/
- garden centre /ˈɡɑːdn sentə/
- greengrocer's /ˈɡriːnɡrəʊsəz/
- hairdresser's /ˈheədresəz/
- jeweller's /ˈdʒuːələz/
- launderette /ˌlɔːnˈdret/
- market stall /ˈmɑːkɪt stɔːl/
- newsagent's /ˈnjuːzeɪdʒənts/
- off-licence /ˈɒf laɪsns/
- 1 stationer's /ˈsteɪʃənəz/
- travel agent's /ˈtrævl eɪdʒənts/

b 🔊 2.22 Listen and check.

ACTIVATION Cover the words and look at the photos. Say the words.

2 PHRASAL VERBS RELATED TO SHOPS AND SHOPPING

a Match the highlighted phrasal verbs to the definitions.

1 A lot of local shops and businesses have closed down because of the recession.
2 A Do you need any help?
   B No thanks, I just want to look round.
3 I wanted to get the coat in a large, but they'd sold out.
4 A Is there somewhere where I can try on this sweater?
   B Yes, the changing rooms are over there.
5 Excuse me, can you help me? I'm looking for a butcher's. Someone told me there was one near here.
6 A Do you have these in a medium?
   B I'm sorry, we're out of mediums at the moment, but we should be getting some in soon.

a not have in stock at the moment
b put something on to see if it fits
c (of a shop) not have any more to sell
d stop trading or doing business
e try to find something
f walk round a place to see what there is

b 🔊 2.23 Listen and check.

ACTIVATION Cover 1–6 and look at definitions a–f. Say the phrasal verbs.

> 🔍 **Shop names with 's**
> The names for many sorts of shops end in 's. This is short for (sb)'s shop, e.g. baker's = baker's shop, chemist's = chemist's shop. In the plural of these shops, there is no apostrophe, e.g. *There are several bakers here.*
>
> Shop names are also often compound nouns, e.g. *bookshop, pet shop, health food store.*
>
> **Other places to buy things in the UK**
> **Charity shops** sell second-hand items (especially clothes) which have been given to them by people to raise money for charity.
>
> **Pound shops** sell a variety of cheap goods which cost one pound.
>
> **Craft fairs** are events where you can buy handmade things, often made by local people.
>
> **Outlets** are shops that sell branded goods at reduced prices.

⬅ p.22

Photography

VOCABULARY BANK

1 DESCRIBING A PHOTO

a Look at the photos and complete the sentences with a word or phrase from the list. Use capital letters where necessary.

behind /bɪˈhaɪnd/ in the background /ˈbækɡraʊnd/
in the bottom right-hand corner /ˌbɒtəm raɪt hænd ˈkɔːnə/
in the centre /ˈsentə/   in the distance /ˈdɪstəns/
in the foreground /ˈfɔːɡraʊnd/   in front of /ɪn ˈfrʌnt əv/
in the top left-hand corner /ˌtɒp left hænd ˈkɔːnə/
on top of /ɒn ˈtɒp əv/   opposite /ˈɒpəzɪt/

Photo 1
1 *In the background*, there's a mountain and some low cloud.
2 _____, there's a grandmother and three children.
3 The boy in an orange T-shirt is standing _____ his grandmother.
4 _____ of the photo, there's a building with lots of steps.
5 There's a small building that looks like a temple _____ a small hill.

Photo 2
6 _____, there's a woman standing on a terrace looking at the view.
7 The woman is standing _____ a low wall.
8 _____ the woman, there's a building with a tower that looks like a church.
9 _____, on the right, you can just see the top of an old building which looks like a ruin.
10 _____, there are some trees.

on top of or at the top of

The bird is **on top of** the photo.   The bird is **at the top of** the photo.

b ▶ 3.10 Listen and check.

ACTIVATION Cover 1–10. Describe where the people and things are in the two photos.

2 TAKING PHOTOS

a Match the sentence halves.
1 e You **use flash** when…
2 ☐ You **zoom in** when…
3 ☐ A photo can **be out of focus** if…
4 ☐ Many cameras have a **portrait setting** to use when…
5 ☐ A photo can be **overexposed** if…
6 ☐ With good cameras you can use different **lenses**, e.g. a wide-angle lens, when…
7 ☐ You **edit** a photo when…

a you're far away from something and you want to take a **close-up** of it.
b you want to take a photo of a **landscape** but you can't get all of it in.
c there's too much light on the subject when you're taking it.
d you want to take a photo of a person.
e you want to take a photo somewhere dark, e.g. indoors or at night.
f you change the size, colour, or brightness.
g your camera isn't automatic and you haven't used the right **settings**.

b ▶ 3.11 Listen and check.

ACTIVATION Cover a–g and look at 1–7. Say the rest of the sentences.

← p.30

Go online to review the vocabulary for each lesson   155

Rubbish and recycling

VOCABULARY BANK

1 RUBBISH: NOUNS AND PHRASAL VERBS

a Read the definitions for *rubbish* and *waste*. Then match the other nouns from the list to their definitions.

nouns
bin /bɪn/   bin bag /ˈbɪn bæg/
landfill site /ˈlændfɪl saɪt/   refuse collector /ˈrefjuːs kəlektə/
rubbish /ˈrʌbɪʃ/   waste /weɪst/
waste-paper basket /ˌweɪst ˈpeɪpə bɑːskɪt/

1 *rubbish* things that you throw away because you don't want them any more (NAmE *garbage* or *trash*)
2 *waste* materials that are not needed and are thrown away, e.g. industrial ~, toxic ~
3 _____ a container that you put rubbish in (also *dustbin*)
4 _____ a plastic bag which you put rubbish in and then throw away
5 _____ a small basket kept indoors where people throw away paper and small things
6 _____ the person whose job it is to take away the rubbish (also *dustman*, informal *bin man*)
7 _____ an area of land where large amounts of waste are covered with earth

b ▶ 4.1 Listen and check.

c Complete the sentences with a phrasal verb from the list.

phrasal verbs
give away /gɪv əˈweɪ/   take away /teɪk əˈweɪ/
take out /teɪk aʊt/   throw away /θrəʊ əˈweɪ/

1 If that pen doesn't work, just _____ it _____. I hate having pens around that don't work.
2 Please could you _____ _____ the rubbish? I did it last week.
3 I'm moving house in a few weeks, and I've decided to _____ _____ a lot of books and clothes to a charity shop.
4 In most countries, people throw away used glass, cardboard, etc. in special bins. Local councils then collect this waste and _____ it _____ to be recycled.

d ▶ 4.2 Listen and check.

ACTIVATION Cover the words and say the definitions and sentences.

2 PACKAGING

a Match the words and photos.

☐ bottle /ˈbɒtl/
☐ can /kæn/
☐ cardboard box /ˈkɑːdbɔːd bɒks/
☐ carton /ˈkɑːtn/
☐ jar /dʒɑː/
☐ lid /lɪd/ (or cap /kæp/)
☐ packet /ˈpækɪt/
☐ plastic bag /ˈplæstɪk bæg/
☐ pot /pɒt/
☐ pouch /paʊtʃ/
☐ sell-by date /ˈselbaɪ deɪt/
☐ tin /tɪn/
☐ (polystyrene) tray /treɪ/
1 tub /tʌb/
☐ wrapper /ˈræpə/

b ▶ 4.3 Listen and check.

ACTIVATION What kind of packaging is normally used for…?

biscuits   cereal   chicken legs   ice cream   milk
olives   pasta sauce   sardines   soft drinks   yogurt

3 THE PREFIX *RE-*

a Complete the sentences with a verb from the list.

reapply /riːəˈplaɪ/   recycle /riːˈsaɪkl/   reheat /riːˈhiːt/
replay /riːˈpleɪ/   rethink /riːˈθɪŋk/   reuse /riːˈjuːz/

1 There's a bottle bank at the local supermarket where you can *recycle* all your glass bottles and jars.
2 All supermarkets in the UK now charge extra for plastic bags. They prefer customers to have shopping bags which they can _____.
3 If you're not sure about the project, you should _____ the whole thing.
4 You can _____ your dinner in the microwave.
5 They'll have to _____ the match next Saturday.
6 You should _____ sunscreen every hour if you have fair skin.

b ▶ 4.4 Listen and check.   ← p.36

Study and work

VOCABULARY BANK

1 HIGHER EDUCATION

a Read the text about University College London (UCL) and complete it with words from the list.

campus /'kæmpəs/   dissertation /dɪsə'teɪʃn/
faculties /'fækltiz/   halls of residence /hɔːlz əv 'rezɪdəns/
lectures /'lektʃəz/   postgraduates /pəʊst'grædʒuəts/
professors /prə'fesəz/   seminars /'semɪnɑːz/
thesis /'θiːsɪs/   tutor /'tjuːtə/
undergraduates /ʌndə'grædʒuəts/   webinars /'webɪnɑːz/

UCL

University College London, also known as UCL, is one of London's most important universities. Founded in 1826, it is based in the Bloomsbury area of central London. The main ¹ _campus_ is located around Gower Street.

UCL currently has around 38,000 students, both ² _____ (students studying for their **first degree**) and ³ _____ (students studying for **further degrees**). Further degrees include a **Master's degree**, usually a one-year course at the end of which students have to write a ⁴ _____, or a **PhD** (doctorate), a three-year (or more) course during which students have to write a doctoral ⁵ _____.

UCL has around 7,000 **academic and research staff**, and 840 ⁶ _____ (the highest ranked university teacher), which is more than any other British university. The research and teaching is divided into ten ⁷ _____, e.g. Arts and Humanities, Engineering Sciences, Medical Sciences, etc.

Many students, particularly first year undergraduates and **overseas students**, live in ⁸ _____. The majority of others find their own accommodation. Students are taught in **tutorials** (small groups of students with a ⁹ _____), or through ¹⁰ _____ (larger classes where students discuss or study with their teacher) or ¹¹ _____ (where a large group of students listen to a talk but do not participate). Some teaching may also be in the form of ¹² _____ (seminars conducted over the internet).

Famous past students range from Alexander Graham Bell, the inventor of the telephone, and Mahatma Gandhi, to all the members of the rock group Coldplay, who met while at university there.

b ◉ 4.13 Listen and check. What do the **bold** words and phrases mean?

ACTIVATION With a partner, say three things which are the same and three which are different about universities in your country.

2 APPLYING FOR A JOB OR COURSE

a Complete the gaps with a noun from the list.

CV /siː 'viː/   experience /ɪk'spɪəriəns/   intern /'ɪntɜːn/
interview /'ɪntəvjuː/   job offer /dʒɒb 'ɒfə/
permit /'pɜːmɪt/   qualifications /ˌkwɒlɪfɪ'keɪʃnz/
reference /'refrəns/   skills /skɪlz/   vacancy /'veɪkənsi/

What you may need to have
- ¹ _qualifications_ (e.g. a degree, a diploma)
- ² _____ (having done some work before)
- ³ _____ (e.g. languages, IT)
- a ⁴ _____ (a letter from a person who would be prepared to recommend you)

What you may need to do
- look for a ⁵ **job** _____ or course
- apply for a ⁶ **work** _____, a place on a course, **a grant / scholarship**
- write a ⁷ _____ and a **covering letter**
- **attend** an ⁸ _____
- get a ⁹ _____ or an offer for a place on a course
- work as an ¹⁰ _____

b ◉ 4.14 Listen and check. What do the **bold** words and phrases mean?

> **attend or assist**
> **attend** = (formal) to be present at an event
> *We strongly recommend that students attend all of their lectures.*
>
> **assist** = (formal) to help sb to do sth
> *Jack was happy to assist Peter with gathering information for the report.*
>
> *apprenticeship or internship*
> **apprenticeship** = a period of time during which sb (usually a young person) works for an employer to learn the skills needed for a specific job
> *The apprenticeship to be an electrician lasts about three years and there is an exam you must pass at the end.*
>
> **internship** = a period of time during which sb (usually a student or recent graduate) gets practical experience of a job
> *Before I got my first job, I did an internship at a publishing company.*

→ p.40

Go online to review the vocabulary for each lesson

Television

VOCABULARY BANK

1 TYPES OF PROGRAMME

a Match the photos to the types of programmes.

- advert /ˈædvɜːt/
- cartoon /kɑːˈtuːn/ (or animation /ˌænɪˈmeɪʃn/)
- chat show /ˈtʃæt ʃəʊ/
- cookery programme /ˈkʊkəri prəʊɡræm/
- current affairs programme /ˌkʌrənt əˈfeəz prəʊɡræm/
- documentary /ˌdɒkjuˈmentri/
- (crime) drama /ˈdrɑːmə/
- live sport /ˌlaɪv ˈspɔːt/
- period drama /ˈpɪəriəd drɑːmə/
- quiz show /ˈkwɪz ʃəʊ/
- 1 reality show /riˈæləti ʃəʊ/
- the news /ðə ˈnjuːz/
- the weather forecast /ˈweðə fɔːkɑːst/

b 🔊 5.2 Listen and check.

> **series, soaps, and sitcoms**
>
> A **series** /ˈsɪəriːz/ is a set of TV programmes about the same subject or with the same characters. It is divided into **episodes**, which usually last between 30 minutes and an hour. When a series first comes out, episodes are usually broadcast once a week. A popular series may return for a second (third, etc.) **season**. **Streaming services** like Netflix now release complete seasons at a time. Sometimes a season is referred to as a **box set**.
>
> A **soap** /səʊp/ (short for *soap opera*) is a story about the lives and problems of a group of people. It is broadcast several times a week, or even every day.
>
> A **sitcom** /ˈsɪtkɒm/ (short for *situation comedy*) is a regular TV programme that shows the same characters in different amusing situations.

ACTIVATION What are the most popular series, soaps, quiz shows, and reality TV shows in your country at the moment?

2 PHRASAL VERBS

a Complete the definitions with a phrasal verb from the list.

be on /biː ɒn/   turn down /tɜːn daʊn/   turn off /tɜːn ɒf/
turn on /tɜːn ɒn/   turn over /tɜːn ˈəʊvə/   turn up /tɜːn ʌp/

1 _____ the TV = press a button, e.g. on a remote control, to start it working (also *switch on*)
2 _____ the TV = press a button to stop it working (also *switch off*)
3 _____ the TV = make the volume louder
4 _____ the TV = make the volume quieter
5 the programme _____ now = it is being shown on TV at this moment
6 _____ to another channel = press a button to watch a different channel (also *change channel*)

b 🔊 5.3 Listen and check.

ACTIVATION Answer the questions with a partner.
Do you ever…?
- choose to stay at home in the evening because there's a good programme on
- turn over to another channel in the middle of a programme
- turn the volume off while you're watching a programme
- turn off a programme as soon as it starts

← p.46

The country

VOCABULARY BANK

1 NATURE

a Match the words and photos.

- [ ] branch /brɑːntʃ/
- [ ] bush /bʊʃ/
- [ ] cliff /klɪf/
- [ ] fence /fens/
- [ ] field /fiːld/
- [ ] gate /geɪt/
- [ ] grass /grɑːs/
- [ ] hedge /hedʒ/
- [ ] hill /hɪl/
- [ ] lake /leɪk/
- [ ] leaf /liːf/ (plural leaves /liːvz/)
- [ ] mud /mʌd/
- [1] path /pɑːθ/
- [ ] rocks /rɒks/
- [ ] sticks /stɪks/
- [ ] stones /stəʊnz/
- [ ] stream /striːm/
- [ ] valley /ˈvæli/
- [ ] well /wel/
- [ ] wood /wʊd/

b ▶ 5.12 Listen and check.

ACTIVATION Cover the words and look at the pictures. Say the words.

> 🔍 **the country and the countryside**
> We normally use *the country* to talk about any area that is not a town or city, e.g. *I live in the country*. We use *the countryside* when we are talking about the scenery in the country, e.g. fields, woods, etc., usually in a positive way, e.g. *We stayed in a little village surrounded by beautiful countryside*.

2 ON A FARM

a Match the words and photos.

- [ ] barn /bɑːn/
- [ ] cockerel /ˈkɒkərəl/
- [ ] cow /kaʊ/
- [ ] donkey /ˈdɒŋki/
- [ ] farmhouse /ˈfɑːmhaʊs/
- [ ] hens /henz/
- [ ] lambs /læmz/
- [ ] sheep /ʃiːp/
- [ ] tractor /ˈtræktə/

b ▶ 5.13 Listen and check.

c Complete the text with a verb or past participle from the list.

grow	harvested	pick	planted

> In the UK, especially in the east of England, a lot of farmers [1]_____ cereals (for example, **wheat**), vegetables, and fruit. Most **crops** are [2]_____ in the early spring and are [3]_____ in the summer, for example, wheat in August, and most potatoes from June onwards. Soft fruits like strawberries are usually **ripe** in June and July, and many farms invite people to come and [4]_____ their own fruit.

d ▶ 5.14 Listen and check. What do you think the **bold** words mean?

ACTIVATION Cover the words in **a** and look at the pictures. Say the words. ← p.51

Go online to review the vocabulary for each lesson

At a restaurant

VOCABULARY BANK

1 THINGS ON THE TABLE

a Match the words and photos.

- bowl /bəʊl/
- candle /ˈkændl/
- corkscrew /ˈkɔːkskruː/
- cup /kʌp/
- fork /fɔːk/
- glass /glɑːs/
- jug /dʒʌg/
- knife /naɪf/
- mug /mʌg/
- napkin /ˈnæpkɪn/ (also serviette /ˌsɜːviˈet/)
- oil and vinegar /ɔɪl ən ˈvɪnɪɡə/
- plate /pleɪt/
- salt and pepper /ˌsɔːlt ən ˈpepə/
- saucer /ˈsɔːsə/
- serving dish /ˈsɜːvɪŋ dɪʃ/
- spoon /spuːn/
- tablecloth /ˈteɪblklɒθ/
- teapot /ˈtiːpɒt/
- teaspoon /ˈtiːspuːn/
- tray /treɪ/
- 1 wine glass /ˈwaɪn glɑːs/

b 🔊 6.1 Listen and check.

ACTIVATION What would you expect to find on a restaurant table in your country? What do you put on the table when you lay it for lunch or dinner?

> 🔍 **food, plate, dish, meal, and course**
> **food** = things that you eat
> **plate** = a round flat object that you put food on when you eat it
> **dish** = 1 a flat container for serving food; 2 food prepared in a particular way, e.g. *the dish of the day, a vegetarian dish*
> **meal** = an occasion when people eat food, e.g. breakfast, lunch, dinner
> **course** = one part of a meal, e.g. *the main course, a four-course meal*

2 THINGS PEOPLE DO IN RESTAURANTS

a Match the verb phrases and photos.

waiters
- lay the table (opp. *clear the table*)
- 1 take an order
- recommend a dish
- carry a tray
- serve customers
- pour the wine

customers
- book a table
- order food
- try the wine
- send something back
- ask for the bill
- leave a tip

b 🔊 6.2 Listen and check.

ACTIVATION Cover the words and look at the photos. Say the phrases.

← p.56

DIY and repairs

VOCABULARY BANK

1 IN A SHED: TOOLS AND OTHER THINGS FOR REPAIRS

a Match the words and photos.

- brick /brɪk/
- bucket /ˈbʌkɪt/
- drill /drɪl/
- hammer /ˈhæmə/
- ladder /ˈlædə/
- nail /neɪl/
- padlock /ˈpædlɒk/
- paintbrush /ˈpeɪntbrʌʃ/
- piece of wood /ˌpiːs ɒv ˈwʊd/
- rope /rəʊp/
- screwdriver /ˈskruːdraɪvə/
- screw /skruː/
- spanner /ˈspænə/
- tap /tæp/
- 1 tile /taɪl/
- wire /waɪə/

b 6.16 Listen and check.

2 IN A DRAWER: USEFUL THINGS AROUND THE HOUSE

a Match the words and photos.

- box of matches /ˌbɒks əv ˈmætʃɪz/
- drawing pin /ˈdrɔːɪŋ pɪn/
- fuse /fjuːz/
- glue /gluː/
- handle /ˈhændl/
- light bulb /ˈlaɪt bʌlb/
- needle and thread /ˌniːdl ən ˈθred/
- penknife /ˈpennaɪf/
- Sellotape /ˈseləteɪp/
- 1 string /strɪŋ/
- tape measure /ˈteɪp ˌmeʒə/
- torch /tɔːtʃ/

b 6.17 Listen and check.

3 VERB PHRASES

a Match verbs 1–9 to phrases a–i.

1. c change
2. ☐ drill
3. ☐ mend
4. ☐ put together (assemble) (opp. *take apart*)
5. ☐ put up
6. ☐ set up
7. ☐ sew
8. ☐ stick
9. ☐ tie

a something together with glue or Sellotape
b a button on a shirt
c ~~a light bulb or a wheel~~
d two things together, e.g. your shoelaces or two pieces of string
e a new wi-fi network or a home cinema system
f shelves or curtains
g a hole in a wall or in a piece of wood
h something that's broken
i flat-pack furniture

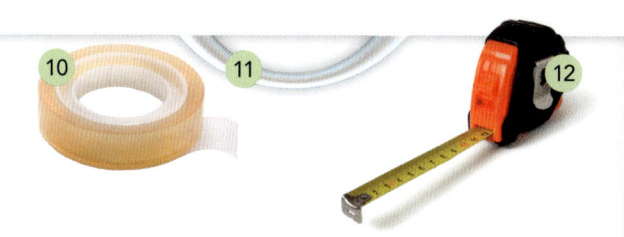

> **Synonyms**
> Synonyms are words with a very similar meaning, e.g. you can *repair*, *mend*, or *fix* something which is broken.

b 6.18 Listen and check. → p.62

Go online to review the vocabulary for each lesson

161

Phrasal verbs

VOCABULARY BANK

> 🔍 **Phrasal verbs revision**
> **Type 1** – phrasal verbs with no object
> The verb and particle are never separated:
>
> *be on* TV, *grow up* on a farm, *move back* to the city, *settle down* to start a family, *turn over* to another channel
>
> **Type 2** – phrasal verbs with an object – separable
> The verb and particle can be separated:
>
> *back up* a file, *close down* a shop, *put together* a piece of furniture, *put up* shelves, *send back* something you bought online, *set up* a wi-fi network, *switch off* a computer, *take out* the rubbish, *throw away* leftover food, *try on* clothes, *turn up / down / on / off* the TV, *keep away* insects
>
> **Type 3** – phrasal verbs with an object – inseparable
> The verb and particle(s) are never separated:
>
> *ask for* the bill, *be out of* a new product, *look for* a cash machine, *look round* a shop, *sell out of* a size, *zoom in on* sth you want to photograph

1 PHRASAL VERBS TO DO WITH MONEY

a Match phrasal verbs 1–6 to definitions a–f.
1 ___ If I lend you the money, can you pay me back next week?
2 ___ I need to take out some money. Where's the nearest cash machine?
3 ___ I won't be able to pay off my student loan until I'm 45.
4 ___ He's so generous. When he won the lottery, he gave nearly all the money away.
5 ___ Nowadays it's difficult for couples to live on only one salary.
6 ___ I had to live off my parents while I was at university.

   a depend financially on
   b finish paying for something
   c give as a present
   d have enough money for what you need
   e return money you have borrowed
   f remove something from somewhere

b 🔊 7.3 Listen and check.

2 PHRASAL VERBS WITH AWAY AND BACK

> 🔍 **The meaning of the particle**
> With some phrasal verbs, the meaning of the particle (the preposition or adverb after the verb) can help you to understand the phrasal verb, e.g. *away* often means *to a different place*, *out of sight*, and *back* often means to *return an action*, e.g. *go back*.

a Complete the sentences with a verb from the list.

be (x2)   call   get   give   put   run   take

away
1 Don't _____ away! I won't hurt you.
2 The boss will _____ away until the end of next week. He's at a conference in Mexico.
3 Please _____ your toys away. They're all over the floor.
4 If you take a paracetamol, it'll _____ the pain away!

back
5 I'm sorry, but I'm confiscating your phone. You'll _____ it back at the end of the day.
6 He's out, I'm afraid. Could you _____ back in about half an hour?
7 A Where are you going?
   B Just to the shops. I'll _____ back in ten minutes.
8 That's my book! _____ it back.

b 🔊 7.4 Listen and check.

3 MORE PHRASAL VERBS WITH TAKE

a Complete the gaps with a particle from the list.

after   apart   on   off (x2)   out   over   up

1 Sorry, I can't come tonight. I'm taking my girlfriend _____ for dinner.
2 They're taking _____ ten new interns at Radio London. Why don't we apply?
3 I take _____ my mother. We're both very outgoing.
4 The plane took _____ twenty minutes late.
5 Unfortunately, my company was taken _____ by a multinational firm, and I lost my job.
6 Take _____ your shoes, please. I've just cleaned the floor.
7 You need to take the keyboard _____ to clean it properly.
8 I need to do more exercise. I think I'll take _____ cycling.

b 🔊 7.5 Listen and check.

↩ p.68

Looking after yourself

VOCABULARY BANK

1 AT THE HAIRDRESSER'S OR BARBER'S

a Match the words and photos.

- bunches /ˈbʌntʃɪz/
- a buzz cut /bʌz kʌt/
- a fringe /frɪndʒ/
- 1 a parting /ˈpɑːtɪŋ/
- a ponytail /ˈpəʊniteɪl/
- plaits /plæts/

have your hair…
- bleached /bliːtʃd/
- curled /kɜːld/
- dyed /daɪd/
- put up /pʊt ʌp/
- straightened /ˈstreɪtnd/

have…
- a blow-dry /ˈbləʊ draɪ/
- a perm /pɜːm/
- a shave /ʃeɪv/
- a treatment /ˈtriːtmənt/
- a trim /trɪm/ (or have your hair trimmed)
- highlights /ˈhaɪlaɪts/ (or lowlights)

b 🔊 8.3 Listen and check.

ACTIVATION How often do you go to the hairdresser's or barber's? What do you usually have done? ⬅ p.76

2 KEEPING FIT

a Match the words and photos for equipment and exercises.

Equipment
- (use) an exercise bike
- (use) a running machine
- (do / lift) weights
- (use) a rowing machine
- (use) a cross-trainer
- (use) a yoga mat

Exercises
- do sit-ups
- do press-ups
- do stretches
- do aerobics
- do spinning
- 1 do Pilates (or yoga)

b 🔊 8.6 Listen and check.

ACTIVATION What equipment or exercises are good if you…?
- want to lose weight
- want to tone your muscles
- want to do cardio exercises
- have a bad back
- want to improve your flexibility

3 BEAUTY TREATMENTS

a Match the words and photos. 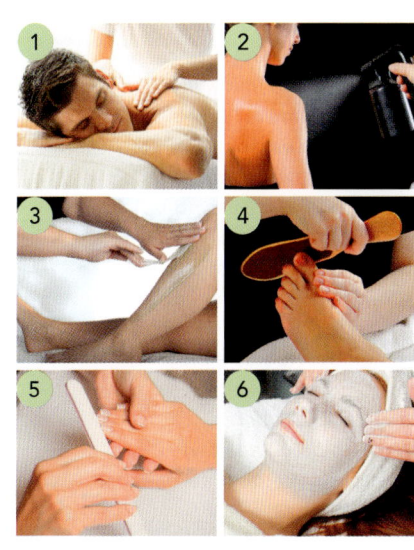
- manicure /ˈmanɪkjʊə/
- pedicure /ˈpedɪkjʊə/
- facial /ˈfeɪʃl/
- massage /ˈmasɑːʒ/
- waxing /ˈwaksɪŋ/
- fake tan /feɪk tan/

b 🔊 8.7 Listen and check.

ACTIVATION Which of these treatments would you enjoy? ⬅ p.78

Go online to review the vocabulary for each lesson

163

Appendix

DEPENDENT PREPOSITIONS

prepositions after verbs

I **agree with** my boss **about** the problem.
He **apologized for** being late.
She **applied for** the job.
We always **argue about** money.
I used to **argue with** my sister a lot.
We **arrived at** the airport at 6.00 a.m.
We **arrived in** Paris in the evening.
I don't **believe in** ghosts.
That bag **belongs to** me.
I can't **choose between** these two shirts.
Our weekend plans **depend on** the weather.
I **dreamt about** my grandfather last night.
They all **laughed at** me when I fell over.

I'm **looking forward to** my holiday.
I'll **pay for** your coffee.
We all **posed for** a photograph.
I **prefer** taking the train **to** flying.
You can always **rely on** your parents.
He **reminds** me **of** an old school friend.
She **shared** her sweets **with** my son.
They **smiled at** me.
I love **spending** money **on** clothes.
They **succeeded in** climbing the mountain.
I **talked to** the hotel manager **about** my room.
Are you **waiting for** someone?
Don't **worry about** it, it's not a problem.

prepositions after adjectives

She's **angry about** her salary.
She's **angry with** her boss.
He's very **close to** his father.
The film is **different from** the book.
I'm really **disappointed with** these photos.
She's **excited about** her new job.
Oxford is **famous for** its university.
I'm **fed up with** waiting. Let's go!
He's very **fond of** his teacher.
I'm **frightened** / **afraid** / **scared of** snakes.
He's **good** / **bad at** remembering names.
Vegetables are **good for** you.
She's **interested in** French literature.
I'm not very **keen on** fast food.
They were very **kind to** me.
He's **married to** my best friend.
I'm very **pleased with** my progress.
I'm **proud of** my children.
I'm **ready for** a holiday.
He's **responsible for** the sales team.
Don't be **rude to** him.
We're **sorry about** what happened.
They're **tired of** working every day.
She's **worried about** her car.

VERB PATTERNS

verb + infinitive with to

afford (*to buy a flat*)
agree (*to help someone*)
arrange (*to meet*)
be able (*to swim*)
choose (*to do something*)
decide (*to buy a new computer*)
expect (*to fail an exam*)
forget (*to lock the door*)
help (*to cook dinner*)
hope (*to go to university*)
learn (*to swim*)
manage (*to escape*)
need (*to leave early*)
offer (*to do the washing-up*)
plan (*to start a family*)
pretend (*to be someone else*)
promise (*to pay someone back*)
refuse (*to cooperate*)
remember (*to buy a present*)
seem (*to be broken*)
try (*to repair the car*)
want (*to go on holiday*)
would like (*to travel abroad*)

verb + gerund (-ing)

admit (*stealing the money*)
avoid (*driving in the city centre*)
can't stand (*queueing*)
deny (*being involved*)
dislike (*going shopping*)
enjoy (*playing tennis*)
feel like (*going home early*)
finish (*having breakfast*)
hate (*being late*)
imagine (*living without the internet*)
keep (*forgetting his name*)
like (*cooking for friends*)
love (*reading*)
mind (*working in the evenings*)
miss (*living in Spain*)
practise (*playing a difficult piece*)
prefer (*running to swimming*)
recommend (*opening a bank account*)
spend (*a long time practising*)
stop (*raining*)
suggest (*seeing a doctor*)

verb + object + infinitive with to

advise (*me to pay cash*)
allow (*us to leave early*)
ask (*her to help*)
invite (*us to go away for the weekend*)
need (*you to fill in a form*)
order (*him to sit down*)
persuade (*me to come to the party*)
teach (*me to play the piano*)
tell (*them to be quiet*)
want (*you to explain*)

verb + object + infinitive without to

let (*me stay up late*)
make (*me tidy my room*)

Irregular verbs

Infinitive	Past simple	Past participle
be /biː/	was /wɒz/	been /biːn/
beat /biːt/	beat	beaten /ˈbiːtn/
become /bɪˈkʌm/	became /bɪˈkeɪm/	become
begin /bɪˈgɪn/	began /bɪˈgæn/	begun /bɪˈgʌn/
bite /baɪt/	bit /bɪt/	bitten /ˈbɪtn/
break /breɪk/	broke /brəʊk/	broken /ˈbrəʊkən/
bring /brɪŋ/	brought /brɔːt/	brought
build /bɪld/	built /bɪlt/	built
buy /baɪ/	bought /bɔːt/	bought
can /kæn/	could /kʊd/	–
catch /kætʃ/	caught /kɔːt/	caught
choose /tʃuːz/	chose /tʃəʊz/	chosen /ˈtʃəʊzn/
come /kʌm/	came /keɪm/	come
cost /kɒst/	cost	cost
cut /kʌt/	cut	cut
do /duː/	did /dɪd/	done /dʌn/
draw /drɔː/	drew /druː/	drawn /drɔːn/
drink /drɪŋk/	drank /dræŋk/	drunk /drʌŋk/
drive /draɪv/	drove /drəʊv/	driven /ˈdrɪvn/
eat /iːt/	ate /eɪt/	eaten /ˈiːtn/
fall /fɔːl/	fell /fel/	fallen /ˈfɔːlən/
feel /fiːl/	felt /felt/	felt
find /faɪnd/	found /faʊnd/	found
fly /flaɪ/	flew /fluː/	flown /fləʊn/
forget /fəˈget/	forgot /fəˈgɒt/	forgotten /fəˈgɒtn/
get /get/	got /gɒt/	got
give /gɪv/	gave /geɪv/	given /ˈgɪvn/
go /gəʊ/	went /went/	gone /gɒn/
grow /grəʊ/	grew /gruː/	grown /grəʊn/
hang /hæŋ/	hung /hʌŋ/	hung
have /hæv/	had /hæd/	had
hear /hɪə/	heard /hɜːd/	heard
hide /haɪd/	hid /hɪd/	hidden /ˈhɪdn/
hit /hɪt/	hit	hit
hurt /hɜːt/	hurt	hurt
keep /kiːp/	kept /kept/	kept
know /nəʊ/	knew /njuː/	known /nəʊn/
lay /leɪ/	laid /leɪd/	laid
learn /lɜːn/	learnt /lɜːnt/ learned /lɜːnd/	learnt learned
leave /liːv/	left /left/	left

Infinitive	Past simple	Past participle
lend /lend/	lent /lent/	lent
let /let/	let	let
lie /laɪ/	lay /leɪ/	lain /leɪn/
lose /luːz/	lost /lɒst/	lost
make /meɪk/	made /meɪd/	made
mean /miːn/	meant /ment/	meant
meet /miːt/	met /met/	met
pay /peɪ/	paid /peɪd/	paid
put /pʊt/	put	put
read /riːd/	read /red/	read /red/
ride /raɪd/	rode /rəʊd/	ridden /ˈrɪdn/
ring /rɪŋ/	rang /ræŋ/	rung /rʌŋ/
run /rʌn/	ran /ræn/	run
say /seɪ/	said /sed/	said
see /siː/	saw /sɔː/	seen /siːn/
sell /sel/	sold /səʊld/	sold
send /send/	sent /sent/	sent
set /set/	set	set
sew /səʊ/	sewed /səʊd/	sewn /səʊn/
shine /ʃaɪn/	shone /ʃɒn/	shone
shut /ʃʌt/	shut	shut
sing /sɪŋ/	sang /sæŋ/	sung /sʌŋ/
sit /sɪt/	sat /sæt/	sat
sleep /sliːp/	slept /slept/	slept
speak /spiːk/	spoke /spəʊk/	spoken /ˈspəʊkən/
spend /spend/	spent /spent/	spent
stand /stænd/	stood /stʊd/	stood
steal /stiːl/	stole /stəʊl/	stolen /ˈstəʊlən/
stick /stɪk/	stuck /stʌk/	stuck
swim /swɪm/	swam /swæm/	swum /swʌm/
take /teɪk/	took /tʊk/	taken /ˈteɪkən/
teach /tiːtʃ/	taught /tɔːt/	taught
tell /tel/	told /təʊld/	told
think /θɪŋk/	thought /θɔːt/	thought
throw /θrəʊ/	threw /θruː/	thrown /θrəʊn/
understand /ʌndəˈstænd/	understood /ʌndəˈstʊd/	understood
wake /weɪk/	woke /wəʊk/	woken /ˈwəʊkən/
wear /weə/	wore /wɔː/	worn /wɔːn/
win /wɪn/	won /wʌn/	won
write /raɪt/	wrote /rəʊt/	written /ˈrɪtn/

Vowel sounds

SOUND BANK

		usual spelling	! but also
🐟	fish	i — risky bin lid tin sitcom since	pretty women busy decided village physics
🌳	tree	ee — sheep screen ea — stream leaf e — recycle thesis	people machine key field receipt
🐱	cat	a — pack campus active cash packet stand	plaits
🚗	car	ar — carton charger starter jar a — craft drama grass	aunt laugh heart
⏰	clock	o — bossy rock top bottom off on	watch want wash sausage because
🐴	horse	(o)or — torch corkscrew al — stall fall aw — awful saw	war quarter pour fought saucer caught audience board
🐂	bull	u — bush butcher's oo — wood cookery look good	could should would woman
👢	boot	oo — spoon zoom u* — glue true ew — screw crew	suitcase cruise shoe move soup through queue
💻	computer	Many different spellings. /ə/ is always unstressed. sp<u>ea</u>ker sp<u>a</u>cious <u>a</u>round cont<u>ai</u>n prof<u>e</u>ssor	
🐦	bird	er — serve prefer ir — dirty circle ur — turn blurred	research work world worse journey
🥚	egg	e — pet hen lens sell fence selfish	friendly already healthy jealous many said

		usual spelling	! but also
⬆	up	u — brush dustman mug mud bucket jug	money front someone enough touch couple
🚂	train	a* — gate baker's ai — nail waiter ay — replay tray	break great weight straighten they grey
☎	phone	o* — remote stone tone rope oa — boat soap	grow show bowl although sew
🚲	bike	i* — tie wire y — dry recycle igh — light bright	buy eyes height
🦉	owl	ou — round out found foreground ow — towel crowd	
👦	boy	oi — noisy avoid oil join oy — enjoy employ	
👂	ear	eer — cheerful volunteer ere — here we're ear — clear hear	really idea period theatre series
🪑	chair	air — airport repair fair hairdresser are — careful square	their there wear area
🧳	tourist	A very unusual sound. euro tour sure manicure luxurious	
/i/		A sound between /ɪ/ and /i:/. Consonant + y at the end of words is pronounced /i/. happy angry thirsty	
/u/		Not a very common sound. education usually situation	

* especially before consonant + e

☐ short vowels   ☐ long vowels   ☐ diphthongs

Consonant sounds

SOUND BANK

		usual spelling		! but also
	parrot	p pp	plate packet adaptor trip opposite apply	
	bag	b bb	bulb bin bag probably tub rubbish robbed	
	key	c k ck	comb score keep trekking brick padlock	chemist's scholarship qualifications account
	girl	g gg	greengrocer's guidebook forgetful vinegar aggressive luggage	
	flower	f ph ff	florist's safari pharmacy photography cliff affairs	enough laugh
	vase	v	valley vacancy travel envious CV shave	of
	tie	t tt	tutor teapot stick start batteries bottle	asked passed
	dog	d dd	drill handle comedy hairdryer addictive middle	planted bored
	snake	s ss ce/ci	swimsuit likes bossy dissertation fence cinema	science scene cycle
	zebra	z s	quiz razor easy newsagent's loves reuse	
	shower	sh ti (+ vowel) ci (+ vowel)	shop toothbrush childish cash ambitious stationer's delicious facial	sugar sure machine chef
	television	Not a very common sound. revision decision massage usually		

		usual spelling		! but also
θ	thumb	th	throw rethink thread path tablecloth maths toothpaste	
ð	mother	th	the that with weather sunbathe together	
tʃ	chess	ch tch t (+ure)	chat chicken stretch match lecture future	
dʒ	jazz	j g dge	jeweller's pyjamas dangerous package hedge bridge	
l	leg	l ll	lay lucky until reliable skill rebellious	
r	right	r rr	result referee profitable story current carry	written wrong
w	witch	w wh	war waste webinar switch whistle which	one once DIY
j	yacht	y before u	yet yellow yoga yourself university argue	
m	monkey	m mm	memory stream mountain moody hammer swimming	lamb climb
n	nose	n nn	needle pond intern barn spinning thinner	knife know
ŋ	singer	ng before k	unpacking flying string bring thanks pink	
h	house	h	hill hiking behind farmhouse unhappy perhaps	who whose whole

☐ voiced   ☐ unvoiced

Go online to watch the Sound Bank videos

OXFORD
UNIVERSITY PRESS

Great Clarendon Street, Oxford, OX2 6DP,
United Kingdom

Oxford University Press is a department of the
University of Oxford. It furthers the University's
objective of excellence in research, scholarship,
and education by publishing worldwide. Oxford
is a registered trade mark of Oxford University Press
in the UK and in certain other countries

© Oxford University Press 2020

The moral rights of the author have been asserted

First published in 2020

2024 2023 2022 2021 2020
10 9 8 7 6 5 4 3 2 1

No unauthorized photocopying

All rights reserved. No part of this publication
may be reproduced, stored in a retrieval system,
or transmitted, in any form or by any means,
without the prior permission in writing of Oxford
University Press, or as expressly permitted by law, by
licence or under terms agreed with the appropriate
reprographics rights organization. Enquiries
concerning reproduction outside the scope of the
above should be sent to the ELT Rights Department,
Oxford University Press, at the address above

You must not circulate this work in any other
form and you must impose this same condition
on any acquirer

Links to third party websites are provided by
Oxford in good faith and for information only.
Oxford disclaims any responsibility for the materials
contained in any third party website referenced in
this work

ISBN: 978 0 19 403906 2

Printed in China

This book is printed on paper from certified and
well-managed sources

ACKNOWLEDGEMENTS

[Acknowledgements text omitted for brevity — extensive list of photo credits, permissions, and source citations covering multiple columns.]